THOMAS GRANTHAM

MERCER
UNIVERSITY PRESS

Endowed by

TOM WATSON BROWN

and

THE WATSON-BROWN FOUNDATION, INC.

THOMAS GRANTHAM

God's Messenger from Lincolnshire

JOHN INSCORE ESSICK

MERCER UNIVERSITY PRESS

MACON, GEORGIA

The James N. Griffith Series in Baptist Studies

This series on Baptist life and thought explores and investigates Baptist history, offers analyses of Baptist theologies, provides studies in hymnody, and examines the role of Baptists in societies and cultures around the world. The series also includes classics of Baptist literature, letters, diaries, and other writings.

—Walter B. Shurden, Series Editor

MUP/ H876

1400 Coleman Avenue
Macon, Georgia 31207

First Edition

Books published by Mercer University Press are printed on acid-free paper that meets the requirements of the American National Standard for Information Sciences—Permanence of Paper for Printed Library Materials.

Mercer University Press is a member of Green Press Initiative (greenpressinitiative.org), a nonprofit organization working to help publishers and printers increase their use of recycled paper and decrease their use of fiber derived from endangered forests. This book is printed on recycled paper.

ISBN 978-0-88146-461-0

Cataloging-in-Publication Data is available from the Library of Congress

To Dempsey and Shelley,
the first Baptists I ever met

Contents

Foreword

Thomas Grantham Redivivus

This book is at the head of a new wave of interest in the English General Baptists of the seventeenth century. General Baptists are the oldest variety of Baptists in England and North America with a unique theological position, a comprehensive polity, and an expanding history of outreach in the East, London, and the Southeast. Seemingly overwhelmed in the numerical advance of Baptists in their first century by the Calvinistic or Particular Baptists, the General Baptists have been lumped with the Particulars or harried out of the narrative by some of their congregations' forays into Unitarianism at the head of the eighteenth century. Their power and influence in the making of Baptist character remains undiminished to the serious student of Baptist Studies because of their bold stances on the sacraments, the nature of the church, and religious liberty. The very earliest English Baptists, John Smyth, Thomas Helwys, and John Murton are accounted among their ranks.

Professor John Inscore Essick is among a new generation of historians of Baptists who moves beyond the bipartite classification of English Baptists. From the nineteenth century onward it was fashionable to develop the narrative around two groups, almost in competition for a Whiggish outcome. Left out were the Seventh Day Baptists, varieties and regions of Calvinistic Baptists, and those who fall into Christopher Hill's description of fluid movements of persons and congregations among several cousin sects like Familists, Levellers, Ranters, and Seekers. The bipartite typology came under close scrutiny in the 1980s, and what emerged was a much-diversified approach. In the 1990s this was linked to a "polygenetic" approach to interpret Anabaptist origins advanced by historians and theologians like James M. Stayer and Arnold Snyder. Others followed in this train of thought, with the results finally showing up in contemporary English historiography. The impact of a Baptist polygenetic approach is to give due scholarly attention to the General Baptists and Seventh Day Baptists, among others.

In an essay several years ago, I suggested that Thomas Grantham was the first systematic theologian among the Baptists. Inscore Essick's book proves the point. Systematic theology among Dissenters was in its nascent stages in the seventeenth century and quite often a crude attempt to gather and connect various ideas into a handbook for churches and personal libraries. Grantham's *tour de force*, *Christianismus Primitivus* (1678), illustrates genuine intellectual progress in connecting ideas and principles, deducing theological principles not only from the Scriptures but also from the literature of the first five centuries, and bringing a unified vision to an often-fractured sect. In his theological analysis of Grantham's literary corpus plus the capstone work itself, Inscore Essick demonstrates that in Grantham one finds an ecclesiology and a doctrine of the Spirit, while also making unique contributions to religious liberty and a usable method of interpreting scripture. I believe Thomas Grantham's work is the finest and most sophisticated theological example of seventeenth-century English Baptist life and thought.

Following the lead of John Nicholson in his seminal 1958 *Baptist Quarterly* essay on the office of messenger, Inscore Essick further develops and analyzes the polity issues of General Baptist connectionalism. He rightly places Grantham's development of the office in the foundation, laid three decades earlier in the work of Edward Barber, William Jeffrey, Thomas Lover, William Rider, and the evolving experience of General Baptists in Lincolnshire, Kent, and Buckinghamshire. This represents the all-important first generation of General Baptist experience. Importantly, Inscore Essick recovers the biblical basis of a threefold ministry that General Baptists of the 1640s were attempting to re-establish based on their reading of the primitive churches. Modern readers will profit from Inscore Essick's analysis as the debate goes forth on Baptist autonomy and interdependence, especially in North America.

Inscore Essick reminds us that Thomas Grantham was one of the great Dissenting controversialists of his era. In an age of modern and mass media, it is hard to comprehend the importance or even relevance of seventeenth-century public disputations. They were spectacles at one level, sometimes concluding in semi-violent outcomes, particularly if they involved brash and impertinent speakers or members of sects like the Quakers or Ranters. At another level, in an age of extraordinary free expression, as Christopher Hill reminded us, the disputes and the literary follow-ups were opportunities to introduce and advance theological ideas in an era that was increasingly literate and awash in biblical literalism. In Grantham's debates and apologetic treatises he was first and foremost a teacher of great conviction, an intellectual evangelist. As Inscore Essick well points out, Grantham brought a sense of unity and legitimacy to the General Baptist movement, as he debated with spokesmen of the Church of England, other Dissenters, and even among his own kind. This would turn out to be the finest years of General Baptist theological creativity and we are grateful for Inscore Essick's acumen in analyzing the historical records of the debates and literature.

There is also a larger reason why Thomas Grantham should be taken seriously. He represents a type of Christian experience that has characterized Baptists at their best. Grantham interacted intentionally with other Christians, claiming close friends among Churchmen. He was well traveled in his own constituency, by no means an obscurantist. He responded to cultural and political realities like the Restoration of the former king. His representation to King Charles II at least twice placed Baptists in a position they rarely achieved in their nonconformity. In this regard Grantham ranks with William Kiffin among the Calvinistic Baptists of London, and Dr. Peter Chamberlen among the Seventh Day Baptists. Repeatedly in a "Tottering Age," as Inscore Essick reminds us, Thomas Grantham represented General Baptists as the King's loyal subjects. Contemporary Baptist leaders worldwide would do well to follow in the footsteps of so able and distinguished, irenic and engaging a leader as Grantham of Lincolnshire.

Inscore Essick brought to his PhD seminars at Baylor University an undergraduate degree from Appalachian State University and a Master of Divinity from Campbell University Divinity School, a theological institution characterized by an evangelical openness to ideas and serious scholarship. He had been introduced to Baptist life and thought in his graduate studies and was well schooled in the current historiography. What set Inscore Essick apart was his relentless inquisitiveness and thoroughness in doing research. I recall chatting with him about the need to resurrect Thomas Grantham from relative obscurity. He took on this formidable project, completing his dissertation in 2008. Setting aside conventional treatments, Inscore Essick went to the primary sources in England and did the hard, thorough work. His bibliography reveals his discovery of Grantham's full literary corpus, plus letters and documentary details previously unknown. His appendices reproduce several key Grantham documents. It is fitting that John Inscore Essick should be the first full-time professor of church history at the Baptist Seminary of Kentucky, setting a high standard of faculty scholarship.

I commend this book as a significant contribution to Baptist Studies and the larger picture of later seventeenth-century Dissent. I especially hope the British Baptist and Dissenting historical communities in particular will find this research useful. We have needed a first-rate accounting of this leading General Baptist figure, and Inscore Essick has with clarity and insight brought Thomas Grantham out of the shadows and back into the prominence he enjoyed during his lifetime.

William H. Brackney BA (hons), MAR, PhD
The Millard R. Cherry Distinguished Professor of Christian Thought and Ethics
Faculty of Theology, Acadia University
Wolfville, Nova Scotia

Acknowledgments

Research, writing, and publishing are communal acts. Without guidance, patience, correction, support, and encouragement from others, this book would still be incomplete. There are so many individuals and learning communities who have helped me along the way, but a few deserve special mention.

I must begin by thanking Cliff and Wanda Atkins, Hubert and Nancy Clark, Geraldine Essick, Julie and Michael Lee, Stephanie Moody Shaffer, and Bill and Cindy Raines. Their generosity kept this book on the path to publication. Assistance and expertise were also provided by Pam Durso, Bryan Keyworth, Robert Kershaw, Kelley Land, Madeline Light, Keith and Thomas Sisman, George Southcombe, Ellen Parks, and Jeff Wood. I am especially thankful for William Brackney's advice concerning matters of content and style. The project he introduced me to is better at completion because of his wisdom and insight.

The Department of Religion at Baylor University housed a community of scholars that taught me much about reading, research, and writing. I am honored and grateful to have studied and written under the direction of Dr. Bill Pitts, a historian whose acumen and generosity bless me still.

A productive research trip to England in spring 2008 was made possible by the Glenn O. and Martell B. Hilburn Endowed Graduate Research Scholarship, given through the Department of Religion at Baylor University. While in England the hospitality of the following libraries and collections allowed for access to important manuscripts: The Lincoln Public Library, Lincoln; Dr. Williams's Trust and Library, London; The Bodleian Library, Oxford; and The Norfolk & Norwich Millennium Library, Norwich. Finally, the kind staff members of St. Stephen's Church in Norwich were helpful in my efforts to locate Thomas Grantham's final resting place.

In the United States my research was made easier by the accommodating staff members at the Moody Memorial Library, Baylor

University; the Bosworth Memorial Library, Lexington Theological Seminary; The James P. Boyce Centennial Library, the Southern Baptist Theological Seminary; and the Ensor Learning Resource Center, Georgetown College; Keith and Thomas Sisman.

Closer to home, the Baptist Seminary of Kentucky has been an inspiring place to work. President Greg Earwood and Dean Dalen Jackson graciously granted me time and resources to see this project through to the end. Mark Medley patiently endured more impromptu conversations and interruptions than I can remember.

Finally, at home Amber, Olin, and little Leif continually teach me about the proper *telos* of research, writing, and publishing: beloved community.

Lincoln Cathedral

Wall hook, Lincoln Cathedral jail

Dungeon at Lincoln Cathedral

Monksthorpe Chapel and baptistry (foreground), Lincolnshire
Photo credit: Keith and Thomas Sisman

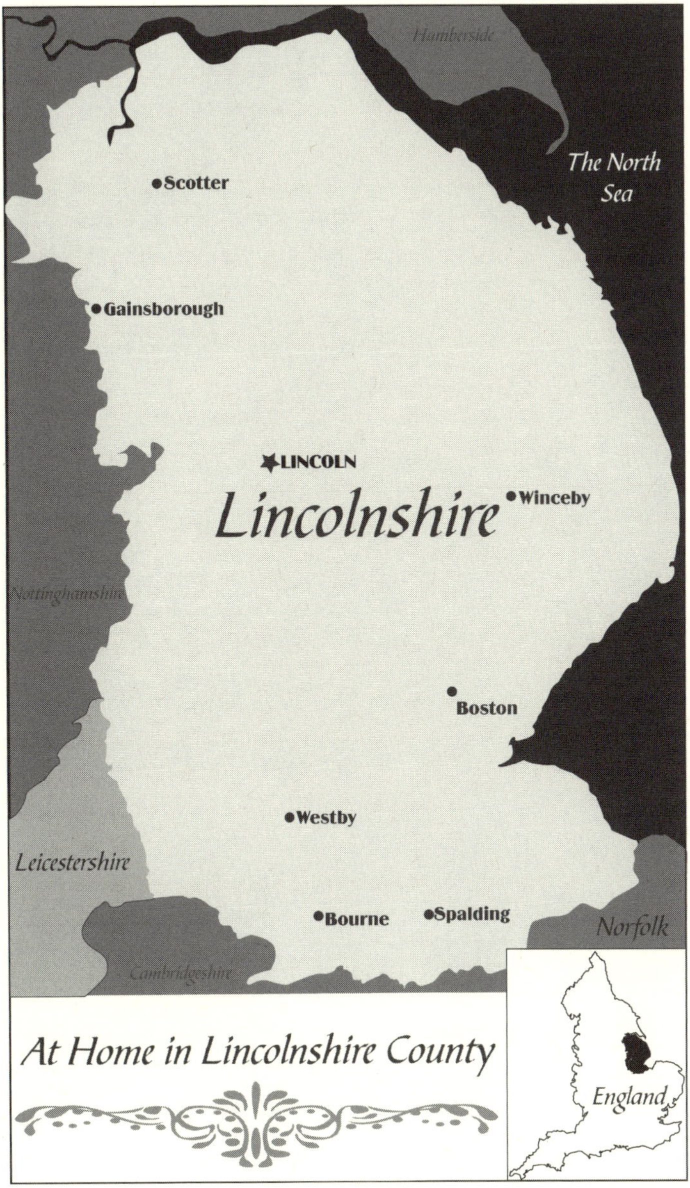

At Home in Lincolnshire County

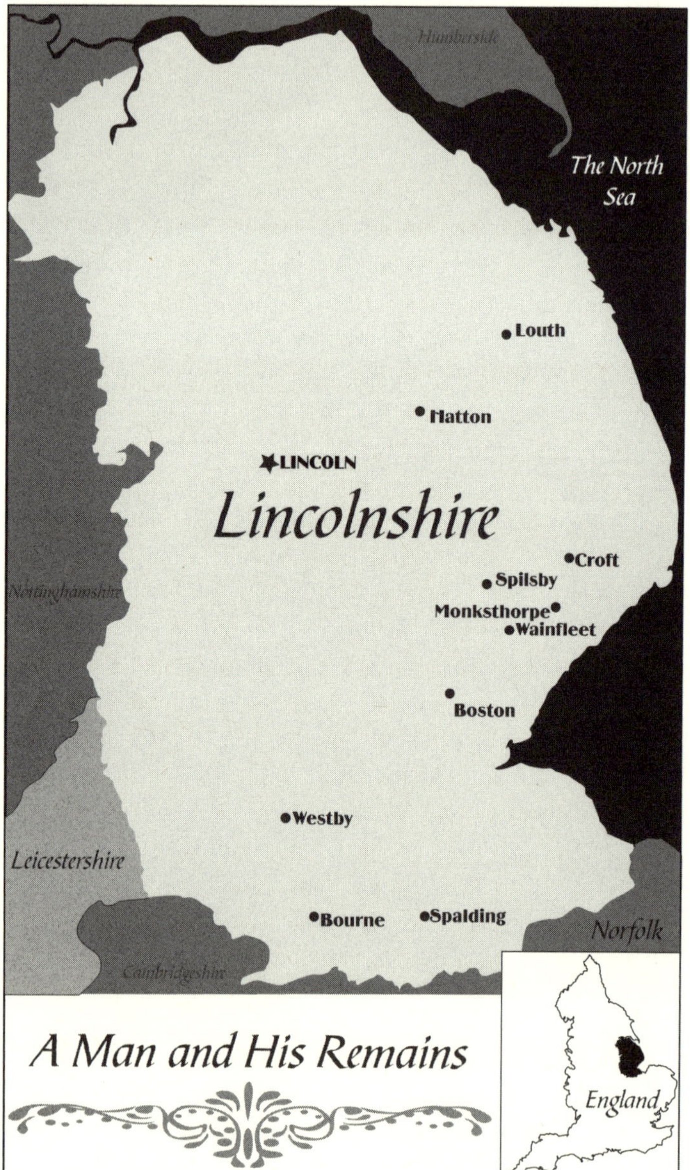
Humberside
The North Sea
Louth
Hatton
LINCOLN
Lincolnshire
Croft
Spilsby
Monksthorpe
Wainfleet
Nottinghamshire
Boston
Westby
Leicestershire
Bourne
Spalding
Norfolk
Cambridgeshire
England
A Man and His Remains

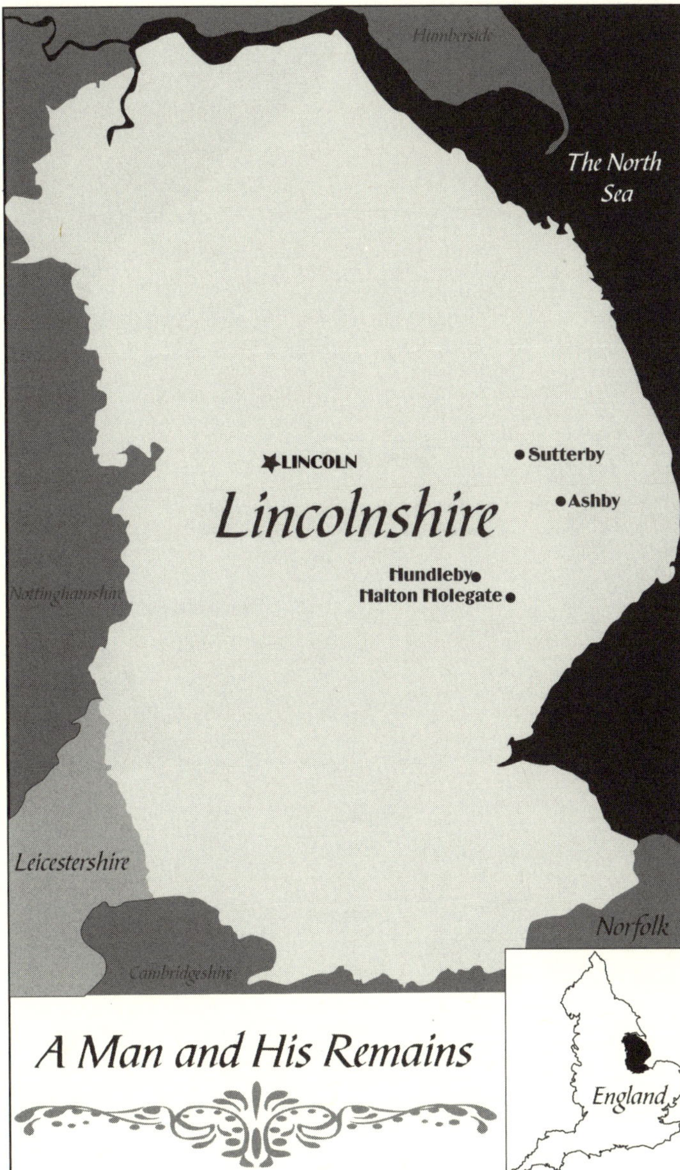
Humberside
The North Sea
LINCOLN
Lincolnshire
Sutterby
Ashby
Hundleby
Halton Holegate
Nottinghamshire
Leicestershire
Norfolk
Cambridgeshire
A Man and His Remains
England

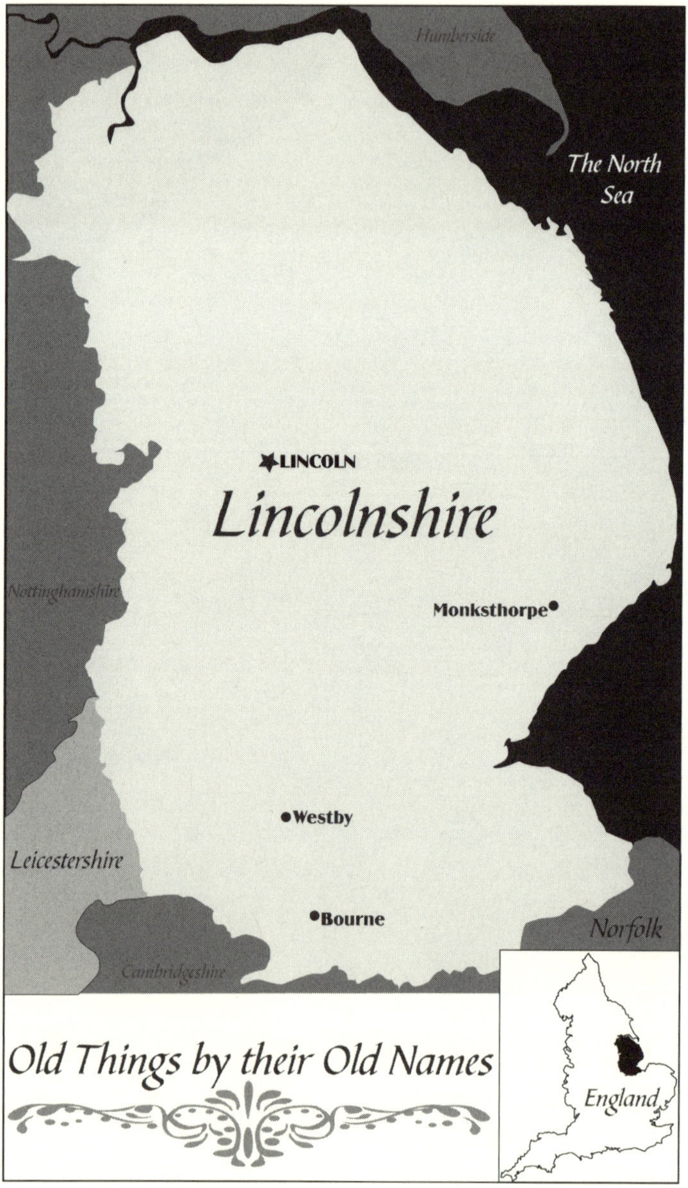
Humberside
The North Sea
LINCOLN
Lincolnshire
Nottinghamshire
Monksthorpe
Westby
Leicestershire
Bourne
Norfolk
Cambridgeshire
Old Things by their Old Names
England

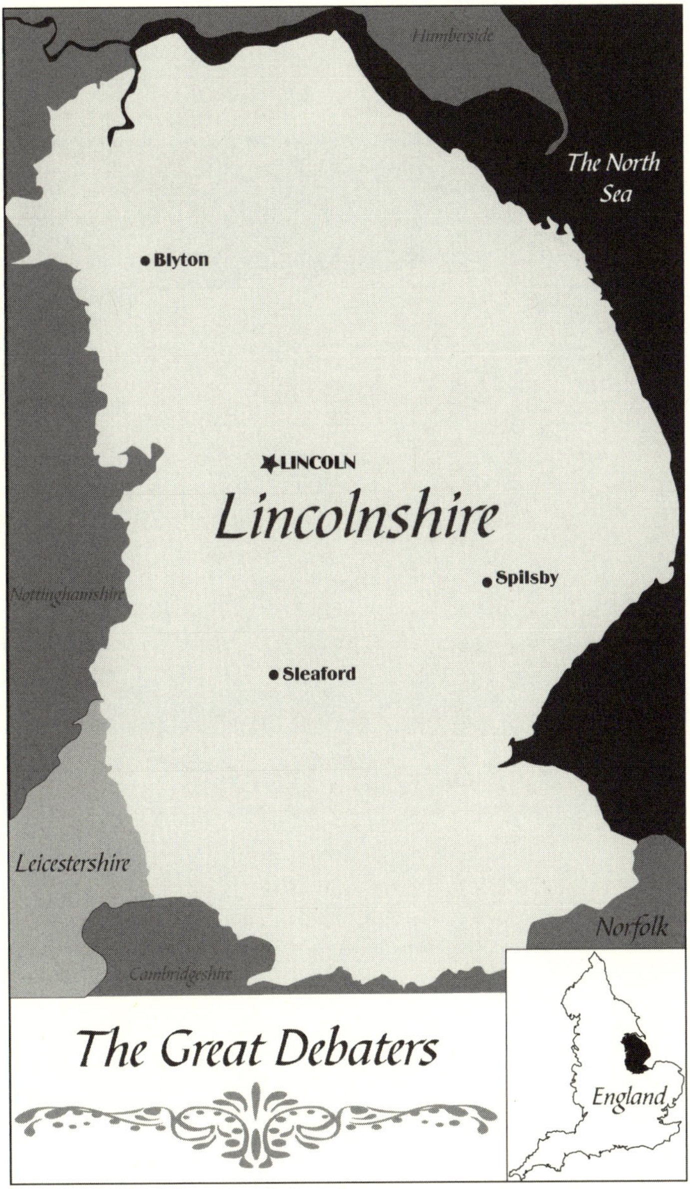

The Great Debaters

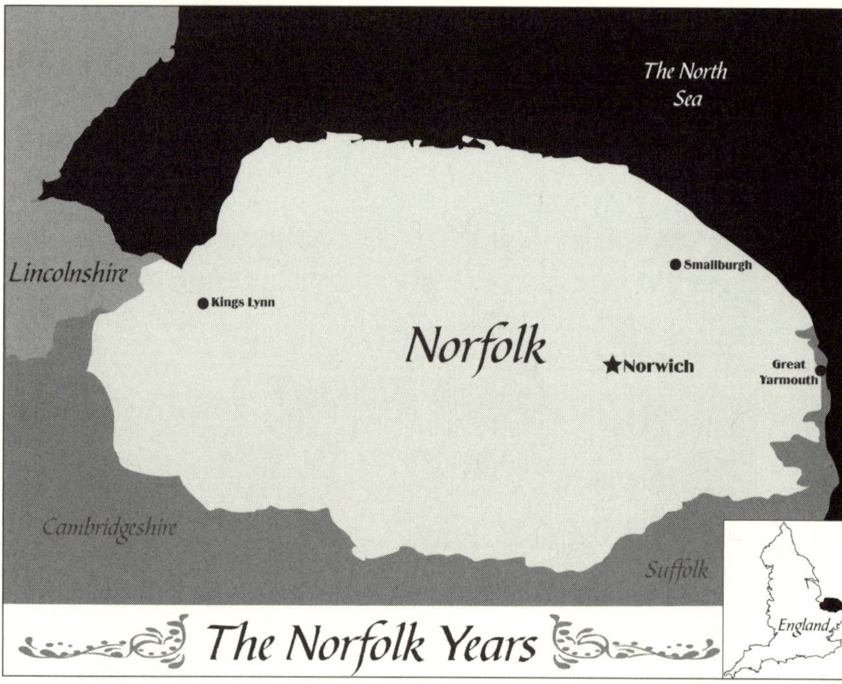
The North Sea
Lincolnshire
Kings Lynn
Smallburgh
Norfolk
Norwich
Great Yarmouth
Cambridgeshire
Suffolk
England
The Norfolk Years

Exterior of St. Stephen's Church, Norwich, western view

Exterior of St. Stephen's Church, Norwich, north tower

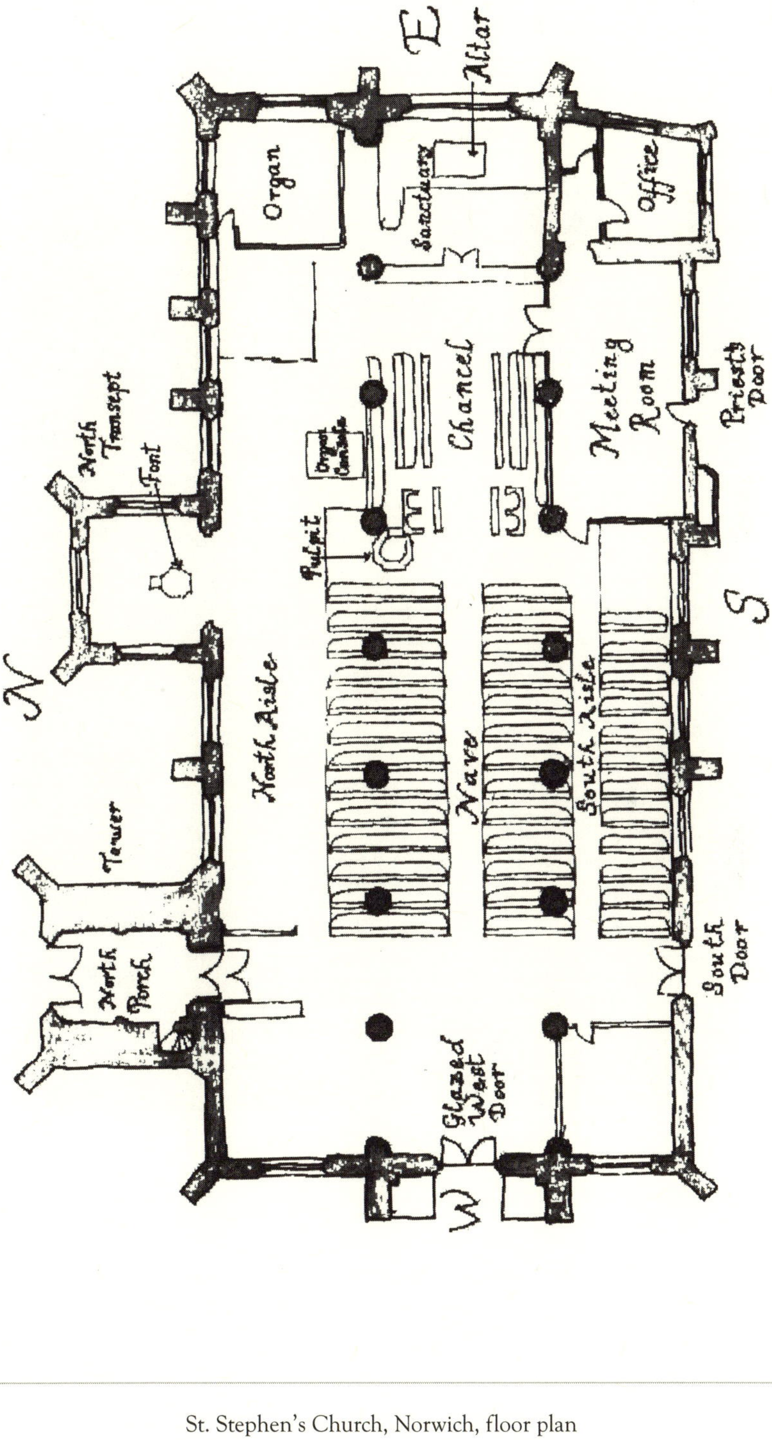

St. Stephen's Church, Norwich, floor plan

Interior of St. Stephen's Church, Norwich, western view

Introduction

Thomas Grantham after Three Hundred Years

This study testifies to the legacy of Thomas Grantham, the depths of which cannot be plumbed in a single volume. The findings presented here are in some sense an invitation to give Grantham a voice in the future, to let the history of which he is a part surprise and challenge. His is a story of a teenager being asked to lead a congregation. His is a story of kings and prisons. His is a story of leadership in the midst of tumultuous and uncertain times. His is a story of telling others there is a better way. Through printing, preaching, debating, and representing congregations in the counties of Lincolnshire and Norfolk, Grantham contributed to the process by which a regional, sectarian affiliation of General Baptist congregations became a legitimate dissenting presence in England by the end of the seventeenth century. Now, more than three hundred years after his death, a history of Thomas Grantham is necessary.

Any account of the life and ministry of Thomas Grantham must locate him in Lincolnshire, the county in which he was born and lived most of his life. The chapter "At Home in Lincolnshire County" surveys life in the large, rural county of Lincolnshire up to the Restoration of 1660. Lincolnshire residents faced a number of economic and political challenges that strained the rural county's relationship with the crown. Because of its size and relatively weak ecclesiastical discipline, Lincolnshire was home to several sectarian religious groups in the seventeenth century. The Baptists were one of the groups to establish a significant dissenting presence in the county.

When Thomas Grantham was baptized into the Baptist congregation gathered at Boston, Lincolnshire in 1652, he joined a sectarian General Baptist movement that had enjoyed a congregational presence in the county since at least 1626. When Grantham began his public career as a minister in the late 1650s, the anti-predestinarian Baptist presence in Lincolnshire claimed multiple congregations, lively theological disagreements, and a vibrant mobile group of capable ministers.

The chapter "A Man and His Remains" provides an updated and thorough biographical and literary sketch of Thomas Grantham's life (see also Appendix I). This study provides the reader with as much biographical information as possible *and* uses the available information to fashion a coherent narrative focused on key aspects of Grantham's ministry. An examination of the local records in Lincolnshire, for example, challenges older claims of his birth place and family history and instead traces Grantham's history to the village of Hatton, Lincolnshire, where he was almost certainly born to one William Grantham in 1633/4. William Grantham's will strengthens his connections to the illustrious General Baptist Thomas Grantham, for in it one finds that William was a tailor by trade and had a son named Thomas. Additionally, the will of Thomas Grantham himself will be introduced for the first time as a valuable resource for knowledge related to Grantham's family background and dynamics. Grantham's own will reveals a great deal about the specifics of Grantham's family and occupation: (1) he was married to Bridget; (2) he had at least five sons; (3) he was a farmer; (4) he owned land in Hundelby, Ashby by Partney, and Halton-Holegeate; and (4) he ratified his will in Sutterby, implying he owned land there as well. When Thomas Grantham died in the county of Norfolk in 1692, he left behind a lifetime of congregational service, ministerial travels, appearances before royalty, imprisonments, public theological disputes, and a distinguished literary corpus. The biographical findings provided in "A Man and His Remains" add much to the historical portrait of Thomas Grantham first begun by Thomas Crosby in the eighteenth century.

Scholars have rightly identified Grantham's wide-ranging literary corpus as a major theological achievement, and there is strong evidence that Grantham's writings greatly affected the trajectory of General Baptist theology in the seventeenth century and beyond. Still, most surveys of Grantham's life have either highlighted select published documents or listed the titles of his published documents. A major benefit of the chapter "A Man and His Remains" is that the interested reader now has a biographical narrative that contextualizes and summarizes all known documents published or signed by Grantham. As a result, it is possible to see Grantham's publication history arranged in the context of his other ministerial activities carried out in accordance with the office of messenger.

Questions and debates concerning church polity persisted throughout Grantham's ministry. The chapter "Old Things by their Old Names" expands on the work of John F. V. Nicholson by examining Grantham's role in consolidating the office of messenger and establishing it as a third ministerial office among the General Baptists in the seventeenth century. Convinced that a correct reading of the scriptures called for a third ordained office, that of "messenger," in addition to deacons and elders, Grantham labored extensively to restore the apostolic office among the baptized believers in his care. It is clear that he considered messengers to be successors of the original twelve apostles, yet he also insisted that messengers did not inherit all aspects of the ministry entrusted to the original twelve. The tasks they did share, Grantham argued, included itinerant elements such as preaching the gospel in all places, founding new churches, and defending the gospel.

Grantham contributed in several ways to the establishment of the office of messenger among many General Baptist congregations between 1660 and 1700. His published defenses of the messenger's office between 1671 and 1692 constitute perhaps the greatest source of information pertaining to the office of messenger and its place among the sectarian General Baptists of the post-Restoration decades. His best and most detailed treatment of the subject was *A Defence of the Offices of Apostles* (originally published in 1671; re-published again in 1674 and 1678 with similar titles). From these documents and the records of his activities as a messenger, it is clear that Grantham was committed to solidifying the office to which he had been ordained.

The congregations with which Grantham worked had a distinct process for electing and ordaining messengers. Ordained messengers served under the authority of their own local congregations, yet their ordination service reflected an inter-congregational cooperation as it consisted of a gathering of elders and other messengers. Ideally, according to Grantham, General Baptist messengers worked in conjunction with local congregations—especially those they planted—to preach, baptize, celebrate the Lord's Supper, ordain, arbitrate, and defend the faith. Due in large part to Grantham's tenacious commitment to his role as a messenger, by the end of the seventeenth century General Baptists were enjoying a strong presence in Lincolnshire and pioneering a permanent presence in the county of Norfolk.

Grantham expended considerable energy as a messenger fulfilling a primary role of the office: defending the gospel against attacks. He developed a reputation as a capable defender of the baptized believers and was called upon to contend with other Christian groups by means of public debates and correspondence. The chapter on "The Great Debaters" focuses in particular on Grantham's apologetic interactions with Anglicans, Roman Catholics, Quakers, and Presbyterians. In the cases of William Fort (Anglican) and an unnamed Roman Catholic, Grantham was encouraged to respond on behalf of the baptized believers in Lincolnshire. As the correspondence with the Presbyterian John Collinges of Norwich shows, Grantham also initiated contact via epistolary correspondence in order to address the ever-popular theological issue of God's sovereignty.

Knowledge of Grantham's debates and interactions with non-Baptist opponents is primarily derived from his own publications, though much helpful information was recorded by his adversaries. He was ever willing to engage opponents in apologetic dialogue and publish transcripts or summaries of the exchanges. As one might expect, Grantham's presentation of the disputes portrayed the Baptist position in a favorable light, but even so it is clear that he had acquired considerable expertise in formal public debate. In the debate with the Anglican William Fort, for example, Grantham exhibited command of debate protocol. When recounting his debate with the Quaker John Whitehead, Grantham described his own debate demeanor as calm and collected opposite

Whitehead's quick temper. Taken together, Grantham's many disputes and the documents describing them point to the public nature of religious discourse among the various dissenting groups of the later seventeenth century.

The chapter "God, Government, and King" examines Grantham's posture towards magistrates and government. His own actions and writings stand as but one example of the actions and thoughts of the General Baptist population he represented throughout his ministry. Practically speaking, Grantham and his congregations saw in the crown a potential guardian. Grantham petitioned King Charles II on behalf of the persecuted General Baptists in Lincolnshire in 1660, 1661, and 1672. In addition, Grantham joined many other Baptist ministers in choosing to accept a government-issued preacher's license under the conditions of the Declaration of Indulgence in 1672. In Norfolk he instructed other Baptists to take a similar path in 1689 and register a meeting place for worship according to the Toleration Act. In all of this, Grantham steadily guided the General Baptists in Lincolnshire and Norfolk to work with the civil authorities in pursuit of peace and order.

Like many Baptists of the period, Grantham's writings evince a willingness to cooperate with civil authorities as much as possible. There is documentary evidence in *The Loyal Baptist* (1674) and *Christianismus Primitivus* (1678) that in both belief and practice the baptized believers sought to be loyal and peaceful citizens. In these documents Grantham unequivocally instructed his readers to avoid revolution or sedition. They were to obey the laws enacted by civil rulers and uphold the common good. He did, however, qualify the loyalty by confessing that Baptists would, if necessary, obey the laws of God if they came into conflict with the laws established by earthly magistrates.

Grantham's writings also addressed General Baptist understandings of civil service, military service, marriage, poor relief, and use of cemeteries. Grantham allowed that Christians could hold government positions and serve in a nation's military. His treatment of General Baptist marriages suggest that his fellow dissenters conducted their own marriage ceremonies because they were excluded from Anglican ceremonies. Grantham argued that because General Baptists, like other citizens, paid taxes for poor relief and the upkeep of cemeteries, they were to enjoy equal access to governmental benefits. Grantham's positions on these issues suggest that many of the Baptists with whom he associated were—or sought to be—integrated into parish life. Far from desiring to overturn society, Grantham argued that the baptized believers supported the welfare of England and its people.

Chapter 1

At Home in Lincolnshire County

A journey around England's eastern county of Lincolnshire would wind through scenic hills and valleys of The Wolds before descending into the delicate marshy Fenlands that border the North Sea. Should one pass near or through cities and towns bearing the names Lincoln, Boston, Spilsby, Hatton, Sutterby, or Louth, be aware that Thomas Grantham (1633/34–92) traversed these very hills and navigated these same marshes in the seventeenth century.

Temptations to contextualize the Baptists and other Dissenters in relation to the crown or parliamentary policies are strong and often justified, but it is imperative to remember that the enforcement of such policies was almost always carried out at the local level.[1] Thus, any treatment of Thomas Grantham must take into account his primary local context: the county of Lincolnshire. To discover the county of Lincolnshire, then, is to locate Thomas Grantham.

Lincolnshire at the Restoration of 1660

James VI of Scotland became King James I of England in 1603, and at that time many local officials wondered to what extent the crown would seek to influence local politics. If the king's religious policy was an accurate predictor of things to come, then James's decision to convene a meeting with bishops and a number of Puritans at Hampton Court Palace in early 1604 indicated his intention to exercise a great degree of control

---

[1] William G. Hoskins (*English Local History: The Past and the Future* [Leicester UK: Leicester University Press, 1966]) and Lawrence Stone ("English and United States Local History," *Daedalus* [Winter 1971]: 128–32) were the principal originators of the modern examination of local history.

over the localities. In response to those Puritan grievances outlined and delivered to the king in the form of the Millenary Petition, James conceded almost nothing and instead insisted that those ceremonies and vestments despised by the Puritans remain in place. The crown further demanded complete conformity to its wishes by 30 November 1604.

William Chaderton, Bishop of Lincoln from 1595 until his death in 1608, encouraged conformity in Lincolnshire but was ultimately unwilling to deprive those nonconforming ministers of their positions and livings. By 1606, central pressures to hold ministers accountable to *The Book of Common Prayer* had subsided in the county to the point that Puritan types such as the clergyman John Cotton (d. 1652) enjoyed some level of toleration.[2] Royal policies were largely unpopular at the local level, and it appears the king's monetary interest in local affairs, which was occasional and sporadic, resulted in a growing suspicion of the crown during the next decade.[3]

The succession of King Charles I in 1625 ushered in new concerns and exacerbated existing ones in counties like Lincolnshire. History of Lincolnshire scholar Clive Holmes detailed several ways in which royal policy during the personal rule (i.e., rule without Parliament) of Charles I directly impacted citizens and rulers in Lincolnshire: fen drainage, ship money, forced loans, the Book of Orders, and the Bishop's War.[4]

An issue particular to Lincolnshire in the opening decades of the seventeenth century was growing external pressure for more agricultural land. Engineers proposed digging a series of canals by which the marshy wetlands known as the Fenlands would become arable land. The proposal to drain the fens was unpopular in rural eastern Lincolnshire, where traditionally the fens had functioned as common land suitable for a pastoral economy. Charles I was himself the lord of two manors in the

---

[2] Clive Holmes, *Seventeenth-Century Lincolnshire* (Lincoln UK: Society for Lincolnshire History and Archaeology, 1980) 96. Cotton served as a minister of the established church in Boston, Lincolnshire, before his Puritan leanings led him in 1633 to depart for America, where he was active in the Massachusetts Bay Colony.

[3] Holmes, *Seventeenth-Century Lincolnshire*, 102.

[4] Ibid., chapter 8.

county, both of which happened to be situated in the midst of fen-heavy areas. In order to increase his own income from those manors, the king opened the way for outside investors to drain the fens, thus altering significant amounts of the common land worked by peasants and other manual laborers.[5] A study of peasant farming in Lincolnshire during this period found that the loss of land through fen drainage was a challenge for Fenland farmers like Thomas Grantham.[6]

In addition to enduring the drainage of their fens, Lincolnshire residents were also forced to support financially a growing military force. England had managed to remain out of the fray of the Thirty Years War until 1624, but eventual involvement prompted Charles I to insist on the formation of a well-trained and well-equipped army. The development of such a fighting force required significant financial support, not to mention considerable energy and local cooperation in collecting the new tax. Landowners in Lincolnshire were required to pay a penny an acre for each muster, or official summoning of troops. Under James I musters were infrequent and the cost manageable, but under Charles I musters occurred weekly and amounted to significant payments.[7] The strain of these royal demands for military support only served to alienate Lincolnshire citizens further from the crown.

An additional factor in the decline in royal popularity among many citizens of eastern Lincolnshire was an increase in yet another financial burden: ship money. Charles's decision to require towns and counties to provide additional money for expenses related to the navy incited strong

---

[5] For a detailed discussion, see Joan Thirsk, *English Peasant Farming: The Agrarian History of Lincolnshire from Tudor to Recent Times* (New York: Methuen, 1957) 108–41. See also Holmes, *Seventeenth-Century Lincolnshire*, 130.

[6] Thirsk, *English Peasant Farming,* 108. See also William Page, ed., *The Victoria County History of Lincoln*, (London: Archibald Constable, 1906) 332–34. The Victoria County History is a series of volumes devoted to documenting the history of people and places in England on a county-by-county basis. Only a single volume on Lincolnshire has appeared (1906), but it was mistakenly numbered in the printing process as volume 2.

[7] Holmes, *Seventeenth-Century Lincolnshire*, 104–5.

negative reactions to the crown in coastal counties like Lincolnshire.[8] Citizens initially refused to pay, and some even resisted to the point of imprisonment, but threats and punishments usually led to payment in full. It has been pointed out that increased attention to the payment of ship money, which affected a larger percentage of a county's population, promoted a greater political awareness among the average citizens.[9]

One aspect of Caroline rule that was received with some respect was the issuance of the Book of Orders in 1631. Though the Book of Orders contained nothing original, it was an attempt by Charles to compel local magistrates to enforce specific but neglected statutes that had been in place for decades. The legislation included poor relief, alehouse licenses, wage rates, enclosure policies, and repairs for roads. Records suggest that the various laws were initially strictly enforced under the Tudor dynasty, but in subsequent years enforcement seems to have waned.[10]

When considered alongside the crown's imposition of fen drainage, muster taxes, and the collection of ship money, the promotion of William Laud (d. 1645) to the position of Archbishop of Canterbury in 1633 (a position he held until his execution) was a monumental if controversial step for Charles I where Lincolnshire was concerned. John Williams (d. 1650), Bishop of Lincoln from 1621 until 1641, had disagreements with Laud dating back to the 1620s. Williams resisted any proliferation of Arminian influence in Lincolnshire, and so under his leadership the diocese fell far short of Laud's vision for the Church of England.

---

[8] Thomas G. Barnes wrote that "no other secular program attempted by Charles and his Council during the 'personal rule' appears so foolhardy as ship money," *Somerset, 1625–1640* (Cambridge MA: Harvard University Press, 1961) 203. See Holmes, *Seventeenth-Century Lincolnshire,* 130–40, for specific reactions to the demand for ship money in Lincolnshire.

[9] Roger Lockyer, *The Early Stuarts: A Political History of England 1603–1642* (New York: Longman House, 1989) 265–67.

[10] For the larger context of the issuance of the Book of Orders, see Barry Coward, *The Stuart Age: England, 1603–1704* (New York: Pearson Education, 2003) 169–70. The unavailability of records related to the implementation of the Book of Orders is unfortunate, but Barnes's study of Somerset may exhibit a pattern present elsewhere (*Somerset*, 172–202). For the impact of the Book of Orders in Lincolnshire, see Holmes, *Seventeenth-Century Lincolnshire,* 109–12.

Williams's hesitancy to enforce and apply Laudian reforms in Lincolnshire led to the bishop's rather public and nasty conviction before the royal court known as the Star Chamber in 1636.[11] In his absence, Laud took over direct control of the diocese himself for a few years until Williams was reinstated for short time in 1640 and 1641. This series of events only exacerbated the growing distance between crown and county.

Finally, the circumstances surrounding what is commonly termed The Bishops' War (1639–40) also did much to erode allegiance to, and popularity for, the crown. Charles I took measures to raise an army in an attempt to stave off the Scottish rebellion. First, many objected to his decision to replace local military leaders with professional soldiers, but there was also doubt that the methods of choosing, training, and sustaining the troops could actually produce a fighting force capable of resisting the Scots. Lincolnshire, like many other counties, experienced various hostile reactions to royal attempts to raise yet more money and recruit soldiers. Leaders ranging from sheriffs to constables actively avoided collecting money or forcing conscription. By the conflict's conclusion, Charles I was without support, and it was clear that the end of his personal rule without parliament was rapidly approaching.

When the realities of civil war appeared in 1641 and 1642, the House of Commons divided over how far it should go in its rejection of Charles I. Of Lincolnshire's twelve ministers elected to Parliament, ten sided with the William Pym-led majority of Ministers to Parliament who favored greater restrictions on royal prerogative.[12] Back in Lincolnshire there was no clear consensus regarding the measures proposed in the House of Commons. Holmes pointed out that popular sentiment at the time is difficult to measure, but the equivocations of many "demonstrate that in Lincolnshire, as in other counties, there was no enthusiastic, universal commitment to either side."[13] Holmes went on to say that county elections in 1640 exhibited a desire for Parliament to enact

[11] For a discussion of the Williams-Laud affair, see Hugh R. Trevor-Roper, *Archbishop Laud, 1573–1645* (London: MacMillan, 1963) 179–84; 325–32.

[12] Holmes, *Seventeenth-Century Lincolnshire*, 142–43.

[13] Ibid., 149.

reforms, but as the year wore on parliamentary support was sapped on account of Pym's increasingly radical plans, the self-interests of the wealth citizens and nobility, and a sense of basic loyalty to the crown.[14] Thus, a young Thomas Grantham spent his childhood in a county frequently caught in a back-and-forth struggle for supremacy in the years leading up to the outbreak of the First Civil War in 1642.

Lincolnshire's place in the larger narrative of the war is noteworthy because, as *The Victoria County History of Lincoln* put it, Oliver Cromwell's "military genius first received public recognition" at the important Battle of Winceby in 1643, which took place in a small village just a few miles from Thomas Grantham's birthplace (see map 1).[15] Parliamentarians held the upper hand in Lincolnshire in the years following the decisive victory at Winceby despite persistent annoyances originating in the royalist stronghold of Newark, located just across the border to the east in Lincolnshire's neighboring county of Nottinghamshire. With Newark as a base, royal supporters engaged in constant raiding and plundering of the Lincolnshire countryside. Thus, when Newark finally fell to the parliamentarians in 1646, the royalist presence in Lincolnshire ceased significantly.

During the First Civil War, the local administration of governmental duties was restructured in the counties to reflect a growing "associational" model of parliamentary cooperation. Thus, after 1645 Lincolnshire was administered by a county committee as a member of the Eastern Association (which also included nearby counties such as Suffolk, Norfolk, and Cambridgeshire). In time, however, these committees came to be hated on account of their oversensitivity to the desires of Westminster and insensitivity to local concerns.[16]

Lincolnshire was not a major battlefield during the Second Civil War (1648–49), though there were two military engagements within the

---

[14] Ibid., 150–51.

[15] Page, *The Victoria County History of Lincoln*, 282–83. Cromwell has often been credited with providing key leadership and direction at the Battle of Winceby in October 1643.

[16] Holmes, *Seventeenth-Century Lincolnshire*, 193.

county. Talk of royalist plots in the county surfaced, prompting Parliament to send additional troops, but whatever plots there may have been never materialized. The end of the Second Civil War in September 1648 and the stunning execution of King Charles I in early 1649 ushered in an eleven-year period during which England had no monarch and was instead generally thought of as a Commonwealth (i.e., a republic) ruled by a Lord Protector (i.e., supreme ruler).

These shifts in leadership were received rather coolly in Lincolnshire, perhaps because of continuing high taxes and burdens related to supporting a persistent presence of soldiers in the county. In addition, that such circumstances created space and freedom for various religious expressions to maneuver, recruit, and grow only served to magnify questions of security and stability. The Commonwealth-Protectorate years of 1649–60 did, however, provide Dissenters of all stripes in Lincolnshire with opportunities for growth and expansion.

Weakened ecclesiastical discipline at the parish level during the war years paved the way for a more pluralistic religious landscape in Lincolnshire. One study found that the Lincolnshire was "eminently suitable" for the proliferation of sectarian groups on account of it size and the meager wages of parish clergy.[17] In fact, it appears that Dissenters in Lincolnshire gained such a foothold during this period that by the time of the Restoration in 1660 there was a "comparatively large body of organized dissent" standing outside the established Church.[18] The Baptists, to whom a teen-aged Thomas Grantham joined himself in the 1650s, were certainly among those groups that gained adherents and influence in the new religious situation. Several Baptists congregations emerged in Lincolnshire during this period, including one in Boston in 1651 where Thomas Grantham was baptized only a year later in 1652.

Parliament offered to make Oliver Cromwell King of England in 1657, but he refused and opted instead to enact a new constitution whereby he ruled in a modified executive role until his death in

---

[17] Jesse Plumb, "Early Nonconformity in Lincolnshire," from the Summary. See also Holmes, *Seventeenth-Century Lincolnshire*, 198ff.

[18] Page, *The Victoria County History of Lincoln*, 67.

September 1658. Cromwell's popularity in Lincolnshire had certainly declined by the time of his death, but it is telling that upon news of his death in a group of approximately 6,000 Lincolnshire men agreed, in an encomium published in the weekly pro-Cromwellian newspaper *Mercurius Politicus*, that Richard Cromwell, Oliver's son, was inheriting a "peaceable and prosperous government."[19]

Richard Cromwell, however, proved far less capable as a Lord Protector than his father. His inability to maintain peace and prosperity resulted in a brief rule of less than nine months, at which point Parliament was recalled, the Protectorate was rejected, and some whispered of the return of a king. When the monarchy was restored in 1660 and Charles II had taken the throne of England, Baptists in Lincolnshire almost immediately petitioned the king for assistance in addressing the injustices being imposed upon them by their enemies. The last name on the petition is that of a young man, Thomas Grantham, who, though only twenty-six years old, delivered the document into the king's hand. Such was the beginning of Grantham's public ministry.

Baptists in Lincolnshire at the Restoration of 1660

Baptist beginnings in the county of Lincolnshire will always be connected to the life and ministry of John Smyth (d. 1612), who has been credited with founding the Baptist movement in 1609 when he baptized himself in Amsterdam. Smyth's relationship with Lincolnshire, however, predates his Baptist days. Not only was he born in the county, but Smyth also held ecclesial positions in two prominent Lincolnshire cities. In the city of Lincoln, the capital of Lincolnshire, he served as city lecturer for the established Church from 1600–02. Smyth soon left the Church of England in 1606 and took a position with a Separatist congregation in the market town of Gainsborough, his last stop before migrating to Holland in 1608.

Despite Smyth's ties to Lincolnshire, the Baptist story in the county does not begin with him. Archival work in Lincolnshire has uncovered

---

[19] *Mercurius Politicus*, 559 (17–24 March 1659): 308.

evidence of a Baptist presence in the county at least as early as 1618. In that year, Thomas Lauton of St. Benedict Parish was brought before a church court as an alleged "Anabaptist" who refused to attend parish worship services.[20] It also seems that an unlicensed school operated by an excommunicated "Anabaptist" named Peter Finch existed in Lincoln by 1623, but details of the school and its curriculum are unavailable.[21] It is not altogether clear that "Anabaptists" such as Lauton or Finch were, in fact, Baptists, but it was a common practice for opponents to label them as Anabaptists. In addition, no fewer than eight extant wills that belonged to known Baptists were ratified in Lincoln between 1628 and 1649.[22] These wills reveal that some of the earliest individual Baptists in Lincolnshire worked as bakers, weavers, brewers, tailors, and musicians.

Clues pertaining to Baptist congregational beginnings in Lincolnshire can be found in (1) the 1626 correspondence between five congregations in England and the Waterlanders (Mennonites) in Amsterdam and (2) extant notes made by the Waterlanders concerning the congregations in England.[23] Several relevant insights about early Baptists in Lincolnshire can be gleaned from these documents. First, the

---

[20] Local historian Robert Kershaw found details of Lauton's court appearance in the official records of the bishop's visitations in 1618, "Baptised Believers: Lincolnshire Baptists in Times of Persecution, Revolution and Toleration, 1600–1700" (Master's thesis, University of Nottingham, 1995) 8. On the question of Baptist origins, there is general agreement among historians that the Baptists first emerged out of the English Separatist ranks, but the question of Anabaptist influence remains. For discussions of Anabaptist influence, see Lonnie Kliever, "General Baptist Origins: The Question of Anabaptist Influence," *Mennonite Quarterly Review* 36, no. 4 (October 1962): 291–321; and Glen H. Stassen," Anabaptist Influence in the Origin of The Particular Baptists," *Mennonite Quarterly Review* 36, no. 4 (October 1962): 322–48.

[21] Kershaw, "Baptised Believers," 8.

[22] Ibid., 9.

[23] The five cities named were London, Lincoln, Sarum (i.e., Salisbury), Coventry, and Tiverton. There was also a letter was sent from Amsterdam to Lincoln in 1630. To read the Waterlander notes in translation, see Benjamin Evans, *Early English Baptists*, 2 vols. (London: J. Heaton & Son, 1864) 2.21–44. See also Barrington R. White, *The English Baptists of the Seventeenth Century* (London: Baptist Historical Society, 1996) 23–24.

city of Lincoln was home to an anti-predestinarian Baptist congregation as early as 1626, though nothing is known of when or how this group formed or if it had links to John Smyth. Second, the Lincoln congregation may not have had its own minister, and if it did not, then it was coordinating with one or more of the other five congregations to schedule a ministerial visit. Third, congregations that did not have ministers apparently only celebrated the Lord's Supper on those Sundays when a minister was present. Fourth, the congregations appeared to have restricted the teaching office to those gifted and able to teach. All of this suggests that Baptist life in the city of Lincoln was established and somewhat organized by at least 1626.

Tracking the growth of Baptist life beyond the city of Lincoln is more difficult. Dissenters enjoyed greater freedom of movement, gathering, and open disagreement during the Commonwealth-Protectorate years (1649–60). Lincolnshire native Hanserd Knollys (d. 1691) was a tireless preacher and leader in his home county before he moved to London and joined a Particular Baptist congregation in the mid-1640s, but his legacy in Lincolnshire is largely a pre-Baptist one.[24] Similarly, Samuel Oates (d. 1683), who broke ties with the Baptists toward the end of his life, actively championed a sectarian General Baptist cause in Lincolnshire in the 1640s.[25]

---

[24] For the life and ministry of Hanserd Knollys in his own words, see his posthumously published autobiography, *The Life and Death of that Old Disciple of Jesus Christ and Eminent Minister of the Gospel, Mr Hanserd Knollys* (London, 1692). Recent studies of Knollys include Dennis Bustin's *Paradox and Perseverance: Hanserd Knollys, Particular Baptist Pioneer in Seventeenth-Century England* (Waynesboro GA: Paternoster Press, 2006) and Michael A. G. Haykin's *Kiffin, Knollys, and Keach: Rediscovering Our English Baptist Heritage* (Leeds UK: Reformation Today Trust, 1996). For details on Samuel Oates, see Stephen Wright's entry "Oates, Samuel (bap. 1614, d. 1683)" in the *Oxford Dictionary of National Biography*.

[25] Murray Tolmie's social-scientific study employed sectarian language when describing the anti-predestinarian General Baptists of the seventeenth century as the only group of separate churches to form outside of the influence of separatist minister Henry Jacob (*The Triumph of the Saints: The Separate Churches of London 1616–1649* [New York: Cambridge University Press, 1977] 3–4). Based on a

By 1646 small Baptist congregations appeared at Scotter in the north and Spalding in the south (see map 1). Extant records of the Baptists gathered at Fenstanton, in neighboring Cambridgeshire, reflect a robust relationship between it and several Baptist congregations in Lincolnshire in the seventeenth century. The Cambridge-educated Henry Denne (d. 1666) was a significant supporter of the General Baptist presence in and around Lincolnshire. He was involved with the establishment of a Baptist presence around Fenstanton in the early 1640s and was later arrested in Spalding, Lincolnshire, in 1646 for baptizing converts in the river.[26] Elsewhere in Lincolnshire, in the area of Bourne (see map 1), Denne assisted the Baptist congregation gathered around Thurlby and Langtoft in a debate with an unnamed "priest."[27]

Leaders like Samuel Oates and Henry Denne were responsible for what little General Baptist momentum there was in Lincolnshire by the 1640s, but it was not until the 1650s that General Baptist numbers and organization began to increase in the county. It was also about this time that divisions began to emerge among the General Baptists themselves. The interaction between the congregations at Westby and Fenstanton

---

predominantly rural membership base, loose organization practices, radical outlook, and a more fluid membership, Tolmie concluded that the General Baptist congregations "stood at the edge of organized sectarianism" (80). Interpreting the General Baptist movement in sectarian terms helps in understanding Thomas Grantham's ministry and leadership in the second half of the seventeenth century. Such conclusions might also shed light on Grantham's apparent lack of interaction or concern with the more Calvinistic Particular Baptists who emerged within the Henry Jacob circle.

[26] Thomas Crosby, *The History of the English Baptists*, 4 vols. (London, 1738) 1.222, 305. Denne had been a Church of England clergyman before joining the Baptists. Denne's influence was far-reaching, for even the independent thinker and writer Lucy Hutchinson (d. 1681), widow of Colonel John Hutchinson (d. 1664), wrote that she found published arguments against infant baptism by Denne and John Tombes (d. 1676) to be biblical and convincing (James Sutherland, ed., *Memoirs of the Life of Colonel Hutchinson* [New York: E. P. Dutton & Co., 1973] 238.

[27] The debate took place in Caistor sometime before 1653. See Edward B. Underhill, ed., *Records of the Churches of Christ Gathered at Fenstanton, Warboys, and Hexham, 1644–1720* (London: Haddon Brothers, 1854) 63–65.

reveal a great deal about the state of Baptist affairs in Lincolnshire in the years just before the Restoration of 1660.

In 1653 the congregation gathered at Westby, Lincolnshire (see map 1), commissioned two messengers, John Lupton and Joseph Wright, to enter neighboring counties and "call in question all persons, and to judge and determine all matters."[28] The Baptists in Westby soon became concerned about the conduct of their messengers and so in August sent a letter of inquiry to the congregation at Fenstanton. In addition to a concern with the messengers, the Baptists in Westby were also troubled by Fenstanton's willingness to maintain communion with those who had not received the laying on of hands and the practice of observing the Lord's Supper *after* the meal.[29] The Fenstanton Baptists insisted in their reply that they always sought to uphold biblical doctrine, but they also expressed a desire to act patiently with those who required further instruction.[30] Outright rejection of those who had not accepted the laying on of hands, they wrote, would only lead to excessive division and separation within the church. Just a few months later the Westby congregation itself had become deeply divided over whether bread was to be broken in remembrance of Christ before or after the meal, at which time the congregation wrote to the Fenstanton church inviting Henry Denne to come mediate and restore unity.[31]

The laying on of hands was also an issue in the Thurlby-Langtoft congregation, gathered in the southern region of Lincolnshire. Henry Denne had assisted the believers there in putting the congregation "into order,"[32] but a dispute later broke out when the pastor Robert Wright avowed views in favor of the laying on of hands. The congregation at large did not agree with Wright, but the two sides were able to coexist for several months. Wright and his wife eventually separated from the congregation and insisted on the necessity of the imposition of hands,

---

[28] *Records of the Churches of Christ Gathered at Fenstanton*, 60ff.

[29] Ibid.

[30] Ibid., 69.

[31] Ibid., 136.

[32] *Records of the Churches of Christ Gathered at Fenstanton*. 64.

foot washing, and partaking of a feast *before* celebrating the Lord's Supper. The Thurlby-Langtoft congregation took measures to discipline Wright and his followers but sought the advice of the Fenstanton congregation before excommunicating them. The episode concluded with representatives from the Fenstanton successfully reconciling the two sides.[33]

It is clear from this brief overview that by mid-century there were a number of General Baptist congregations in and around Lincolnshire. They were not all of one mind. Disagreements centered on the questions regarding the role and number of ordained officers in the church, the imposition of hands, the place of foot washing, the placement of the feast in relation to the Lord's Supper. Church offices and the laying on of hands were two critical issues on which General Baptists continued to disagree throughout the remainder of the seventeenth century. Yet it is clear that the congregations communicated with one another, sought advice from one another, assisted one another in debates and internal disputes, and were even hesitant to take drastic disciplinary measures without consulting other congregations. Evident in these circumstances were the seeds of associational patterns of inter-congregational relationship and a vibrant traveling ministry. The efforts of Denne, Oates, and others to assist a large number of regional congregations in the 1640s and 1650s were indicative of the mobile leadership given by General Baptist messengers in the following decades.

Given the fluid organizational and theological nature of the young sectarian General Baptist movement, one wonders about the opinions of those baptized believers with whom Grantham first interacted in the south marsh area of Lincolnshire. Details regarding his initial interaction with Baptists are limited, but his own theological and ecclesial womb was probably not unlike that of the Westby congregation. Like those baptized believers in Westby, Grantham advocated for the imposition of hands and granted considerable authority to the office of messenger. Grantham did not necessarily create new categories so much as he

---

[33] Ibid., 70–71.

strengthened and established those habits and practices already at work among many General Baptists in Lincolnshire. Historians Thomas Crosby and Adam Taylor thought it impossible to talk about seventeenth-century Baptists in Lincolnshire without referencing Grantham. They were correct, but the reader should bear in mind that Grantham was a son of Lincolnshire and the progeny of the General Baptists in that county. Grantham was born into a large, rural county with a history of heavy taxation and religious dissent. He was also born into a county with a small but growing number of General Baptists. Thomas Grantham was at home in Lincolnshire, so any examination of his remains must begin there.

Chapter 2

A Man and His Remains

Reconstructing the life of Thomas Grantham is no simple task. There is no known autobiography or biography written by one of his contemporaries. In the case of Grantham, however, the historians have access to more than twenty original writings. Though predominantly polemical in nature, these documents and those of Grantham's opponents provide many biographical details. Thomas Crosby's *History of the English Baptists* (1738–40)[1] includes the earliest known attempt at reconstructing the life and ministry of Thomas Grantham. The work of William Richard, Adam Taylor, and Joseph Ivimey from the early nineteenth century builds on and augments Crosby. While the historical interpretations of these authors are not always reliable, they constitute important sources for information related to the life, times, and legacy of

---

[1] Thomas Crosby, *The History of the English Baptists* (London, 1740) 3.75ff. A bibliography of Grantham's publications is available in William T. Whitley, ed., *A Baptist Bibliography, 1526–1837*, 2 vols. (London: Kingsgate Press, 1916–1922); and Edward C. Start, ed., *A Baptist Bibliography*, 25 vols. (Rochester NY: American Baptist Historical Society, 1947–1976) 9.101–6. A standard source for information regarding English publications during the second half of the seventeenth century is Donald Wing's *Short-Title Catalogue of Books Printed in England, Scotland, Ireland, Wales, and British America and of English Books Printed in other Countries 1641–1700*, 2nd ed. 4 vols. (New York: Modern Language Association of America, 1982) 2.157–58. For more information on documents cited in this study that were published prior to 1641, see A. W. Pollard and G. R. Redgrave, *A Short-title Catalogue of Books Printed in England, Scotland, and Ireland and of English Books Printed Abroad, 1475–1640*, 2nd ed. (London: Bibliographical Society, 1976). For a helpful introduction to the variety and locations of sources related to Baptist history in particular, see Susan J. Mills, "Sources for the Study of Baptist History," *Baptist Quarterly* 34, no. 6 (April 1992): 282–96.

Thomas Grantham. Perhaps the most important contribution made by the authors centers on the fact that they had before them documents and sources no longer available.

More recent biographical sketches, including the entry in the *Oxford Dictionary of National Biography* (hereafter *ODNB*) and the work of Robert Kershaw, are also helpful and provide a general framework for this chapter. The following reconstruction of Grantham's life and ministry is built on birth records, wills, Grantham's publications, the writings of his opponents, unpublished letters, and the studies by Crosby, Richard, Taylor, Ivimey, Kershaw, and the *ODNB*.[2]

---

[2] In addition to Crosby's *History of the English Baptists*, see the biographical introductions in an anonymous, thirty-two page, handwritten manuscript housed in Dr. Williams's Congregational Library, *Brief Notes Containing Memoirs of the Ministerial Acts, Particularly Such as relate to the Writings of that Servant of Christ, the Reverend Mr. Thomas Grantham Messenger of the Baptized Churches in Lincoln Shire of Blessed Memory*, (n.p., ca. 1690s); Adam Taylor, *The History of the English General Baptists* (London: T. Bore, 1818) 1.127–37, 185–218, and 307–17; the three-part article "A Memoir of Thomas Grantham," *General Baptist Repository and Missionary Observer* 4, no. 44 (1 August 1825): 281–86; 4, no. 45 (1 September 1825): 321–26; and 4, no. 46 (1 October 1825): 361–67; the four-part article by William Richard, "Biography of Thomas Grantham," *Universal Theological Magazine* 3, no. 13 (January 1805): 1–10; 3, no. 14 (February 1805): 57–68; 3, no. 15 (March 1805): 109–17; and 3, no. 16 (April 1805): 165–71; Joseph Ivimey, *A History of the English Baptists* 2.262–83; Edmund Oldfield, *A Topographical and Historical Account of Wainfleet and the Wapentake of Candleshoe, In the City of Lincoln* (Boston: Printed by John Noble, 1829) 355ff.; Alexander Gordon, "Grantham, Thomas (1634–1692)," *Dictionary of National Biography* (hereafter *DNB*), eds. Stephen and Sidney Lee, 63 vols. (London: Smith, Elder, & Co., 1890) 22:410–12; W. L. Johnson, Jr., and Richard L. Greaves, "Grantham, Thomas (1634–1692)," *Biographical Dictionary of British Radicals in the Seventeenth Century*, ed. Richard L. Greaves and Robert Zaller, 3 vols. (Brighton, England: Harvester Press, 1983) 2:23–24; A. C. Underwood, *A History of the English Baptists* (London: Kingsgate Press, 1947) 110–111; Barrington R. White, *The English Baptist of the Seventeenth Century* (London: Baptist Historical Society, 1996) 118–19; Robert R. Kershaw, "Baptised Believers: Lincolnshire Baptists in Times of Persecution, Revolution and Toleration, 1600–1700" (Master's thesis, University of Nottingham, 1995); Oscar C. Burdick, "Grantham, Thomas (1633/4–1692)," *Oxford Dictionary of National Biography*, http://www.oxforddnb.com/view/article/11298?docPos=2

Finding Thomas Grantham (1633/34–50)

Determining birth dates for those born in seventeenth-century England is an inexact science. Parish records and bishop's transcripts are the primary sources for this biographical information, but unfortunately these records are often incomplete, missing, or ambiguous. Where Thomas Grantham is concerned, the parish records and bishop's transcripts for this period in Lincolnshire include at least two different birth entries for "Thomas Grantham" in late 1633 and early 1634.[3] Both births occurred near Spilsby, a market town in a rural region of eastern Lincolnshire (see map 2). The *ODNB*, an oft-cited secondary source for information on Grantham, identified the "Thomas Grantham" born to Ralf and Elyzabeth Grantham in Spilsby on 15 April 1633 as a probable match.[4] These details of Grantham's birth have been repeated and assumed true in recent decades, yet there is reason to question the *ODNB*'s conclusion.

(accessed 3 September 2008); and Keith E. Durso, *No Armor for the Back* (Macon GA: Mercer University Press, 2007) 154–62. Later writers tended to draw heavily on Crosby, Taylor, and Ivimey.

[3] Though no existing primary source identifies either of these as Grantham's birth years, it is possible to determine his birth date by counting backward from his death in January 1692. His published dying words stated that he died at the age of fifty-eight. Determining precise birth dates for this period, for methods of dating could fluctuate depending on the context. C. R. Cheney's helpful *Handbook of Dates for Students of English History* (London: Offices of the Royal Historical Society, 1981) provides an introduction to date calculation methods during this period. It was common until 1752 to use 25 March (the day on which the Annunciation was also celebrated) as the beginning of the year, though in the seventeenth century 1 January was also a common starting point. Thus, Grantham occasionally specified which day it was on both calendars. So, those born in December 1633 and February 1634 can be considered to have the same birth year, though not the same Gregorian calendar year.

[4] Bishops Transcripts for Spilsby (1633/34), Lincolnshire Archives, Lincoln UK. Burdick, in his article for the *ODNB*, pointed to Spilsby, while Richard pointed to Halton, "Biography of Thomas Grantham," *Universal Theological Magazine* 3, no. 13 (January 1805): 2.

A survey of the bishop's transcripts for Hatton, a small village just under twenty miles to the northwest of Spilsby, reveals that a different "Thomas Grantham" was born to William Grantham and baptized on 27 January 1633/34.[5] A 1692 entry in *The Lincoln Date Book*, a record of notable events and people in Lincolnshire history up to circa 1866, included an obituary for one Thomas Grantham, "…born at Hatton near Spilsby, in 1634."[6] These two pieces of information are important for at least three reasons. First, the obituary itself includes a lengthy account of Grantham's activities in the years immediately following the Restoration of 1660. Second, the recorded location and date of birth in the bishop's transcript supply clues to Grantham's origins, for there were several men by the same name in Lincolnshire during the seventeenth century. Finally, this entry highlights the importance later Lincolnshire historians afforded the dissenting General Baptist Thomas Grantham. For Grantham to have been granted almost an entire page in this county history—along with bishops, ministers to parliament, knights, sheriffs, and others—is a monument to his immediate and long-term impact on religious life in Lincolnshire.

A second reason to question the *ODNB*'s conclusions about Grantham's birth is an extant Lincolnshire will for a William Grantham, dated 19 January 1657.[7] In this will, William Grantham named two sons, Thomas and Richard, as co-executors of his will. Perhaps more importantly, this will shows that William was employed as a tailor. This fact provides a strong connection to our Thomas Grantham, who wrote that in his youth he had the same employment as his father, "who was both a

---

[5] Bishops Transcripts for Hatton (1633/34), Lincolnshire Archives, Lincoln UK. The handwriting is unclear after William, but it does confirm that Thomas was born to a William in Hatton. Richard wrote that Grantham's house was still standing in the early nineteenth century ("Biography of Thomas Grantham," 2).

[6] *The Date Book for Lincoln and Neighbourhood* (Lincoln UK: R. E. Leary, 1866) 155.

[7] The Will of William Grantham, 19 January 1657 (W1662/i/364), Lincolnshire Archives, Lincoln UK.

Farmer and a Taylor."[8] Thus, it seems more than plausible that the William Grantham responsible for signing this will was Thomas Grantham's father.

If this hypothesis is correct, William's will may also indirectly provide a clue as to Thomas's place in the larger Grantham lineage in Lincolnshire. In his will, William left his best suit to his brother, also named Thomas Grantham. It is difficult to identify exactly which Thomas Grantham could have been William's brother. At least two Ministers to Parliament from Lincolnshire during the seventeenth century also were named Thomas Grantham.[9]

These few shreds of biographical detail may shed further light on Grantham's allusion to his family background and pedigree in the Dedicatory to his *Christianismus Primitivus*, which was addressed to his family:

> To my kinsmen according to the flesh, in the next place I address my Self; I mean the ancient of family of the Granthams in the county of Lincoln especially. How welcome such a Dedication will be to you I know not, and therefore shall not name you particularly, you being persons of Quality in this World, and my extraction being immediately from your poor Kindred, yet such as were acknowledged by your Progenitors. And though I am one of the lowest of my Father's House, yet let it not displease you to hear my Voice, whilst in these several Tractates I only bespeak you for God; and in order thereunto, beseech you to consider your standing in relation to Christianity, in respect of its Primitive Institution.[10]

From this excerpt it appears that Grantham's family held some place of esteem in Lincolnshire, though Grantham himself likely was among

[8] Thomas Grantham, *The Infants Advocate the Second Part* (London: 1690) 8. Grantham's humble origins were similar to those of other Baptist leaders such as William Kiffin and Benjamin Keach.

[9] See Clive Holmes, *Seventeenth-Century Lincolnshire* (Lincoln UK: History of Lincolnshire Committee for the Society for Lincolnshire History and Archaeology, 1980) 103–104, 140–43.

[10] Thomas Grantham, *Christianismus Primitivus* (London, 1678) 1.1.

those who were less wealthy. Giles Firmin (d. 1697), a theological opponent from Grantham's later years in Norwich, noted that he had been told that Grantham's family suffered "much loss for the king" during the civil war.[11]

In the end, it is clear that Thomas Grantham was born in Lincolnshire, probably winter 1633 or spring 1634. Based on the discussion above, he was probably born to William Grantham in the village of Hatton, a region of Lincolnshire where the wolds—the fens around Boston—and the coastal marsh converge.[12]

Details of Grantham's childhood are scant. Grantham's immediate or extended family may have had limited wealth at some point, yet it seems that spiritual tendencies and gifts were soon manifest as he "began to seek the Lord very early."[13] Grantham's father apparently disapproved of this spiritual bent, however, and so he unsuccessfully attempted to extinguish his son's fervor in childhood by apprenticing him to a tailor.[14] This parental nudge may have failed, for Firmin said that upon completion of "his service" as a tailor, Grantham "gave himself to learning."[15] At about age fourteen or fifteen (ca. 1650) Grantham came to "repentance and faith."[16] This serious young man eventually found a permanent spiritual home among the General Baptists of Lincolnshire.

Baptizing Thomas Grantham: 1650–60

Joseph Ivimey probably overstated the case when he claimed that with Grantham "almost all the events in relation to the Baptists in

---

[11] Giles Firmin, *Scripture-Warrant Sufficient Proof for Infant-Baptism* (London, 1688) A2.

[12] Kershaw, "Baptised Believers," 32.

[13] Crosby, *The History of the English Baptists,* 3.75–76. Crosby did not provide a source for this claim.

[14] Firmin, *Scripture-Warrant*, sig. a2v–a3r. See also Firmin's *The Answer of Giles Firmin* (London: n.p., 1689).

[15] Firmin, *Scripture-Warrant*, sig. a2v–a3r.

[16] Thomas Grantham to John Connould, 21 April 1691. The letters passed between Grantham and Connould are housed at The Beinecke Rare Book and Manuscript Library, Yale University Library, New Haven CT.

[Lincolnshire] are connected," but he was certainly right to include Grantham among the major Baptist figures there.[17] Nothing is known of Grantham's first exposure to Baptists or Baptist principles, and his movements in the years following his conversion are unclear, but sometime between 1651 and 1653 he found in Boston, Lincolnshire, "a people congregate upon the profession of the foundation principles of Christ's doctrine [in] Hebrews 6:1–2."[18] Strangely, more biographical information becomes available at this crucial point in Grantham's life, but organizing it is complicated. Although Grantham was baptized in the Baptist church at Boston in 1653, all accounts of his life point to an earlier connection with a young but growing congregation of baptized believers in the south marsh area of Lincolnshire (see map 2). Since the beginning of Grantham's public ministry is intricately involved with the "South Marsh Church," a brief account of the church's history is in order.

In about 1644, a reform-minded church had formed in the south marsh area of Lincolnshire.[19] This congregation rejected signs and sponsors but retained sprinkling as the preferred mode of baptism.[20] The separatist congregation was persecuted for admitting no sponsors and rejecting ceremonies such as making the sign of the cross.[21] The nature of English separatism was conducive to division, however, and disagreements eventually divided the congregation. By 1651 it appears the

---

[17] Ivimey, *A History of the English Baptists,* 2.262.

[18] Thomas Grantham to John Connould, 21 April 1691. Crosby wrote that Grantham was baptized at "about the 19th year of his age" in the gathered church at Boston, Lincolnshire (*History of the English Baptists*, 3.76–78). Crosby went on to say that Grantham was later ordained as a pastor in 1656 at age twenty-two. Richard wrote that Grantham embraced immersion and Baptist principles in 1651, at about age nineteen, and joined the Boston church ("Biography of Thomas Grantham," 3). The *ODNB* said this occurred about 1652.

[19] Crosby's account of this congregation came from Grantham's no–longer extant *Christianitas Restaurata*, *History of the English Baptists*, 3.77. There seems to be no other version of the manuscript available after Crosby.

[20] Apparently those in the congregation had already rejected making the sign of the cross and allowing parents to function as "sponsors" for their infants at baptism.

[21] Crosby, *History of the English Baptists*, 3.77

church consisted of a group of four, all of whom embraced baptism by immersion.[22]

It is possible that Grantham may have already attached himself to this young congregation in the south marsh area as early as 1651, not long before being baptized in Boston in 1653.[23] If this were the case, then Taylor may have been correct in identifying Grantham as one of the four to separate over the issue of immersion in 1651.[24] That Grantham was baptized in the Boston church instead of the South Marsh congregation is curious. Is it possible that the South Marsh Church was without its own minister and the congregations shared a minister, as was the case with the Lincoln gathering earlier in the century? If so, this might explain Grantham's early work of procuring preachers for the South Marsh Church while he "exercised his own gifts among them privately."[25]

Grantham's potential for ministry did not remain hidden long, for in 1656 the South Marsh congregation chose him as pastor, a post he would hold for the next thirty years.[26] When reflecting on his ordination later in

---

[22] Crosby believed this nucleus formed the foundation of the General Baptist presence in Lincolnshire, though it is unclear whether the four were men and if there families were considered part of the church.

[23] Kershaw, "Baptised Believers," 32. Kershaw followed the order of events found in Crosby, Richard, and Taylor instead of the *DNB* entry.

[24] Taylor, *The History of the English General Baptists*, 1.128. Regardless of whether Grantham was one of the original four, Taylor rightly described the seventeen-year old Grantham as a "principal instrument" and chief supporter of believer's baptism in the South Marsh Church.

[25] Crosby, *History of the English Baptists*, 3.77.

[26] Ibid. Grantham would have been about twenty-two years old when he became the pastor. The *ODNB* held that Grantham's first pastorate was at Boston, but Kershaw argued that Grantham's first pastorate was not at Boston but rather with the South Marsh Church in 1656 ("Baptised Believers," 32). Monksthorpe Baptist Church's history (see Bryan Keyworth, "History of Monksthorpe Baptist Church," Monksthorpe Baptist Church, http://homepage.ntlworld.com/bh.keyworth/ History.htm [accessed 12 November 2008]) suggested that the "South Marsh" church might have been a false name used to protect the identity of the actual Monksthorpe location, an argument Kershaw also advanced ("Baptised Believers," 34–35). If so, then Grantham was instrumental in the foundation of Monksthorpe Baptist Church,

life, Grantham recalled his reluctance and doubts in the face of the congregation's decision:

> [I]n all faithfulness, nothing seemed more terrible to me. The greatness of the work, and my poor and low capacity, and great unfitness for so sacred a work, did cause me to strive much against many pressures in my spirit, which yet I hope were from the Lord. I remained silent under a heavy burthen, with much begging of God that I might be excused; but if not, that it would then please him to fit me for, and bless me in the work. And he was stronger than I, and prevailed. Then I opened my mouth with great trembling and fear: (the Lord knows it.) I had rather been sent to any drudgery in the world, than to preach. Howbeit, it pleased God to bless my weak beginnings to the edification of some, and to the illumination, and, I hope, true conversion of others. This being observed by some leading men among the baptized churches, for to them I was now related, I was chosen, though God knows unwillingly, to the office of presbyter, to take the oversight of a small congregation; and solemnly ordained, by fasting and prayer, and laying on of hands, of such as were ordained before me.[27]

Grantham developed into a capable and influential minister. The church grew under his leadership and eventually dispatched a string of General Baptist preachers.

Most of the events described above took place during the Protectorate years in English history (1653–59), which tended to be a period more tolerant of Dissenters than previous or subsequent years. Yet Baptists did encounter persecution during Cromwell's reign; they were often taken before judges because of their absenteeism and choice to gather independently of the official parish congregation.[28] This was true for the South Marsh congregation. Local magistrates and mobs openly sought opportunities to disturb meetings and disrupt worship, but somehow the church obtained meeting space at Northelm Chapel,

---

which remains an active and worshipping community to this day. The Monksthorpe records, however, make no mention of Grantham.

[27] See Thomas Grantham's letter to John Connould, 11 June 1691.

[28] Crosby, *History of the English Baptists*, 3.86.

Wainfleet.[29] In time, the number of General Baptist congregations increased to the point that the historian William T. Whitley felt justified in describing Lincolnshire as a General Baptist "stronghold" during the seventeenth century.[30]

Husband, Father, and Husbandman?

Before turning to Grantham's public career as a General Baptist messenger and advocate, it is useful to provide a few details that are available regarding his family life and secular occupation(s). This is a difficult task because Grantham left few clues about his personal life, and *Christianitas Restaurata*, the one document that apparently contained some information, is no longer extant.[31] However, working with the slivers of data available and relying on various public records one can draw a few conclusions with some confidence.

Perhaps the best source for information about Grantham's family and life in Lincolnshire is a will signed by one Thomas Grantham on the ninth day of May 1690. Although none of the published sources related to Grantham mention this document, there are sufficient internal and external connections to conclude that it is the will of the Thomas Grantham under consideration here.[32] Several family members and situations stand out in the will.

The will suggests that Grantham considered Sutterby, Lincolnshire, to be his home and that he was a husbandman. He also owned land in Hundelby, Ashby by Partney, and Halton Holegate.

Bridget is mentioned as the deceased wife of Thomas Grantham, though it is unclear how long she had been dead.

---

[29] Taylor, *History of the English Baptists*, 1.131. Crosby recorded that the university-educated John Watts was a notable convert who joined the congregation during this period (*History of the English Baptists*, 3.78–79).

[30] William T. Whitley, *A History of British Baptists* (London: Kingsgate Press, 1923) 168.

[31] Crosby, *History of the English Baptists*, 3.77.

[32] The Will of Thomas Grantham, 9 May 1690 (W1691/ii/255), Lincolnshire Archives, Lincoln UK. For the full text of the will, see Appendix A.

Benjamin, one son of Thomas Grantham, was to receive his father's land in Hundelby.[33]

Benjamin and two other sons, John and Abel, were to receive a portion of the money obtained from the sale of Thomas Grantham's land in Ashby by Partney.

Thomas Grantham left twenty-one pounds to John Hill, a kinsman, who was to use the money to pay a debt owed by Mary Grantham.

Mary Grantham was the widow of the deceased Thomas Grantham of Ashby. The implication here is that Thomas Grantham had a son named Thomas (perhaps the eldest?), but that he died before the completion of the will, widowing Mary Grantham.

If Mary Grantham had already paid the debt, then John Hill was to divide the twenty-one pounds equally between Thomas and Abner when they turned twenty-one. Thomas and Abner were the sons of the deceased Thomas and (presumably) Mary Grantham.

Thomas Grantham asked John Hill and Mark Smith, a son-in-law, to oversee the sale of the Ashby land and distribution of the proceeds from that sale.

Thomas Grantham asked John Hill and Mark Smith to oversee the sale of his land in Halton Holegate. With the money received, they were to pay Mary Grantham's twenty-one pound debt if it remained unpaid. If that debt had already been paid, they were instructed to give the twenty-one pounds to Thomas Grantham's grandchildren Thomas and Abner.

Mark Smith and John Hill were then instructed to take the remaining money from the sale of the Halton Holegate land and divide half of it among the four children of Thomas Grantham's other deceased son, Abner, and then to give the rest to a pious and charitable cause.

Based on the contents and details of this will, Thomas Grantham was a husband, father, and grandfather at the time the will was written.

---

[33] A manuscript of Grantham's, *The Quaeries Examined* (London, 1676), held in the British Library has a handwritten note on the last the page that the book is the property of Benjamin Grantham. The note is dated 1684. A copy of Grantham's *The Loyal Baptist* (London, 1684), also held at the British Library, bears the same name and date.

His wife, Bridget, had already died by this time, as had at least one son.[34] He worked as a husbandman (farmer) and owned at least three plots of land in close proximity to each other (Hundelby, Ashby by Partney, and Halton Holegate) (see map 3). Sutterby, where he ratified his will, is several miles north of Hundelby, while his birthplace, Hatton, is a greater distance to the northwest of Hundelby.

That this will was written for the Thomas Grantham under consideration here seems even more likely upon discovery that he was the trustee of a 1679 will for John Tailor. In this will, it is said that Grantham's children, Abner and Mary, were both under the age of twenty-one.[35] Moreover, there is a reference to Grantham's work as a tailor and his farming at Ashby by Partney, where he reared a family. The few pieces of information gleaned from John Tailor's will confirm the likelihood that the Thomas Grantham mentioned is the same man responsible for the Sutterby will of May 1690. The mention of family members named Abner and Mary is significant, as is the reference to his work as a tailor and farmer in Ashby by Partney.

There are still more biographical clues available in Grantham's writings. Grantham wrote in the late 1670s that God had blessed him with "many" children and "that all that are yet capable, have been Baptized."[36] A decade later, he referred in writing to his wife and family, noting that some of his children had died as infants.[37] It is clear that by 1663 he was earning a living "by the labour of [his] hands, and never

[34] Though no details are given, based on common marital patterns among Baptists in the seventeenth century, it is likely that Bridget was herself a Baptist. Baptists were strict about enforcing endogamous marriages. See further, Bill Stevenson, "The Social Integration of post-Restoration Dissenters, 1660–1725," in *The World of Rural Dissenters, 1520–1725*, ed. Margaret Spufford (New York: Cambridge University Press, 1995) 361.

[35] See the *ODNB*.

[36] Thomas Grantham, *The Controversie about Infants* (London, 1680) 47.

[37] Grantham refers to children who died in infancy in *The Infants Advocate* (London, 1688) 16.

saluted the schools to gain knowledge of their arts."[38] Elsewhere he wrote that farming had been his primary occupation.[39] All of these details accord with those in his presumed will, but there are certainly blank spots in the portrait.

Why, for example, would an overtly religious and pious figure like Thomas Grantham include almost no religious language in his will? There is the line "Into the handes of almighty God I commit my Soul, and to the earth my Body in hope of a Happie Resuerection to Life eternal through Jesus Christ" at the outset and the mention of "Pious and Charitable uses" at the end, but that is the only religious language in the document.[40] It seems unlikely that Grantham would have been concerned with trouble from the established church, for the Toleration Act (1689) granted certain freedoms. Technically speaking, institutional structures that might have impacted the language and nature of dissenting wills in the past were no longer in place. At the same time, one could make the case that Grantham knew all too well that freedom could be illusory and fleeting in the seventeenth century. He had seen two declarations of indulgence come and go; perhaps he thought the third would end in a similar fashion. While any overt religious or Baptist language in the will is curiously absent, it does not seem like a serious obstacle to concluding that this is Thomas Grantham's will.

Another question relates to Grantham's presence in Lincolnshire at the end of his life. Thomas Grantham moved to Norwich around 1686, which means he would have been required to return to Sutterby just

---

[38] Grantham wrote *The Baptist against the Papist* (London, 1663) during a stint in prison. Grantham was self-taught, for in the opening pages of the work he reminded readers that he worked for his food and had no formal education. Grantham's vocation was consistent with what is known of most post-Reformation Dissenters. Bill Stevenson has shown that most Dissenters during this period "lived and worked in the countryside" ("The Social and Economic Status of post-Reformation Dissenters, 1660–1725," 357). Kershaw found that several leading General Baptists in Lincolnshire from 1660–1700 were husbandmen/farmers, "Baptised Believers," Table 3.

[39] Grantham, *The Infants Advocate, the Second Part,* 8.

[40] The Will of Thomas Grantham, 9 May 1690.

before his death to sign and ratify the will in May 1690. Is it possible that he would have made this journey late in life? While it may seem unlikely at first, the records show that Grantham was active in his last years. For example, he traveled to London in 1689 for the General Baptist Assembly, where he recorded the minutes. While it does seem odd to find him in Sutterby in 1690, given his other travels it was by no means an impossible trip.

There are questions about the family genealogy, particularly regarding the sons, grandsons, daughters, and a daughter-in-law named Mary. The questions likely result from a lack of details. Similarly, "Ann Grantham" was present when Thomas died in Norwich, her place in the family is not clear. It is likely this she was Grantham's daughter, but again, the picture is incomplete. When taken together, however, the significant overlap of names, places, and occupations convince this author that this will for Thomas Grantham did, in fact, belong to that prominent General Baptist minister and messenger.

Grantham Goes Public (1660–72)

The General Baptist cause in Lincolnshire prospered in the late 1650s, which engendered some hostility against the movement in the wake of the Restoration in 1660. In March 1660, forty-one General Baptists met in London to compose and issue a "Confession of Faith," which was "[o]wned and approved by more than twenty thousand."[41] At least one representative from Lincolnshire signed the document: William Pann.[42] This statement of faith was revised on several occasions and came to be known as the *Standard Confession*. By 1700 it had become the foundational General Baptist statement of faith. Grantham, who has been identified as the author even though he was not even a signatory, was

---

[41] The text is available in Crosby, *History of the English Baptists*, vol. 1, appendix, 87–90. For the context of the *Standard Confession* see William L. Lumpkin, *Baptist Confessions of Faith* (Philadelphia: Judson Press, 1959) 220ff.

[42] William Pann's family name appears as "Paine" in some documents.

probably not the author of the confession.[43] He was, however, soon to become a representative for the Lincolnshire General Baptists.

Dissenters in Lincolnshire were not immune from the tumult. General Baptists appealed to local magistrates for help but received little or no protection. Finding no relief locally, they appealed directly to Charles II for assistance. In July of 1660, several General Baptists (most of them from Lincolnshire) formulated and signed a *Narrative and Complaint*, the first address or petition to the king protesting their ill treatment at the hands of local magistrates.[44] Grantham, though only twenty-six years old, and Joseph Wright, a messenger of the Westby congregation, were assigned the task of delivering the petition into the king's hands (see map 2). They obtained an audience with the king and presented the petition and a copy of the confession that was signed in March.

The *Narrative and Complaint* was a petition that described local hostilities in detail and recounted how adversaries disturbed peaceful Baptist meetings.[45] Some Baptists were imprisoned and even fined for not attending weekly Anglican worship. Others were unjustly indicted at the Quarter Sessions.[46] The petition was primarily a narrative account of the harassment suffered by the General Baptists in Lincolnshire; it made no specific request of the king. The king responded favorably to the petition, saying "[t]hat it was not his mind, that any of his subjects, who lived peaceably, should suffer any trouble upon the account of their judgements or opinions in point of religion."[47] Charles II promised to watch over these loyal subjects and assigned a Member of Parliament to

---

[43] William J. McGlothlin, ed., *Baptist Confessions of Faith* (Philadelphia: American Baptist Publication Society, 1911) 109.

[44] This petition is available in Henry Jessey's *The Lords Loud Call to England* (London: Printed by H. J., 1660) 15–16. Grantham included the confession in *Christianismus Primitivus*, 3.7–9.

[45] See "God, Government, and King" for further discussion of the various petitions signed and delivered by Grantham in the early 1660s.

[46] The Quarter Sessions were periodic county courts that convened at least four times per year.

[47] Jessey, *The Lords Loud Call to England*, 17.

look into the matter.[48] Little else is known of this promise or the identity of the Member of Parliament, but Thomas Venner's three-day uprising in London in January of 1661 halted any momentum sectaries may have secured in 1660. The government responded quickly and decisively to the uprising. On 10 January 1661, the king forbade Anabaptists, Quakers, and Fifth Monarchy men to meet. Thus it should come as no surprise that some Baptists, commonly referred to as "Anabaptists," submitted *The Humble Apology of Some Commonly Called Anabaptists* to the king on 28 January 1661. This apology was signed by prominent Particular Baptists such as William Kiffin, Christopher Blackwood, John Spilsbury, and the printer Francis Smith.

The baptized believers in Lincolnshire made a separate appeal to the king in the form of the *Second Humble Address*. Dated 23 January 1661, Grantham was one of thirty signatories representing a large number of Baptists in Lincolnshire.[49] The submission of two appeals in rapid succession suggests that Baptists throughout England were concerned enough to remove any hint of disloyalty in light of growing hostility against them. Thomas Grantham was chosen by his fellow Baptists in Lincolnshire to lead the way in this endeavor.

It did not take long for hostility toward Baptists to become more forceful. Sometime between the *Second Humble Address* on January 1661 and 23 February 1661, Grantham was arrested at a Baptist meeting in Boston and taken to Lincoln Castle, which also housed a jail. From this jail, Grantham and seven others composed *The Third Address* to Charles II, dated 23 February 1661.[50] The address maintained the prisoners' innocence and requested that they be free to worship God as they were persuaded by scripture. The appeal apparently came to nothing, for Grantham spent more than a year in the castle jail. Ever the

---

[48] Ibid.

[49] Thomas Grantham et al., *The Second Humble Address* (London: Printed by Simon Dover, 1661).

[50] Grantham was one of eight signatories on *The Third Address* (London, 1661). The same eight, along with twenty-two others, had signed *The Second Humble Address*.

apologist, Grantham used his time in prison to publish *The Prisoner against the Prelate* (1662) and *The Baptist against the Papist* (1663).[51]

The Prisoner against the Prelate recounted a dialogue composed in verse between a personified Jail ("Prisoner") and the Lincoln Cathedral ("Prelate"). In this prison treatise, Grantham took the perspective of the Prisoner and offered various reasons for separating from the established church. Among the issues addressed are toleration, believer's baptism, infant baptism, imposition of hands, the end of all things, and organ music. It is of some importance that Grantham included the text of the confession submitted to Charles II in July 1660, but in *The Prisoner against the Prelate* he dealt with the various articles in more detail and even employed a "test of antiquity" to support his positions. Though Taylor thought it had "little merit as a poem,"[52] *The Prisoner against the Prelate* does reveal the range of Grantham's interests and his willingness to converse with ancient sources regarding contemporary liturgical practices. *The Prisoner against the Prelate* was a jail cell view onto the issues faced by General Baptists in Lincolnshire.

Some time later during this same stint in the Lincoln jail, rumors began to circulate of Grantham being a closet papist and perhaps a Jesuit. Local clergy questioned him about his identity and beliefs, and in response to their questions Grantham published *The Baptist against the Papist*. Grantham went on the record as a supporter of the same freedom for Roman Catholics that he sought for himself, but his main goal in

---

[51] Almost all of Grantham's published treatises were printed as pamphlets. Pamphlets were short treatises printed in quarto, or on sheets of paper folded twice. Pamphlets were often bundled for circulation with pamphlets written by the same author or other authors. Existing manuscripts of Grantham's writings reveal they were bundled with various and even unrelated treatises by other authors. The number of folds typically suggested the status attached to a particular publication. Most of Grantham's publications were of the smaller size. The notable exception in the corpus is *Christianismus Primitivus* (1678), which was printed in a folio style (a sheet of paper folded once). For the production and importance of pamphlets in the seventeenth century, see Joad Raymond, *Pamphlets and Pamphleteering in Early Modern Britain* (New York: Cambridge University Press, 2003) 4ff.

[52] Taylor, *The History of the English General Baptists*, 1.198.

publishing this short treatise was to prove that he was no papist. His published correspondence with the anonymous Roman Catholic outlined several ways in which the "present Papal Church" could not be the true church of Christ.[53] The Roman church was unable to prove its status as the true Church. It had no true baptism. It was a national church. It increased its membership by means of the "carnal sword." It was made up of unregenerate members. Grantham's willingness to engage Roman Catholics in conversation and advocate for their freedom to worship since they, too, were susceptible to imprisonment, was on full display in this prison document.[54] Grantham's confinement lasted for at least two Assizes (periodic criminal courts), and then in 1663 he was brought before the bar and dismissed without charge after fifteen months of imprisonment.[55] He may have returned to his South Marsh Church upon release, but his freedom was short lived.[56]

When, in 1664, religious gatherings of more than five people—apart from the jurisdiction of the Church of England—were forbidden, soldiers were sent into the countryside with orders to enforce the act and disarm Dissenters who continued to convene.[57] Grantham was among those arrested in Lincolnshire for failure to comply, though it seems that no weapons were found among the General Baptists. Crosby reported that during the regional roundup those in noncompliance, notably Baptists, were made to "run along like lacqueys" beside the authorities' horses.[58] For the first night of their imprisonment, Grantham and his companions

---

[53] Grantham, *The Baptist against the Papist*, 34–46.

[54] Grantham included the full text of *The Baptist against the Papist* in the fourth book of *Christianismus Primitivus.*

[55] For a detailed analysis of the Assizes during Grantham's lifetime, see J. S. Cockburn, *A History of English Assizes 1558–1714* (New York: Cambridge University Press, 1972) 23–48, 153–87.

[56] Ivimey recorded that Grantham and those with him returned to their respective churches upon release, *A History of the English Baptists,* 2.267.

[57] The Conventicle Act of 1664 forbade any religious gathering of more than five people outside the Church of England. It was intended to discourage dissent and strengthen the established Church.

[58] Crosby, *The English Baptists of the Seventeenth Century*, 3.81.

were lodged in an inn, where they were subjected to filthy language and swearing.[59] The following morning, they were asked questions intended to trap them and invited to take an oath to the Church of England. As a result of Grantham's steadfastness, he spent the next six months in the jail at Louth, a market town in the northeastern region of Lincolnshire (see map 2).[60]

Grantham's enemies kept his case from being heard at the local Assizes, but he was eventually examined and released at the Quarter Sessions. Shortly after his release, a spurious suit was brought against Grantham accusing him of baptizing a woman and then beating her.[61] This case, like those previously, was thrown out, and Grantham was released. The pattern of harassment and slander continued throughout his life and probably contributed to the ten imprisonments he endured.[62]

Few details regarding Grantham's life are available for the later 1660s, but it is clear that he was ordained as a messenger of the baptized churches in 1666. Grantham and the place of messengers in General Baptist life will be taken up in the next chapter; he was instrumental in transforming the office into a regional and inter-congregational position. In letters to an Anglican friend later in life, Grantham wrote of his ordination: "I was elected by the consent of many congregations, and ordained to the office of a messenger by those who were in the same office before me, and … the place where I was thus ordained was in mine own mansion or dwelling house [the place where the church usually met]…"[63] The reference to the meeting place is noteworthy here, for Grantham revealed that Baptists were in the habit of congregating for

---

[59] Ibid.

[60] Ibid.

[61] Ibid.

[62] Charles B. Jewson, *The Baptists in Norfolk* (London: Carey Kingsgate Press Limited, 1957) 29. Grantham's grandson, Grantham Killingworth, erected a memorial monument to his grandfather in Norwich. The monument has since been removed, but the wording may be found in Oldfield, *A Topographical and Historical Account of Wainfleet and the Wapentake of Candleshoe*, 361–62. The full text of the memorial is included as Appendix C.

[63] Thomas Grantham to John Connould, 21 April 1691.

worship in his home at the time of his ordination. In addition to describing the ordination itself and the role of a messenger, a later letter mentioned that becoming a messenger amounted to an appointment to a "larger trust" than that of pastor, which involved oversight of "churches in divers places that had need of help."[64] The office of messenger was a controversial topic among Christians in England, however, and Grantham would often find himself defending his office.

Grantham's first known published document after his ordination to the office of messenger was a short document that explained how the fourth commandment was of a "different nature from the other nine."[65] In *The Seventh-Day-Sabbath* (1667) Grantham developed seven main points:

1. Nothing moral is impossible; it would be impossible for the entire universe to observe the Sabbath command. Therefore, observing the Sabbath command must not be a moral imperative.

2. Moral precepts take precedent over ceremonial precepts. Grantham makes the point that observation of the Sabbath often gave ground to other ceremonies like circumcision.

3. All purely moral commands may be dispensed with in cases of necessity. Grantham is convinced that saving the life of a beast or human is more necessary than observing the Sabbath.

4. Grantham employed the warning against judging others in Colossians 2:16.

5. The Sabbath day was a sanctifying sign given to the "Church of the Jews" and not necessarily to the whole world.

6. Jewish festivals were ceremonial; therefore, the seventh-day Sabbath is also ceremonial.

7. Grantham asserted that if the fourth command were to be enforced, then so would the punishment for breaking it: death.

---

[64] Thomas Grantham to John Connould, 11 June 1691.

[65] Thomas Grantham, *The Seventh-Day-Sabbath* (London, 1667).

The particular context of this short work is unknown, yet it appears that idiosyncratic views of Sabbath observance among some Baptists were enough of a concern to Grantham to warrant a published treatise attacking them. That John Lupton, a signatory to both *The Second Humble Address* and *The Third Address*, wrote the Epistle Dedicatory for this treatise and recommended it to the General Baptist churches suggests that the issue was not unimportant. Seventh-Day Baptists, though never large in number during this period, existed as a distinct Baptist strain and exhibited a rugged biblicism that even Thomas Grantham's General Baptists found to be troubling.

About this time, the Lincolnshire Dissenters encountered another wave of resistance from local clergy and conforming parishioners. Local leaders denied Baptists burial plots in the typical areas, even digging up corpses and then leaving them in front of the deceased's homes.[66] Grantham narrated the story of the desecration of Robert Shalder's corpse in the late 1660s. Shalder, of Croft (see map 2), had been baptized in 1666 only to die a couple of years later. Grantham recorded Shalder's epitaph in order "to keep in memory that sordid action..."[67] Grantham and his fellow Baptists were appalled at such indecent actions, but this kind of treatment was not unusual.

A short time later, the Lincolnshire clergyman Robert Wright delivered a speech defending the sprinkling of infants and attacking believer's baptism. Wright's speech was especially offensive to the Lincolnshire General Baptists since he had formerly been a minister among them. Wright had been excluded from a Baptist congregation in the past for "irregular life and conversation."[68] Without income, Wright was forced to seek employment elsewhere. He requested a benefice from the bishop in exchange for denying his former convictions and preaching

---

[66] Grantham, *Christianismus Primitivus*, 3.56. Crosby also included this account (*The History of the English Baptists*, 2.239). See also Daniel Neal, *History of Puritanism*, 5 vols. (1732; repr., Bath UK: R. Crutwell, 1795) 4.492–93.

[67] Ibid.

[68] Crosby, *The History of the English Baptists*, 2.242.

against the Baptists. The bishop agreed, and Wright made good on his promise.

Wright assumed the local Baptists would wilt under the power of his rather public denunciation and attacks. He underestimated Thomas Grantham. In March 1670, Grantham signed and posted four fliers, addressed to all Lincoln residents, challenging Wright to a "friendly conference in the place where he preached…"[69] Two papers were posted at the top of the steep hill into which a portion of Lincoln was built, and two were posted at the bottom. The two up the hill were promptly removed and likely delivered to the bishop and judge while the two down the hill were read by many throughout the city before being removed by clergy that afternoon. It is unclear what, if anything, was done to Grantham immediately, but the bishop's chaplain, William Silverton, sent a rather "angry" and "ill-natured" letter to Grantham and the Baptists, outlining his disdain for their meetings and practices.[70] Grantham again functioned as the Baptist spokesperson and responded:

> Finally, whereas Mr. Silverton saith, he will defend his proposition; it is hereby certified, that if he will either publish any thing upon the last two proposals, or dispute of them peaceably in a free audience, some of those whom he in the height of his wit [styles], *erroneous antick Baptists*, are resolved in the strength of Christ, to hear and try that which he shall declare, time and place being convenient.[71]

William Pann delivered this letter to Silverton, but nothing came of the invitation to public discourse. Given Grantham's public and steadfast response to these attacks, it is possible that the entire episode may have resulted in a six-month imprisonment.[72]

Baptists faced considerable external opposition during the early 1670s, but there was also significant internal disagreement and strife.

---

[69] Ibid., 2.242–43. Crosby included the text of the flier and added that they were posted by William Pann.

[70] Crosby, *The History of the English Baptists*, 2.243.

[71] Ibid., 244.

[72] William Richard, "Biography of Thomas Grantham," *Universal Theological Magazine* 3, no. 14 (February 1805): 65.

The necessity of the imposition of hands, or the laying on of hands signifying the gift of the Holy Spirit, was a controversial issue among the General Baptists during these years. Adam Taylor wrote that Baptists were far too eager to devour one another in the early 1670s over the issue of imposition of hands, which is probably why Grantham chose the title *A Sigh for Peace* (1671) for his defense of the practice.[73] Grantham addressed *A Sigh for Peace* to the "Church of Christ London, with the General Assembly of Messengers" in hopes that it might bring "brotherly concord, peace and truth" to a polarized situation.[74] Grantham proposed that all sides agree that imposition of hands "is one of the principles of Christ's doctrine, and part of the foundation."[75] Grantham also appended an explanation of why apostles, or messengers, were still necessary and imperative.

Grantham published *The Paedo-Baptist Apology for the Baptized Believers* in 1671 on the occasion of "unkind usages which the Baptized Churches have received from the Paedo-Baptists, by violently dispersing their Assemblies, by defacing and taking away their meeting places, by imprisoning their persons, seizing and wafting their estates, by injuring them in their trade by means of excommunications...and penal proceedings..."[76] Grantham, like many Baptists of his day, attacked any understanding of circumcision as a type of baptism and denied claims that baptism cleansed children from original sin. This was the first of several documents written by Grantham in support of believer's baptism and against infant baptism.

Charles II's Declaration of Indulgence in 1672 prompted some General Baptists in Lincolnshire to again send a message to the king. Charles attempted to extend some level of religious liberty and mitigate the persecution of Dissenters by offering preaching and worship licenses in exchange for a name, location, religious affiliation, and promise to

---

[73] Taylor, The History of the English General Baptists, 1.119.

[74] Thomas Grantham, *A Sigh for Peace* (n.p., 1671) Epistle Dedicatory, A2.

[75] Ibid., A4.

[76] Thomas Grantham, *The Paedo-Baptist Apology for the Baptized Believers* (n.p., 1671) To the Reader, A2.

avoid seditious behavior. In light of the declaration, Grantham (with another unknown messenger) was sent to wait on the king with "A Humble Address, or Remonstrance."[77] This address expressed gratitude for the toleration but also noted the ways in which the Indulgence still infringed upon Baptist liberty. In addition to delivering the address to Charles, Grantham was among those Dissenters who obtained a license under the terms of the Indulgence.[78] Grantham was given a license recognizing him as a "Baptist teacher," but, curiously, he registered for it in the town of Rouston (or Raiston), Leicestershire—a county bordering Lincolnshire to the west (see map 2). Possessing an official license ensured relative safety and peace for a time, but Parliament pressured Charles into retracting his indulgence on 8 March 1673. The licenses were recalled in 1675.[79] It is possible that Parliament would have been willing to tolerate Protestant dissenters, but the clauses allowing freedom for Roman Catholics were considered detestable.[80]

Grantham's other known activities during this period included public disputes with Quakers. At least two such debates occurred in Lincolnshire in 1672, one at Spilsby and another at Sleaford in the south-central region of the county.[81] Grantham's *The Baptist against the Quaker*, which is only found in the fourth book of Christianismus

---

[77] For a more detailed discussion of the response to the Declaration of Indulgence and *A Humble Address and Remonstrance,* see the chapter "God, Government, and King."

[78] Three basic types of licenses were offered under the Indulgence: (1) one could register for a license as a teacher, preacher, or minister of a particular group; (2) one could register as a teacher in general, and (3) one could register one's home as a Nonconformist meeting place. All information related to licenses requested and granted under the 1672 Declaration of Indulgence can be found in volume 1 of George L. Turner's *Original Records of Early Nonconformity under Persecution and Indulgence*, 3 vols. (London: T. F. Unwin, 1911–14).

[79] See Frank Bate, *The Declaration of Indulgence, 1672: A Study in the Rise of Organised Dissent* (London: University Press of Liverpool, 1908) 130–43.

[80] Barry Coward, *The Stuart Age: England, 1603–1704* (New York: Pearson Education, 2003) 308.

[81] Robert Ruckhill, *The Quakers Refuge* (n.p., 1673) 40. See chapter on "The Great Debaters" for further discussion of Grantham's debates with Quakers.

Primitivus (1678), recounted how he and John Whitehead debated issues ranging from the authorship of the Pentateuch to the nature of Jesus' resurrected body. In addition, *The Baptist against the Quaker* was a direct refutation of Quaker claims in *The Quakers Refuge* (1673).

In the context of toleration granted and then revoked, many Baptists once again fell prey to the harassment of ecclesiastical and secular authorities. Grantham was imprisoned along with other Lincolnshire Baptists during this period. At the behest of his fellow Baptists, Grantham penned an unpublished account of these ordeals and titled it *The Baptist Complaint against the Persecuting Priests*.[82] Based on the excerpt in Crosby's *History of the English Baptists*, one gets the picture of a sustained effort on the part of Lincolnshire General Baptists to live in relative peace with members of the Church of England, only to receive persecution and insult in return. Grantham, using the biblical Job as an example, claimed that, "to complain against malicious, debauched, and cruel practices, is part of the work of those, who are to bear a testimony for God."[83] The cruel practices included being dragged before judges in the time of Cromwell and having possessions taken and never restored. The Baptists estimated their imprisonments during the previous decades at no less than one hundred incidents and their levies at three hundred pounds. Furthermore, they claimed the cost of their imprisonments and related appearances at the Assizes and Quarter Sessions came to more than a thousand pounds. Finally, the excerpt noted that hundreds had been presented to commissary courts and excommunicated as a result.[84] This account of Baptist sufferings in Lincolnshire shows how local actors were often responsible for persecution and that the threat and presence of persecution solidified a young General Baptist population. Grantham's central place in the story of seventeenth-century Lincolnshire General Baptists was undeniable.

---

[82] The exact date or context is unclear, but Crosby apparently had access to a copy and included a lengthy excerpt (*The History of the English Baptists*, 3.84–90).

[83] Crosby, *The History of the English Baptists*, 3.85.

[84] Commissary courts were ecclesiastical courts; each diocese had its own commissary court.

The Maturing Theologian (1673–85)

Little is known of Grantham's personal life from 1673–1685. His activities as an author increased as he published no fewer than nine treatises, most notably the massive and monumental *Christianismus Primitivus* (1678). Sometime prior to 18 September 1673, William Fort, a parish minister in Blyton, appeared at Baptist meetings in the town and sought to disrupt the proceedings.[85] Fort aimed to dispute with the baptized believers, but most Baptists had no experience with such things. Thus, they requested that Grantham debate Fort on 18 September 1673. Based on Grantham's own account of the dispute, which was later published in dialogue form as *A Religious Contest* (1674), the two men debated the nature of authentic baptism. The debate ended in a friendly manner as both sides "went away in peace."[86]

Appended to *A Religious Contest* was Grantham's response to Edward Stillingfleet's *A Rational Account of the Grounds of the Protestant Religion* (originally published in 1665).[87] Stillingfleet was bishop of Worcester during the second half of the seventeenth century and a well-known preacher and writer. Stillingfleet's opponents were Anglicans who had converted to Roman Catholicism, but Grantham accused him of doing harm to the larger cause by affirming the validity of infant baptism.

The year 1674 also saw Grantham publish a work titled *The Loyal Baptist*. The entire treatise, which was presented in the form of two sermons, argued that in 1 Peter 2:17 were found the four great duties of "a constant conformist to the scriptures": (1) to honor all people, (2) to

[85] Thomas Grantham, *A Religious Contest* (London, 1674) Epistle to the Reader. The *ODNB* claimed that Grantham had a dispute with a Quaker named Fort, but that appears to be a mistake since the only known "Fort" Grantham interacted with was an Anglican minister.

[86] Grantham, *A Religious Contest*, 20. See the "The Great Debaters" chapter for a more detailed treatment of *A Religious Contest* and the impact of Grantham's participation.

[87] Grantham's response to Stillingfleet was titled *Brief Animadversions upon Dr. Stillingfleet's Digressions about the Baptising of Infants* (London, 1674).

love the brotherhood, (3) to fear God, and (4) to honor the king.[88] These attributes of a loyal citizen were deemed important because they exhibited to the magistrates and king that Baptists should not be considered a threat to the social order.

At the same time Grantham was urging his fellow believers to be loyal citizens, he was also involved with internal General Baptist disputes over the place of imposition of hands in the worshipping life of the baptized congregations. In *A Treatise of Laying on of Hands* (1674), Henry Danvers had recognized the ability of all believers to lay on hands in appropriate situations (e.g., healing, conferral of charismatic gifts, and ordination).[89] Grantham agreed in part, but sought to correct Danvers's mistakes by publishing *The Fourth Principle* (1674), which amounted to a sustained discussion of the proper understanding of the fourth of six principles found in Hebrews 6:1–2.[90] Grantham affirmed the necessity of the imposition of hands, but contended that not all believers were given the authority to perform the act. Rather, the act of imposition was confined to those who occupied the appropriate office and were thus imbued with authority.[91]

Infant baptism remained one of the controversial issues for Grantham in the 1670s. There is evidence of what appears to have been a rather testy exchange between Grantham and an Independent minister in Norfolk named John Horne (d. 1676). Horne, who was himself born in Lincolnshire, had made his way to King's Lynn in the 1640s and ministered at All Saints Church in the city until being ejected from his living for nonconformity in 1662. Grantham would make his own way to King's Lynn a few years later. Details of the exchange between these

---

[88] Thomas Grantham, *The Loyal Baptist* (London, 1684) title page. The title page of the 1684 edition shows that *The Loyal Baptist* was first published in 1674.

[89] Henry Danvers, *A Treatise of Laying on of Hands* (London, 1674).

[90] Thomas Grantham, *The Fourth Principle* (London, 1674). The reader should note that the previously published *A Defence of the Offices of Apostles*, which had been appended to *A Sigh for Peace* in 1671, was also appended to *A Fourth Principle* but with a slightly different title: *A Discourse of the Successors of the Apostles*.

[91] Ibid., 20.

two natives of Lincolnshire are limited to Horne's published treatise, *The Cause of Infants Maintained* (1675), but in that work he included lengthy quotations of a now-lost publication by Grantham entitled *Mr. Horne Answered.*[92] Grantham had sought a public debate with Horne, who had previously engaged Quakers in debate, but Horne's poor health prevented such a vocal and public affair.[93]

Grantham had to look elsewhere for a theological opponent. At some point in 1675 the Cambridge-educated Presbyterian minister John Barret published *Fifty Queries*, which was composed of fifty questions from Richard Baxter's *Plain Scripture Proof of Infants Church-membership and Baptism* (1651), for any who would deny the validity of infant baptism.[94] Baxter originally published *Plain Scripture* in the context of his debates with the Baptist John Tombes, but the question was by no means settled in 1675. Grantham took up Barret's challenge in 1676 with *The Quaeries Examined.* In this short treatise Grantham responded to each of Barret's questions in detail. Attached to the end was a three-page postscript detailing Grantham's answers to related baptismal questions posed by an Anglican minister. Barret returned the favor in the 1678 with *Much in a Little*, which was a direct rebuttal of Grantham's treatise. Early in the work Barret referred to Grantham as "your champion," sarcastically revealing Grantham's esteem and reputation among the General Baptists.[95]

---

[92] Adam Taylor, who had access to an extant copy of this treatise, gave the long title as *Mr. Horne answered; or, Paedo-rantism not from Zion: wherein is shewed his mistake about the reason of his writing; and the insufficiency of his evidence alledged to prove Infant Baptism descended from Zion, briefly discovered: together with twelve arguments by way of preface plainly shewing: that it as reasonable to baptize persons asleep or dead as it is to baptize infants*, *The History of the English Baptists*, 1.482.

[93] John Horne, *The Cause of Infants Maintained* (London 1675) 3.

[94] John Barret, *Fifty Queries, Seriously Propounded to those that Question, or Deny Infants Right to Baptism* (London, 1675); Richard Baxter, *Plain Scripture Proof of Infants Church Membership and Baptism* (London, 1651).

[95] John Barret, *Much in a Little* (London, 1678) 7. Joseph Whiston also reacted to Grantham's baptismal views in *Infant-Baptism Plainly Proved* (London, 1678) Letter to the Reader.

Grantham later responded to Barret in *The Controversie about Infants* (1680), but as was often the case, Grantham's theological attention was divided between non-Baptist opponents and divisions among the General Baptists themselves. In 1678 he must have devoted a significant amount of time and attention to the final draft of *Christianismus Primitivus*. As the title of this 600-page tome suggests, Barrington R. White was correct in writing that Grantham intended "to get behind the traditions of the Reformers, of the Medieval Church, of the Fathers, to the New Testament model."[96] By far Grantham's largest and most detailed publication, *Christianismus Primitivus* was written at the request of several churches in Lincolnshire as a compilation of new material and previously published treatises. The new material was included as books I–III and comprises what is probably Grantham's mature theology. He addressed a variety of issues from across the theological and ecclesiastical spectrum including, among others, the authority of the scripture, biblical translations, the divine attributes, Christology, eschatology, angelology, worship, baptism, the Lord's Supper, church polity, Christian discipline, sabbatarianism, the Christian's relationship with civil authorities, the question of whether Christians may hold civil offices, the roles of women in the church, marriage and familial roles, and the proper understanding of the Jewish people. According to William H. Brackney, the range of issues and the manner in which Grantham dealt with them in *Christianismus Primitivus* establishes that Grantham was a most important figure who bequeathed to the Baptist evolutionary process "a set of factors that qualified [it] as a maturing evangelical Protestant tradition."[97]

The fourth and final book of *Christianismus Primitivus* included material that Grantham had already published, with one possible exception. The previously published documents were *The Baptist against*

---

[96] Barrington White, *The English Baptists of the Seventeenth Century*, 117.

[97] William H. Brackney, "Thomas Grantham, Systematic Theology, and the Baptist Tradition" in *From Biblical Criticism to Biblical Faith: Essays in Honor of Lee Martin McDonald*, eds. William H. Brackney and Craig A. Evans (Macon GA: Mercer University Press, 2007) 199–216.

the Papist (1663); *The Baptist against the Quaker* (no longer extant); *The Paedo-Baptists Apology* (1671); *The Quaeries Examined* (1676); and *The Fourth Principle* (1674). The sixth treatise, *Gospel-Separation Maintained*, appears to have been new in 1678, but given the textual evidence that the other treatises had already been published, it is quite possible that *Gospel-Separation* was actually published at some earlier point. That Grantham addressed the work to the English nation, his own family, and the baptized Christian churches, reveals the comprehensive nature of his undertaking.

Little is known of *Christianismus Primitivus*'s immediate reception among Grantham's fellow General Baptists or others of the period.[98] That his *magnum opus* was published in folio form implies that the work and author were highly regarded in some circles. In 1701, Joseph Hooke cited it when defending the office of messenger,[99] and it was popular enough to be included among theological treatises found in America in the same year. Benjamin Laker (d. 1701), a prominent Baptist who had signed the 1663 edition of the *Standard Confession* and who later emigrated to the Carolinas, bequeathed a copy of *Christianismus Primitivus* to his daughter, Sarah Harvey.[100] Grantham's importance in the post-*Christianismus Primitivus* years can also be deduced from the sheer number of writings produced and disputes entered on behalf of the General Baptists. Grantham's activity level in the years following the publication of *Christianismus Primitivus* increased greatly, and his growing reputation regularly translated into more involvement in matters of controversy.

---

[98] It was quoted occasionally in the eighteenth century. The philosopher and theologian William Whiston (d. 1752), who was friendly with "eminent" General Baptists such as Grantham Killingworth (Thomas Grantham's grandson), included a statement from Grantham regarding the possibility that miracles continued into the present, *Memoirs of the Life and Writings of Mr. William Whiston* (London, 1753) 1.371–2.

[99] A fuller discussion of Hooke's relationship to Grantham follows in the next chapter, "Old Things by their Old Names."

[100] George Stevenson, "Laker, Benjamin," in *Dictionary of North Carolina Biography*, 6 vols. (Chapel Hill: University of North Carolina Press, 1991) 4.3–5.

There was also considerable Christological controversy among the General Baptists in 1678. Partly in response to the heretical teachings of Matthew Caffyn, who had come to hold Hoffmanite[101] conceptions of Christ, Thomas Monk led fifty-four other General Baptists from the Midlands in drafting and publishing the *Orthodox Creed.* The creed was intended to "unite and confirm all true protestants in the fundamental articles of the Christian religion..."[102] The first eight articles dealt extensively with the nature of the Trinity, which betrayed the underlying concern with articulating a correct Christology.

The *Orthodox Creed* was not the only document submitted during this period. In a little-known letter to the gathering of General Baptists known as the General Assembly, likely dated from the same period, Thomas Grantham and other Baptists from the Isle of Axholme, Nottinghamshire, and Peterborough also expressed great concern at the "grievous" impurity infiltrating the churches.[103] The letter, which was reprinted in the eighteenth century, urged the assembly to allow no "New or Strange Doctrine to obtrude upon the Churches, and more especially concerning the Godhead, from whence the whole Body of Christian doctrine hath its true Value and Usefulness."[104] The excerpt ended with

[101] Anabaptist theologian Melchior Hoffman (d. 1543) believed that while Christ had real human flesh, it was a heavenly flesh that originated in heaven. Hoffman's views had a profound impact on later Low Country Anabaptists such as Menno Simons (d. 1561).

[102] The quotation is taken from the title page. See Lumpkin, *Baptist Confessions of Faith*, 297.

[103] A portion of this letter was reproduced by Joseph Hooke in *Creed-Making and Creed-Imposing* (London: Printed by J. Darby and T. Browne, 1729) 37–38. Hooke did not date the letter, but internal evidence in the excerpt he quotes suggests that it was written around the time that the General Assembly struggled with how to deal with Caffyn. It is possible that the letter was written while Grantham ministered in Norfolk after circa 1686. There was renewed controversy during this time as Joseph Wright tried to have Caffyn censured. It is also noteworthy that as late as 1729 Hooke was employing Grantham's legacy and writings to uphold a Trinitarian understanding of God.

[104] Hooke, *Creed-Making and Creed-Imposing*, 37.

an affirmation of the dual natures of Christ, which of itself was an endorsement of the Chalcedonian definition.

In 1680 Grantham published *The Controversie about Infants* in response to Barret's *Much in a Little* (1678). Grantham's reply consisted of two main points. First, he denied that any infant dying before baptism was destined for damnation. The second portion of the treatise recorded Grantham's answers to Barret's more than sixty questions in *Much in a Little*.[105] Upon closer examination, it appears that Grantham had already printed a response to Barret in 1679 entitled *The Querist Examined, The Second Part*, but included it as part two of *The Controversie about Infants* in 1680. The eternal fate of dying infants was an issue that Grantham would debate in the coming years, especially as he increasingly came into dialogue with Presbyterian ministers.

Grantham was not out of touch with the Church of England during this time, for he also published in 1680 the irenic *A Friendly Epistle to the Bishops and Ministers of the Church of England* calling for more congenial relations between the established church and the Baptists. In this intriguing treatise, Grantham penned a prayer for concord among Christians, echoed concerns from both sides regarding the division among Christians, and even examined questionable tenets of the Thirty-Nine Articles. Grantham concluded with a plan for unity: (1) petition the king or Parliament for a meeting between Dissenters and Church of England clergy; (2) if the proposals did not meet the standard of "the good old way of Christianity, then we desire they may be rejected, and that you would be pleased to propose things which may be more effectual to procure the unity desired"; and (3) if unity could not be achieved, the Dissenters were to be granted freedom from the suffering they had endured.[106] Grantham was confident the proposal would be "little regarded by many," but he alluded to a sermon by the aforementioned Edward Stillingfleet that lamented the division among

---

[105] See page 27 of *The Controversie about Infants* (London, 1680), which is actually a title page for *The Querist Examined, The Second Part* (printed in 1679).

[106] The proposal for unity is found on pages 37–40 of *A Friendly Epistle to the Bishops and Ministers of the Church of England* (London, 1680).

dissenting Christians.[107] Joseph Hooke was not the only one who appealed to Thomas Grantham's writings and legacy in the eighteenth century. In 1763, almost a century after it first appeared, *A Friendly Epistle* was appended to the end of *Reformation in Religion, Greatly subservient to National Prosperity*, a publication thought to be authored by Grantham Killingworth (d. 1778), Thomas Grantham's grandson.[108]

The peaceful spirit evident in *A Friendly Epistle* was also on display during this period as Grantham participated in a "very Christian conference" in London with Dr. William Lloyd, Bishop of St. Asaph (not to be confused with the William Lloyd who served as the bishop of Norwich in the late 1680s).[109] Lloyd had a reputation for being tolerant and even conversant with Dissenters in his diocese, which did not necessarily increase his standing with other bishops.[110] In addition to his conversation with the General Baptist Grantham, the bishop met with Quakers on 22 September 1681 and 6 August 1682, and with Presbyterians on 27 September 1681 and 28 August 1682. Where or how Lloyd and Grantham met is unclear, but if the two originally met in St. Asaph, then it is curious that Grantham would have been so far away from Lincolnshire.[111] Where dating is concerned, Grantham's conference with Lloyd likely occurred sometime after Lloyd was appointed bishop in October 1680.

Whatever peace Dissenters had experienced early in the decade evaporated upon discovery of the Rye House Plot in 1683.[112] Protestant involvement in the plot prompted a new wave of persecution against those who had largely fallen out of favor with the king after throwing

---

[107] Ibid., 40.

[108] *Reformation in Religion, Greatly Subservient to National Prosperity* (London, 1763).

[109] Knowledge of this conference comes by way of Thomas Grantham's letter to John Connould, 10 May 1691.

[110] Michael Mullett, "Lloyd, William (1627–1717)," *ODNB*, http://www.oxforddnb.com/view/article/16860?docPos=2 (accessed 10 July 2008).

[111] St. Asaph is located in North Wales.

[112] While not everyone agrees there was such a plot, Dissenters were mistreated and harassed as a result of the "discovery."

their support behind the Exclusion Bill in 1679.[113] Ever since, Charles had harassed and persecuted those he formerly sought to protect.[114] In this environment of royal hostility, Grantham republished *The Loyal Baptist* in 1684. Thus it should come as no surprise that Grantham reiterated the four great duties of "a constant conformist to the scriptures": (1) to honor all people, (2) to love the brotherhood, (3) to fear God, and (4) to honor the king.[115]

In the same year Grantham published *The Second Part of the Apology* in response to Nathaniel Taylor's arguments in favor of infant baptism. Grantham also took issue with the lack of discipline in the Church of England and claimed that Matthew 18 was the normative example of discipline among believers. Grantham concluded the treatise with a threefold test of truth: antiquity, reason, and scripture. It seems that *The Second Part of the Apology* was the last known work Grantham published while ministering in Lincolnshire. It was his transition from Lincolnshire to Norfolk that signaled the final years of Grantham's ministry and life.

Losing Thomas Grantham: Norfolk (1686–92)

Almost nothing is known of the circumstances surrounding Grantham's removal to Norfolk sometime between 1686 and 1690 (see map 4). The various published histories offered no explanation for his departure. There was no hint that health concerns were behind his move, nor did his church-planting or writing activities abate. He remained mobile and influential until death. That his health and reputation were intact is evidenced by his secretarial role at the General Baptist Assembly in London in 1689.[116] It is probably safe to assume that as a messenger of the South

---

[113] The "Exclusion Crisis" involved efforts to exclude Charles II's brother, James, from succeeding to the throne because he was a Roman Catholic.

[114] Michael R. Watts, *The Dissenters*, 2 vols. (Oxford: Oxford University Press, 1978) 1.253.

[115] Grantham listed these duties on the title page of *The Loyal Baptist.*

[116] William T. Whitley, ed., *Minutes of the General Assembly of the General Baptist Churches in England*, 2 vols. (London: Kingsgate Press, 1910) 1.28.

Marsh Church, Grantham would have needed permission to leave, but there is no record of a formal mission to Norwich or the surrounding areas. What, then, might have led to his unexpected move to Norfolk?

One possible reason for Grantham's transition to Norfolk may have had to do with his relationship with William Pann, who was from nearby Halton Holegate in Lincolnshire. Grantham and Pann were colleagues, if not friends, and it was Pann, who was the other signatory from Lincolnshire on the 1660 petition to Charles II. It was the same Pann who posted Grantham's fliers inviting the Bapist-turned-Anglican Robert Wright to debate in 1670.[117] Adam Taylor described Pann as Grantham's "co-adjutor and fellow-messenger," and it was none other than Pann who "succeeded [Grantham] in the care of the churches" in Lincolnshire.[118] Given his reputation and relationship to Grantham, Pann's public fall from grace in 1693 was surprising to many General Baptists.

Published histories seem unaware of the event, but records show that Pann presided over an associational meeting at Spalding in April 1693, but by August of the same year he was on "trial" in Gunby.[119] At least fifteen witnesses were brought in from various towns, and Pann was eventually found guilty of fornication, verbally abusing Lincolnshire representatives to London, lying, denial, and false accusation. The association excommunicated Pann, and the church records mention him no more. Citing the troubling William Pann episode in 1693, Robert Kershaw wondered whether Grantham may have been impacted by Pann's tarnished reputation and departed Lincolnshire on negative terms in the late 1680s.[120] But Grantham had already been active in Norfolk well before Pann's disgrace, and there is no evidence for any clear connection between Grantham's departure and Pann's later problems.

---

[117] Crosby, *The History of the English Baptists*, 2.241–44.

[118] Adam Taylor, *The History of the English General Baptists*, 1.316–17.

[119] Details are available in the *Burgh & Monksthorpe Church Book, 1692–1825*, held in the Angus Library at Regent's Park College, Oxford, UK. See also Kershaw, "Baptised Believers," 35.

[120] Kershaw, "Baptised Believers," 35. It was last reported by John Hursthouse that Grantham left because of the unnamed "false brethre *An Epistle to the Baptized Churches in Lincolnshire* (1729).

Regardless of the reasons, toward the end of his life Grantham turned his attention to the county of Norfolk.

In his history of Baptists in Norfolk, Charles Jewson spoke to the issue of Grantham's presence in the county.[121] Calvinistic Baptists were the first to put down roots in Norfolk. General Baptists and Particular Baptists rarely succeeded in occupying the same area,[122] but just before the Revolution in 1688, General Baptists from Lincolnshire began to extend efforts into the region.[123] Jewson identified Grantham as the principle figure in this effort, but noted that he made little or no effort to work with Particular Baptists in the area.[124] It is possible that insufficient records survive regarding the details of this move and that Grantham was released by the South Marsh Church to work as a messenger planting churches in Norfolk.[125] Regardless of how or why Grantham ended up in Norfolk, once there he worked tirelessly to fulfill the mandates incumbent upon his office, debate local ministers, and publish.

Ordering Grantham's exact movements during these years is difficult, but his legacy includes planting churches in Norfolk county locations such as Norwich, the coastal towns of Great Yarmouth and King's Lynn, and the small village of Smallburgh. Norwich, the county capital and most populous of the four towns, was home to Julian (1342–ca. 1416), the great English anchoress and mystic. The origins of the church Grantham founded in Norwich—the second Baptist church in the city—are unclear. Tradition has assigned it an earlier date than 1686, perhaps 1670, but there is no evidence to support this claim.[126] Meetings

---

[121] Jewson, *The Baptists in Norfolk*, 29–37.

[122] Whitley, *Minutes of the General Assembly of the General Baptist Churches in England*, 1.l.

[123] James Marham, a General Baptist minister in Lincolnshire in the 1670s and early 1680s, moved to Norfolk in 1685 and began proclaiming Baptist principles. Grantham worked extensively with Marham in 1688 and 1689.

[124] Jewson, *The Baptists in Norfolk*, 31.

[125] Ibid., 29.

[126] Jewson, *The Baptists in Norfolk*, 29. Jewson did consider it a possibility that the church was planted during an unrecorded visit by Grantham to Norwich at an earlier date.

were held at the White Friars' Convent, where the congregation had evidently secured long-term use of the premises and land for burial.[127] Grantham's grandson, Grantham Killingworth, erected a monument there to his grandfather that described his early career and work in Norfolk.[128] Neither the monument nor White Friars exists today. In Great Yarmouth, Perry Gauci found during this period that a General Baptist church had been reconstituted as recently as 1686, which suggests that Grantham was at least partially responsible for the revival of the church.[129] Grantham is also reported to have preached in the town hall in King's Lynn and has been credited with establishing a General Baptist presence there.[130]

The year 1687 brought winds of change and controversy for Grantham and all Dissenters. In April, King James II issued a Declaration of Indulgence that suspended all penal laws related to church attendance, permitted Dissenters to worship in private houses or other buildings, and did away with required oaths for civil or military service.[131] While this was a huge turn of events for Dissenters in general, it also carried the potential for open and public infighting among the various dissenting

---

[127] Jewson, *The Baptists of Norfolk*, 29. A printing house now stands on the site of the former convent. See also Richard Copsey, *The Medieval Carmelite Priory at Norwich: A Chronology*, http://www.carmelite.org/chronology/Norwich.pdf (accessed on 7 July 2008); John Kirkpatrick and Dawson Turner, eds., *History of the Religious Orders and Communities and of the Hospital and Castle of Norwich* (Yarmouth: C. Sloman, 1845) 150–95; and Francis Blomefield and Charles Parkin, eds., *History of Norwich*, vol. 4 of *An Essay towards a Topographical History of the County of Norfolk*, (London, 1805) 416–23.

[128] See Appendix C for the full text inscribed on the monument.

[129] Perry Gauci, *Politics and Society in Great Yarmouth, 1660–1722* (New York: Oxford University Press, 1996) 166.

[130] *The Lyn Persecution* (n.p., 1692/3) 11.

[131] The Declaration of Indulgence issued by the openly Roman Catholic James II in 1687 (which was revised and reissued in 1688) was similar to that issued by Charles II in 1672 insofar as both sought to alleviate pressure on religious dissenters. Both the 1672 and 1687 declarations circumvented Parliament, which helps explain why they lasted only a short time before being retracted. James II had hoped to win the support of the Dissenters with such moves in 1687 and 1688, but his actions ultimately led to the so-called "Glorious Revolution" and the end of his reign.

groups. Reversal of the declaration in 1688, however, would have certainly put Dissenters on edge, and not until the Act of Toleration in 1689 would relief became permanent. Even in 1689, however, toleration was not extended to Roman Catholics, and in 1689 Dissenters were again required to register their meetinghouses.

In early 1687, Samuel Petto wrote *Infant baptism of Christ's Appointment* as a defense of infant baptism and an attack on the Baptist baptismal position.[132] Petto was a local independent Congregationalist minister and fellow dissenter in Norfolk, which is why Grantham was perturbed that he had written against the Baptists. "It is no convenient time," Grantham wrote, "for Dissenters to write one against another; friendly conferences might do much better."[133] There was to be no friendly conference, however, because Grantham thought men like Petto were "averse to such meetings." Still, Grantham felt some response was necessary, so he offered *Presumption no Proof* (1687) as a defense of believer's baptism and critique of infant damnation. In addition to dealing with Petto, Grantham also used *Presumption no Proof* as an opportunity to respond to *The Plea of the Children of Believing-Parents for their Interest in Abraham's Covenant,* written by Giles Firmin some four years earlier.[134]

In October 1687, Petto responded with *Infant-Baptism Vindicated from the Exceptions of Mr. Thomas Grantham*; Firmin followed suit with *Scripture-Warrant Sufficient Proof for Infant-Baptism* in 1688. The circumstances surrounding Firmin's reply are telling. In the opening pages, Firmin recounted that he had been recently informed by a "young furious Zealot against Infant Baptism" from London that his previous book, *The Plea of the Children*, had been answered by a "great" and "learned" writer by the name of Thomas Grantham, who would

---

[132] Samuel Petto's prefatory letter, released in London, was dated 29 March 1687, *Infant baptism of Christ's Appointment* (London, 1687).

[133] Thomas Grantham, *Presumption no Proof* (London, 1687) To the Reader.

[134] Cf. discussion of Firmin above. Since Firmin's work predated that of Petto, Grantham opened with a preface that doubled as a short response to Firmin.

undoubtedly prove to be a "formidable" adversary.[135] The young zealot even purchased a copy of *Presumption no Proof* for Firmin. This exchange and the conflict surrounding it reveal that Grantham adopted the role of apologist in Norfolk, just as he had done in Lincolnshire. Grantham had become a significant figure not only in Lincolnshire, but word of his abilities had made its way from London to Norfolk. General Baptists had come to expect great things from Thomas Grantham.

In the midst of the literary disputes with Petto and Firmin, Grantham found time to publish *St. Paul's Catechism* (1687), a catechetical pamphlet for children that was written as a conversation between a father and son. The main force of his argument was that the six principles found in Hebrews 6:1–2 were foundational for all Christian churches and necessary for the young to learn.[136] Children were not to be baptized, Grantham believed, but they were to be taken seriously as little theologians.

In 1687 Grantham also published three separate treatises under one title: *Hear the Church: Or, An Appeal to the Mother of us All* (1687).[137] Written as an appeal to all Christians to embrace the Jerusalem Church as the mother of all churches, Grantham took specific aim at the "papists," though the treatise did occasionally broach disagreements with paedo-baptists in general. The first treatise described the state of the primitive Christian church and outlined why it was reasonable to appeal to it as an example. The second treatise, originally written in 1685, consisted of a

---

[135] Giles Firmin, *Scripture-Warrant*, To the Reader, A2–A3.

[136] Thomas Grantham, *St. Paul's Catechism, or, A Brief and Plain Explication of the Six Principles of the Christian Religion, as Recorded Heb. 6.,1,2* (London, 1687). The six principles were: (1) repentance from dead works, (2) faith towards God, (3) the doctrine of baptisms (Grantham asserted three baptisms: the baptism of repentance for remission of sins, the pouring out of the Spirit, and the afflictions that accompany Christian commitment), (4) the laying on of hands, (5) the resurrection of the dead, and (6) the eternal judgment. See further, Stephen Wright, *The Early English Baptists, 1603–1649* (Rochester NY: Boydell Press, 2006) 138ff.; White, *The English Baptists of the Seventeenth Century*, 36–40; and Ernest Payne, "Baptists and the Laying on of Hands," *Baptist Quarterly* 15, no. 5 (January 1954): 203–15.

[137] Thomas Grantham, *Hear the Church: Or, An Appeal to the Mother of us All* (London, 1687).

comparison between Baptist and Roman Catholic views on baptism and the Lord's Supper.[138] The third and final treatise of *Hear the Church* has a rather interesting history. Grantham introduced the treatise by informing the reader that the unnamed adversary in *The Baptist against the Papist* (1662) never replied in print, but did send him seven questions in manuscript form. So, finally, in 1687, Grantham found opportunity to publish the papist's questions and his own answers. The disagreements centered on scripture, the Eucharist, and the marks of the universal church. *Hear the Church* exhibited Grantham's understanding of, and disagreements with, the Roman church.[139]

Grantham's activities were not limited to Norwich in these final years, however, for in 1687 he was present at a meeting in the church at Bourne, Lincolnshire (see map 2). The Bourne church book reports that Grantham was present for the ordination of Joseph Hooke on 7 September 1687.[140] Grantham continued to fulfill the mandate of his office: Hooke was ordained "by Fasting and Prayer, with Laying on of Hands, by Thomas Grantham, then Messenger of the Baptized Churches in Lincolnshire."[141] An entry in the records for 30 June 1688 is a five-page list of the congregation's officers and members. Grantham's name and the title "Messenger" appear first, followed by elders and then

---

[138] The final page of the second treatise on standing firm in the midst of persecution records that it was written in 1685 (*Hear the Church* [London, 1687] 40). Page 20 (the second page of the second treatise) referenced "St. *Paul's Catechism*." Though *St. Paul's Catechism* was not published until 1687, the reference here implies Grantham had been thinking through the idea for some time. The second treatise had a postscript titled: "Concerning the Original Manuscripts of the Holy Scriptures."

[139] *Hear the Church* and *The Baptist against the Papist* are discussed in some detail when outlining Grantham's interaction with Roman Catholics in the chapter on the "The Great Debaters."

[140] The entry can be found on page 7 of the church book. The record was entered in 1720. For commentary, see F. J. Mason, "The Old Minute Book of Bourne Baptist Church," *The Baptist Quarterly* 15, no. 5 (January 1954): 226.

[141] Mason, "The Old Minute Book," 226.

wives.[142] Grantham is also found among the names in the Warboys church book (a congregation in the county of Huntingdonshire, which was a county to the west of the county of Norfolk), where it was written that he baptized two new members in 1688.[143] It is clear from these entries that Grantham remained active and influential as a messenger of the Lincolnshire General Baptists even after his move to Norfolk. It does not appear that he was exiled to Norfolk or that he was estranged from the Lincolnshire General Baptists.

Back in Norfolk, Grantham initiated another round of debate with Giles Firmin in 1688. It was noted above that Firmin published *Scripture-Warrant* in early 1688 as a rebuttal to Grantham's *Presumption no Proof* (1687), so Grantham, not content to let the matter die, retorted with *The Infants Advocate* (1688). Firmin returned the favor some months later in the short, sardonic, and exasperated treatise *The Answer of Giles Firmin*. Grantham replied again a year or so later in *The Infants Advocate, The Second Part* (1690). This would not be the end of this rather lengthy and increasingly bitter spat.

Baptists' baptismal views were a constant source of irritation for their opponents, and in 1689 Grantham published yet another critique of infant baptism, *Truth and Peace*. Grantham was ever willing to engage opponents, and this time his attention turned to an unnamed "Doctor of the Church of England."[144] Grantham intended for *Truth and Peace* to be his last contribution to the controversy, and his main point was that nothing short of the restoration of sacred baptism could revive ancient Christianity in all nations. That Grantham added a postscript detailing the

---

[142] The date actually appears as June 31 in the church book. Adam Taylor (*The History of the English General Baptists,* 1.215ff.) raised a question concerning Grantham's place on this list. He was unsure whether Grantham was included and at the head of the list because he presided over the meeting (the option he believed most likely), or whether Grantham may have removed his membership from the South Marsh Church to this church at some point.

[143] Edward B. Underhill, *Records of the Churches of Christ gathered at Fenstanton, Warboys, and Hexham, 1644–1720*, 2 vols. (London: Haddon Brothers, 1854) 1.282.

[144] Thomas Grantham, *Truth and Peace* (London, 1689) title page.

nature of marriage among baptized believers is revealing, for freedom to worship did not necessarily pave the way for civil or religious equality where marriage was concerned. Grantham claimed that the law of the land did not nullify or void marriages of baptized believers, but actually established them. He doubted that marriages were necessarily to be performed by an official minister and equated the giving and receiving of rings as a baseless Roman Catholic superstition. The nature of conformity and nonconformity may have been different in 1689, but marriage remained an issue nonetheless.

At some point in late 1688 or early 1689 the General Baptist James Marham, who had previously ministered in Lincolnshire but had made his way to King's Lynn after the death of his wife, invited Grantham to preach in King's Lynn (see map 4).[145] Grantham's preaching gained several followers, and the congregation began to grow. Upon Grantham's recommendation, Marham secured a place for public worship by registering a meeting place as specified in the Toleration Act. In this way, a General Baptist presence was established in King's Lynn.[146]

In March of 1689, Grantham attended the General Baptist General Assembly in London, where he likely participated in the lively discussions concerning ordination and congregational singing.[147] The assembly's minutes, which were recorded by Grantham, note that he was especially vocal in opposition to singing recent compositions in a mixed congregation of men and women.[148]

Little is known of Grantham until he was present in Sutterby, Lincolnshire, to ratify his will in May 1690. This may have been his last visit to Lincolnshire. Taylor wrote that Grantham unsuccessfully sought to return to Lincolnshire in 1691, but he gives no source for this claim.[149]

---

[145] *The Lyn Persecution* (n.p., 1692/3) 7–11.

[146] Ibid., 11–12. See also William Richard, "Biography of Thomas Grantham," *Universal Theological Magazine* 3, no. 15 (January 1805): 111.

[147] Whitley, *Minutes of the General Assembly of the General Baptist Churches in England*, 1.1.

[148] Ibid., 1.28.

[149] Taylor, *The History of the English General Baptists*, 1.313–14.

Upon returning to Norwich, Grantham continued to advance the anti-predestinarian cause in the face of growing Calvinistic momentum.[150] Grantham appears to have shown little interest in the Particular Baptists, at least in his published works, but it is clear that he sought to build bridges, albeit unsuccessfully for the most part, with other dissenting groups. Toward that end, Grantham wrote to Dr. John Collinges, a local Presbyterian minister, in September 1690. In the letter, Grantham reacted to a passage in Collinges's *A Discourse of Divine Love* that ostensibly supported God's sovereignty in election: "God cannot seriously act, and be finally opposed."[151] Collinges, who seems to have been unfamiliar with Grantham, immediately penned a response questioning Grantham's common sense and knowledge of God. Collinges had little desire to enter into any kind of sustained dialogue, and his death in January of 1691 ensured its impossibility. Martin Finch, a Congregational minister in Norwich, presided at Collinges's funeral. Such an unlikely friendship between competing churches would likely have been impossible in the past, but Collinges had recently orchestrated a union of Presbyterians and Congregationalists in Norwich. It is little wonder that Grantham felt Calvinism was taking hold of his city.

In February 1691, only a month after Collinges's death, Grantham daringly published *A Dialogue between a Baptist and a Presbyterian*, which included the Grantham-Collinges correspondence and a contrived conversation between a Baptist and a Presbyterian.[152] Finch, who may have been compelled to defend his friend, published *An Answer to Mr. Thomas Grantham's Book* in June. Grantham appears to have been upset that Finch did not seek a more personal meeting first, but Finch defended his reserved nature and hesitancy to engage in discussion with a most intriguing statement:

[150] Thomas Grantham, *A Dialogue between the Baptist and the Presbyterian* (London, 1691) 3.

[151] Ibid., 4ff.

[152] Grantham concluded the treatise with a short poem directed at John Calvin and appended Henry Haggar's popular anti-predestinarian treatise *The Order of Causes* (the fifth edition of 1659) to the end of *A Dialogue*.

> Sir, I perceive you take it ill, that I do not seek acquaintance and familiarity with you, truly it is my natural temper to love retirement, and not to have much acquaintance, but as to your self, I confess I do not desire intimacy with you, because I told you the first time, I ever spake with you about fifteen years since, that one of your own judgment about baptism, had charged you in print, that you set the houses of God on fire, where ever you came, and that you pretended to be an archbishop, and to have jurisdiction over other churches, or words to that purpose; and since you came to live at Norwich, you have been so quarrelsome with those of your own persuasion about baptism, and likewise with my worthy friend Dr. Collinges…[153]

One should proceed cautiously when looking for truth in statements from opponents, but the allusions to division among the Baptists (General/Particular?) and Grantham's possible propensity to overstep the bounds of his office are intriguing.

In April 1691 another meeting of the General Baptist Assembly convened in London. Those present discussed the republication of the *Standard Confession* and the appropriate monetary stipend for traveling messengers. In addition, two messengers were approved and there was a decision to send a "Brother Foxwell" to "assist Thomas Grantham in Norwich in the ministerial work of the gospel."[154] The minutes provide no details on the reasons for Nathan Foxwell's assignment, but it is clear that Grantham required some manner of assistance.

Back in Norfolk, Grantham persisted in attacking Calvinism despite a string of antagonistic encounters with his opponents. In August 1691 he published *The Forerunner to a Further Answer*. In this short treatise Grantham began with an anti-Calvinistic excerpt by George Wither (d. 1667), an eclectic seventeenth-century author, before resuming what had been to that point a one-sided debate with Finch.

---

[153] Martin Finch, *An Answer to Mr. Thomas Grantham's Book* (London: Printed by T. Snowden[?], 1691) 146.

[154] Whitley, *Minutes of the General Assembly of the General Baptist Churches in England*, 1.30ff.

Grantham's frosty interactions with Collinges and Finch were balanced by his remarkably amicable relationship with John Connould, vicar of St. Stephen's in Norwich. Grantham's efforts in Norwich caught Connould's attention when his own parishioners were attracted to the Baptist meetings. In light of this, Connould wrote to Grantham inquiring about his ordination and rejection of infant baptism.[155] The ensuing letters reveal that Connould and Grantham developed a fairly close relationship. Grantham was allowed access to Connould's library, where he may have encountered Michael Servetus's *Restitution of Christianity* (1553).[156] In the aforementioned *A Dialogue between a Baptist and a Presbyterian* (1691), Grantham referenced Servetus several times, marking a notable early reference to him in English.[157] It also became apparent in this correspondence that reports of Grantham's ability to work with eight or nine languages were likely exaggerations.[158]

Theological debates and controversies were not Grantham's only concern in 1691; he was also forced to defend his innocence and integrity against numerous allegations and accusations. In *The Slanderer Rebuked* (1691), Grantham described a disagreement with a "Mr. Toathby," a "seller of wool" and former magistrate in Norwich. According to Grantham, when he was still living in Ashby, Lincolnshire, in 1677, he paid to have his ram shorn. The shearer, however, mistakenly sheared the ram of a nearby poor man. When it was later discovered that it was not Grantham's ram, Grantham paid the poor man one-half the cost of the

---

[155] John Connould to Thomas Grantham, 17 April 1691.

[156] John Connould to Thomas Grantham, 8 May 1691.

[157] The *ODNB* claimed that Grantham accessed the document in Connould's library, while Jewson believed Grantham accessed the manuscript in the library of John Moore, Bishop of Norwich (*The Baptists in Norfolk*, 37).

[158] In a letter to Connould dated 5 May 1691, Grantham mentioned that he had limited knowledge of Latin and requested that Connould refrain from employing lengthy Latin quotations in his letters. William Richard reported that Grantham Killingworth said his grandfather worked in Latin with some ease, "Biography of Thomas Grantham," *Universal Theological Magazine* 3, no. 16 (January 1805): 166. The *DNB* entry for Grantham noted that Grantham may have been proficient in eight or nine languages, but this appears to be incorrect based on Grantham's request to Connould.

ram to settle the matter. After some time, Grantham's enemies encouraged the man to sue Grantham, but it does not seem the matter ever went to court. When Grantham finally moved to Norwich, Toathby confronted Grantham about the incident in May 1691. As a relatively new resident, Grantham found himself without anyone to vouch for his innocence. To clear his name, Grantham had several men from Ashby who were living in Ashby at the time of the incident write letters confirming his testimony and honesty.[159] The mayor of Norwich was convinced of Grantham's innocence and dismissed any charges. The motivation for smearing Grantham's name and reputation is unclear, but it is probable that the accusations were religiously motivated.[160]

In October 1691, Grantham was again accused of stealing sheep. *The Grand Imposter* (1691) tells how John Willet, rector of Tattershall in Lincolnshire, testified in writing that he had seen Grantham spend two hours in the Louth pillory for ordering his servant to brand seven of his neighbor's sheep as his own.[161] When he was called upon to testify before Thomas Blofield, mayor of Norwich on 6 October 1691, Willet broke down and admitted to concocting the entire story. Willet also confessed to lying when he accused three men, one of which was Connould, of encouraging him to lie by giving him too much wine and a payment of two shillings. Blofield was disgusted with these actions and fined Willet, but Grantham took pity on him and paid the fine himself. Grantham also wrote in *The Grand Imposter* that some thought him to be a papist, others a drunkard, and still others called him a "Whoremonger."[162] Grantham dismissed all these accusations, noting that he had

---

[159] Grantham included the letters in *The Slanderer Rebuked* (n.p., 1691). See further, George Southcombe, "The Responses of Nonconformists to the Restoration in England" (DPhil thesis, University of Oxford, 2005) 177–78.

[160] A point made by Southcombe in "The Responses of Nonconformists to the Restoration in England," 178. See also *The Grand Imposter*, 3ff.

[161] Thomas Grantham, *The Grand Imposter* (n.p., 1691) 4. An anonymous pamphlet written by a Calvinist opponent was published in light of this episode; *A Brief and Plain Discourse upon the Decrees of God Wherein Mr. Grantham's Query Is Considered and Answered* (London: Printed by T. Snowden[?], 1692).

[162] Grantham, *The Grand Imposter*, 10.

been the husband of one wife.[163] Grantham's years in Norfolk were filled with conflict and friendship, a testimony to the complex relationships among Dissenters in late seventeenth-century England.

Thomas Grantham took his last breath on 17 January 1692 at age fifty-eight. The cause of death is unknown. Eight people were present at his passing: John Mingo, Andrew Pegg, William Sidwell, Thomas Gambell, Thomas Miller, John Clarke, Alice Clarke, and Ann Grantham.[164] John Clarke's personal copy of *Christianismus Primitivus* contains several handwritten compositions that reflect Grantham's importance in Norwich and the devoted, personal relationships he developed there. Grantham's dying words were transcribed into the manuscript shortly after his death; they were later made public and printed as *The Dying Words of Mr. Thomas Grantham.*[165] Grantham's final thoughts were strikingly coherent and pastoral given his "weak condition." He reminded his friends that "preaching and printing" were his primary contributions. Furthermore, he spoke of his many skirmishes with opponents and claimed to have forgiven them all.

In addition to Grantham's dying words, two acrostic poems written on the occasion of his death can be read in the manuscript. The poems conveyed the grief and sadness resulting from the death of friend, but also expressed confidence in God's presence and future restoration of all things.[166] Two poetic epitaphs are found in the manuscript along with the acrostics and dying words. The epitaphs emphasized Grantham's labors as "A preacher, Bishop, and Evangelist" and encourage the readers to find solace in the coming day of resurrection.[167] There is a thirteen-stanza

---

[163] Ibid.

[164] *The Dying Words of Mr. Thomas Grantham* (n.p., 1692/3). It seems likely that Ann Grantham was the wife of David Killingworth. See Jewson, "The Old General Baptist Church at Norwich," *Baptist Quarterly* 9 (1938-39): 432. The Millennium Library in Norwich holds a manuscript copy of *Christianismus Primitivus* that was owned by a Richard Clarke. It is possible that Richard was related to Alice and John and that all three were members of Grantham's church.

[165] Grantham's dying words are included below as Appendix B.

[166] The acrostic poems are included below as Appendix D.

[167] The epitaph is included below as Appendix E.

poem titled "The Christians dayly Exercise." It seems likely that Grantham authored this poem, but it is impossible to confirm his authorship.[168] The poem urged the Christian to take advantage of the opportunities each day provides, control the passions, think on heavenly things, speak wisely and kindly, pray daily as an individual and family, and close the day with a benediction.

Finally, Clarke's manuscript includes the handwritten text of two eulogies that were likely delivered at Grantham's funeral. The first is a fascinating and anonymous piece titled "An Elegy on the Death of that Eminent and faithful Servant of Christ; and unwearied Labourer in the Gospell Mr Thomas Grantham."[169] The eulogy lauded Grantham and lamented his passing, but it also recounted his multi-faceted ministry. The writer described the irreplaceable nature of Grantham's ability: "Thus whilst our souls were filled, with painfull griefe Rouling from place to place to finde Reliefe. Thinking whoe now was left still to defend. Christs Glorious truth, whoe able to contend. With courage, Argument & dextrous wit. 'Gainst all opposers of the wayes of it." The eulogy went on to praise Grantham's humility and intellectual capacity. It drew attention to *Christianismus Primitivus*, which, as the eulogy claims, was a "famous work" known to "every readers eye." In the remainder of the eulogy Grantham was remembered for attacking Rome and defending believer's baptism.

There is a second eulogy included in the manuscript believed to have been delivered by Connould himself.[170] Regardless of who delivered it, the touching remembrance called attention to Grantham's arguments against infant baptism, his care for the churches, his desire for

---

[168] Jewson believed that Grantham was the likely author of the poem since it was composed "in Grantham's tradition" (Jewson, *The Baptists in Norfolk*, 34). See Appendix F for an excerpt from the poem regarding appropriate "Discourse."

[169] The eulogy takes up almost an entire folio page and was written in a two-column format. It is unclear how many copies of the eulogies survive.

[170] Taylor, *The History of the English General Baptists,* 1.315; Jewson, *The Baptists in Norfolk*, 36.

unity, and his loyalty to the king. It concluded with the observation that "this day has a very great man fallen in Israel."

It was reported that Grantham's enemies attempted to "abuse his corps" after his burial, so Connould had the body interred inside St. Stephen's nave to protect it from desecration.[171] When Connould died in 1708, he requested that he be laid to rest next to his dissenting friend, Thomas Grantham.[172] By all accounts, the death of Thomas Grantham was a difficult loss for the General Baptists cause, especially in Lincolnshire and Norfolk.

---

[171] Taylor held that Grantham was interred in the middle aisle (*The History of the English General Baptists,* 1.315); Jewson wrote that his body was placed inside the west door (*The Baptists in Norfolk,* 36). Benjamin Mackerell's account of the monuments in St. Stephen's reads "Thomas Grantham, an Anabaptist Teacher, was buried under two rows of small broken stones, near to the south porch, Jan. 19, 1691" (*St. Stephen's Parish In the City of Norwich, with some Observations on the Same* [n.p., 1729?] 63).

[172] The current stones in the floor are different from those of the eighteenth century. Connould's stone has been moved from its original position and now rests near the chancel. Thus, Grantham's burial site is likely under an unmarked stone slab at the west end of St. Stephen's nave.

Chapter 3

"Old Things by their Old Names": Grantham and the Office of Messenger, 1660–1700

Baptists from the beginning affirmed a twofold ministry of pastors (also referred to as elders) and deacons. In time, some Baptist congregations began to utilize a third office, that of "messenger," in varying ways. Particular Baptists predominantly used messengers as congregational representatives to convey messages to other congregations or carry out missionary work, but they never embraced or affirmed the office as a third order of ministers. Many General Baptists, on the other hand, believed the office of messenger to be biblical, and the office gradually became an important institution among their congregations.

More than fifty years have passed since John F. V. Nicholson, a Baptist messenger himself and acquainted with the office, published the "The Office of 'Messenger' amongst British Baptists in the Seventeenth and Eighteenth Centuries."[1] Nicholson's seminal work remains the foundational study concerning the office, but little has been done in the way of expansion or critique. The pages to follow will expand Nicholson's work and primarily focus on Grantham's place in the process by which messengers became an established ministry among the General Baptists of the seventeenth century.

---

[1] John F. V. Nicholson, "The Office of 'Messenger' amongst British Baptists in the Seventeenth and Eighteenth Centuries," *Baptist Quarterly* 17, no. 5 (January 1958): 206–25. Following Nicholson's pattern, "messenger" will only be capitalized when a quoted source does so or when the term is used as the minister's official title. For a more recent theological discussion of church offices in Baptist life, see Paul S. Fiddes, *Tracks and Traces: Baptist Identity in Church and Theology* (Waynesboro GA: Paternoster Press, 2003) 83–106.

It is common to encounter the name of Thomas Grantham in small amount of scholarship that is related to the emergence of the office, and there appears to be little doubt that Grantham played an important role in solidifying the office in General Baptist life by the time of his death in 1692.[2] Thus, any explanation or inquiry as to how the office of messenger evolved into an accepted third ministerial office must account for Thomas Grantham, whom Nicholson singled out as the "main source for evidence"[3] of the office among the General Baptists from 1660–1700.

Baptist Messengers Prior to the Restoration of 1660

Nicholson's discussion began with the office of messenger as mentioned in a confession of faith titled the *Faith and Practice of Thirty Congregations* (1651). There are, however, two earlier references to the office in the 1640s: *The London Confession* (1644) of the Calvinistic Baptists and Edward Barber's *A True Discovery of the Ministry of the Gospel* (1645). Nicholson rightfully identified three major sources for information pertaining to the office of messenger (i.e., confessions of faith and minutes of assemblies of Baptist churches, the published writings of individual Baptists, and the records of individual churches[4]), but he dealt with the records of individual churches last. The following examination proceeds in a slightly different order, dealing first with the confessions of faith and minutes of assemblies of Baptist churches, then to the records of individual churches, and finally to the published writings of individual Baptists.

Affirmation of an itinerant and travelling ministry similar to that of the original Apostles was evident among the Familists, the followers of Henry Niclaes (d. 1540), who were present in England by the end of the sixteenth century.[5] No direct link between the Baptists and Familists can

---

[2] Barrington R. White, *The English Baptists of the Seventeenth Century* (London: The Baptist Historical Society, 1996) 117.

[3] Nicholson, "The Office of 'Messenger'," 211.

[4] Ibid., 207.

[5] See Christopher Hill, *The World Turned the World Upside Down: Radical Ideas During the English Revolution* (New York: Penguin Books, 1991) 26ff.

be made with regard to the origins of the messenger's office among the Baptists, but it should be noted that the presence of a mobile ministry was not unprecedented. In addition, the term "messenger" among the Baptists carried different connotations depending on the context. It could refer to a person sent from one church to another with a message or simply someone representing a congregation. In other contexts, a messenger referred to an evangelist or preacher who was responsible for planting new churches in a particular region. While it may be difficult to assign a specific date or time to the genesis of the office among the Baptists, there is little doubt that scripture, and especially its example of the primitive church found therein, was the point of departure for any discussion of the office.

Adam Taylor wrote that an emphasis on scripture led the General Baptists of the seventeenth century to the conclusion that there was indeed a third ministerial office. Based on their close reading of the scriptures,

> [I]t was not long before they supposed that they had discovered in the primitive churches an officer superior to an elder...and that in various passages they are called apostles, or in English, messengers of the churches...They introduced an officer into their systems whom they styled a messenger. He was generally chosen by an association of the representatives of the churches in a certain district, and ordained by those of his own order with great solemnity, the various churches keeping seasons of prayer and fasting. Sometimes a particular church chose a messenger; but in that case his business appears to have been confined to preaching the gospel where it was not known, and regulating such churches as he might be made instrumental in planting. It is indeed probable that at the first this was the chief object of their appointment.[6]

Taylor highlighted at least three important characteristics of the early attempts to appoint and ordain messengers. First, an emphasis on

---

Niclaes was said to have worked with Thomas Müntzer in Germany in the sixteenth century.

[6] Adam Taylor, *The History of the English General Baptists*, 2 vols. (London: T. Bore, 1818) 1.413–14.

scripture led the General Baptists to consider the validity of a new and superior ecclesiastical office. Second, the messenger-system was somehow contingent upon the cooperation and involvement of a number of local congregations. Third, preaching the gospel and planting new churches were the primary tasks of those appointed to this office.

Taylor's identification of scripture as the foundational roadmap was significant, but it is important to remember that he was describing a pattern that only crystallized among some Baptists over a period of decades. In 1644, "elders and messengers" representing seven churches gathered and issued a confession declaring their right to congregate. Barrington White recognized such a meeting as perhaps the first reference to a gathering of this kind among Baptists,[7] while Stephen Wright remarked that in 1644 "the act of association which the confession embodied" was important.[8] The *London Confession* of 1644 is critical in our context because it reveals the presence of "messengers" at a Baptist gathering. No mention is made of their status or role, but signatories such as William Kiffin and John Spilsbury were influential pastors.

A notable omission from the list of signatories in 1644 is the name of Edward Barber, who was apparently in the process of adopting views more consistent with general atonement and laying on of hands.[9] The next year, Barber's reading of Ephesians 4:8–14 led him to the conclusion that the office of "apostle" had not ceased with the death of the last Apostle.[10] In *A True Discovery of the Ministry of the Gospel* (1645), he examined the various gifts described in Ephesians: apostles, prophets, evangelists, pastors, and teachers. He provided no fewer than

---

[7] White, *The English Baptists of the Seventeenth Century*, 68.

[8] Stephen Wright, *The Early English Baptists, 1603–1649* (Rochester NY: Boydell Press, 2006) 136.

[9] Ibid. For a discussion of the complicated journey of Edward Barber, see Wright, *The Early English Baptists, 1603–1649*, 99–140.

[10] Nicholson identified Thomas Lover's *The True Gospel Faith* (London, 1654) as the "first reference to the office in a published work" ("The Office of 'Messenger'," 208), but Edward Barber's *A True Discovery of the Ministry of the Gospel* (London, 1645) predates Lover's work.

thirty-six qualifications for those who would be "Apostles, or Messengers; the Master-builders, or layers of the foundation; Fathers or begetters to the faith..."[11] Barber insisted that messengers must have already submitted to believer's baptism and must belong to a true church.[12] Barber cautioned churches against sending forth those too young or inexperienced,[13] and similarly instructed the messengers to rely on the Spirit instead of books or university training.[14] Envisioning that Baptist messengers, like the original Apostles, would face stiff resistance, he demanded in several places that messengers be willing to endure hardship and persecution.[15] Barber also pointed out that messengers should "strive to make the Gospel free" by finding their own employment.[16] He painted the contemporary messenger primarily as an evangelist who is to preach, baptize, and grow churches, but it is important to note that his discussion stopped short of offering a full-blown picture of a tri-fold ministry of messengers, elders, and deacons. At the same time, he provided no distinction or differentiation between the original Apostles and later apostles.

Barber signed the document "servant to the churches of Christ," prompting Wright to question whether Barber himself may have been "recognized as such an apostle or messenger by churches other than his own."[17] Regardless of whether Wright was correct, one can conclude

---

[11] Barber, *A True Discovery of the Ministry of the Gospel*, 1. See also, White, *The English Baptists of the Seventeenth Century*, 30–31.

[12] Barber, *A True Discovery of the Ministry of the Gospel*, 1.

[13] Ibid., 2.

[14] Ibid., 3.

[15] Ibid. The hostility came in various forms, so a messenger had to be willing to endure the following: be seen as "mad and out of his wits" (3); "preach the gospel boldly in time of opposition" (6); "bear all sorts of affliction with patience" (7); "be mean and poor" in the eyes of the world" (8); "Not to hide their heads, nor flee their countries for fear of persecution" (8); and even to "lay down their lives for the publishing and defense of the gospel" (8).

[16] Barber, *A True Discovery of the Ministry of the Gospel*, 7.

[17] Wright, *The Early English Baptists, 1603–1649*, 139. See also Thomas Edwards, *Gangraena, OR A Catalogue and Discovery of many of the Errours, Heresies, Blasphemies and Pernicious Practices of the Sectaries of this Time*

with him that Edward Barber successfully planted "the seeds" for a third and distinct order of ministry with some kind of inter-congregational responsibility.[18] Yet to assume that General Baptist conceptions of the ministry were fixed or static during this period would be incorrect, and it is perhaps because of this state of affairs that the office of messenger assumed a more prominent position among the General Baptists.

Gauging the extent of Barber's sentiments on the office of messenger in the late 1640s is probably impossible, but it is possible to obtain some sense of the process by which the seeds planted in the 1640s germinated and spread in the 1650s. Taking a closer look at the three main sources identified by Nicholson, one is able to reconstruct with some detail a picture of the various roles assigned to messengers in the years leading up to the Restoration and the beginning of Grantham's public ministry.

As evidenced by the convening of joint meetings of representatives from across a particular region, the General Baptists took advantage of increasing governmental leniency in the early 1650s.[19] The agendas for these meetings included a variety of tasks ranging from theological discussions to financial matters to church discipline. Occasionally the representatives would issue a statement or confession as the need arose. Such a confession was issued by thirty congregations in the region of the Midlands in 1651, but it is in vain that one looks for any reference to messengers. There was acknowledgment of the need to set apart gifted ministers to preach the gospel and the need for mutual aid.[20]

When Baptist congregations in Lincolnshire, Kent, and Buckinghamshire sought to distance themselves from the Fifth Monarchy movement in 1654, they did so by dispatching "many of the Messengers,

(London, 1646) 104–5; and E. P. Winter, "The Administration of the Lord's Supper among the Baptists of the Seventeenth Century," *Baptist Quarterly* 18, no. 5 (January 1959): 196–204.

[18] White, *The English Baptists of the Seventeenth Century*, 31.

[19] Ibid., 47.

[20] William L. Lumpkin, *Baptist Confessions of Faith* (Philadelphia: Judson Press, 1959) 174–88.

Elders and Brethren belonging to several of the Baptized Churches in this nation" to compose, sign, and issue a statement reflecting their support of civil authorities.[21] The extent of the messengers' authority is unclear from the minutes, but their presence and the title are unmistakable.

Additional details can be found in the minutes from a 1656 meeting, which bear the signatures of ten messengers and include two comments related to the function and limits of the office. Messengers were expressly forbidden to select other messengers without the consent of the local congregation, but it was plainly stated that messengers and elders constitute "ye presbittery of the church..."[22] A few lines later, the process by which congregations in need requested aid included sending "sufficient testimony" to another congregation by means of "a messenger appointed for that purpose."[23] It is evident from these brief references that "messengers" could refer to ministers of an "official order" or those with the task of communicating a message to a neighboring congregation.[24]

Details from the various General Baptist church books in the 1650s suggest that there was no consensus regarding the tasks of a messenger.[25] Nicholson identified a reference to a messenger in a Calvinistic Baptist church at Hexham in Northumberland in 1652 as the earliest use of the term in any church record.[26] The records show that Thomas Tillam was commissioned as a minister and messenger of one of the seven churches in London, but his role was apparently that of missionary to several

---

[21] William T. Whitley, ed., *Minutes of the General Assembly of the General Baptists*, 2 vols. (London: Kingsgate Press, 1909) 1.1, 5.

[22] Ibid., 6.

[23] Ibid.

[24] Nicholson, "The Office of 'Messenger'," 208.

[25] Ibid., 209–10. Most of the examples included below are also cited in Nicholson but with less background or commentary.

[26] Edward B. Underhill, *Records of the Churches of Christ gathered at Fenstanton, Warboys, and Hexham, 1644–1720* (London: Haddon Brothers, 1854) 289.

northern counties. In later entries, the term "messenger" apparently denoted a representative role.[27]

The Fenstanton records suggest that a messenger's task could vary and that one's status as a messenger could be temporary or permanent. For example, in 1652 the church appointed members as "messengers" to visit those guilty of backsliding.[28] A more famous episode including messengers occurred in 1653, when the church in Westby, Lincolnshire (see map 5) sent messengers John Lupton and Joseph Wright into the county of Huntingdon "to call into question all persons, and to judge and determine all matters."[29] Such presumption of authority sparked so great a disagreement when the messengers arrived at Fenstanton that before the two proceeded to the next town Messenger Wright removed the offending line from the letter he was carrying. When the Westby congregation discovered its messengers had acted in this way, the congregation sent a letter to the Fenstanton church about the matter and also inquired as to why that church maintained communion with those who had not received the laying on of hands.

Henry Denne was also chosen and ordained as a messenger in 1653, but his particular task was "to divulge the gospel of Jesus Christ."[30] There was apparently some concern by 1654 and 1655 that Baptist ministers not engage in public ministry without the formal backing of their base church.[31] Furthermore, messengers were reluctant to make serious decisions without first consulting their own congregation.[32]

An entry from the Fenstanton records in 1656 provides valuable insights related to financial support of messengers during this period.[33] A

---

[27] Ibid.

[28] Ibid., 40.

[29] Ibid., 68ff.

[30] Ibid., 72.

[31] Ibid., 98–113.

[32] Ibid., 138–56. This is the case of Edmond Mayle and John Denne in 1655. The two were sent to assist John Miles in Wisbeach but would not agree to stay on longer unless granted permission by the Fenstanton church.

[33] Underhill, *Records of the Churches of Christ gathered at Fenstanton, Warboys, and Hexham, 1644–1720*, 196–98.

group of Baptists meeting at Stamford (in the Midlands) decided to send John Fairbrother and William Reignolds into the western parts of England as messengers. In order to offset the cost of their expenses, an appeal was made to the churches for support. The Fenstanton church refused to participate on two grounds: questionable collection methods and the background of one of the messengers. Financial assistance was also discussed in a meeting at Chatham in Kent in 1657, where "messengers, elders, and brethren" affirmed the evangelistic role of messengers and insisted that their families should receive financial support in their absence.[34]

The entries above from the church records in no way provide a complete picture of the origins of the office in the 1650s. Yet it does seem that the local church may have been *the* determining factor in how messengers functioned among General Baptists in the 1650s. Nicholson notes that local churches evidently desired to retain control of their own messengers and looked upon messengers from other churches with some suspicion.[35]

The ideas of Edward Barber were encountered above, but when one turns to discussions of the office in the works published by individuals during the 1650s, it is not surprising that the theoretical and theological explanations reflect the variety of positions evident in the confessions, joint statements, and church records.

The process of sending messengers was vaguely outlined in Thomas Lover's *The True Gospel Faith* (1654). Article 22, citing Acts 1, asserted that Christians "have the power to choose Messengers, Pastors, and Teachers from among themselves." Lover noted that in English "Apostles" were called "Messengers," and their task was twofold: to "set in order the things that are wanting" and to "ordain Elders in every Church."[36]

---

[34] "Two Association Meetings in Kent, 1657," *Transactions of the Baptist Historical Society* (1912–13): 247–50. See also White, *The English Baptists of the Seventeenth Century*, 49–50.

[35] Nicholson, "The Office of 'Messenger'," 209.

[36] Lover was referencing Acts 6:3 (*The True Gospel Faith*, 9).

Thomas Collier (d. circa 1691), a Particular Baptist, articulated an opposing interpretation of Ephesians 4:8–14 in 1655 when he wrote that the church had only two offices: elder and deacon.[37] Collier affirmed the gifts of Apostles but basically limited their expression to the primitive church. Where the other gifts are concerned, Collier contended that with the exception of Apostles, the various gifts named in Ephesians are exercised through the office of elder. Thus, one elder may have exhibited gifts of teaching and ruling whereas another only possessed the gift of teaching.[38]

William Rider, a General Baptist writing in 1656, rejected Collier's twofold understanding of the ministry.[39] Instead, Rider was convinced that "in the word Elders is comprehended all offices in the Church…and so Elders is distinguished into several offices in the Church, as Bishops and Deacons…"[40] Having made room for multiple offices, Rider denied that the office of apostle had ceased and noted that whoever did the work of an apostle (i.e., laying a foundation) was an apostle. It is noteworthy that Rider did not employ the term "messenger" as a title or description of the office of apostle.

One final publication from the 1650s illustrates an emerging pattern of the ministry of messengers among the General Baptists. Messenger William Jeffrey from Kent, who was a signatory to the declaration in 1654, published *The Whole Faith of Man* in 1659. *The Whole Faith of Man* includes perhaps the most organized and detailed defense of the office in the 1650s. Given the comprehensive nature of Jeffrey's discussion of the office in *The Whole Faith of Man* and the close association of the congregations in Kent and Lincolnshire, it is likely that Thomas Grantham's conception of the office of messenger was directly or

---

[37] Thomas Collier, *The Right Constitution and True Subjects of the Visible Church of Christ* (London: Printed by Henry Hills, 1654) 20.

[38] Ibid.

[39] William Rider, *Laying on of Hands Asserted* (London, 1656) 15ff.

[40] Ibid., 16–17.

indirectly influenced by Jeffrey's defense of the office and the prevailing pattern of church polity it represents.[41]

Jeffrey's treatment is important for several reasons. First, it establishes that among the General Baptists of the late 1650s, "apostles" and "messengers" were synonymous titles for the same office in the region around Lincolnshire.[42] Second, Jeffrey provided clear details of how messengers were to be chosen: "they are to be chosen out of the congregation by the congregation…" and they are to be elected by the "free consent" of the church.[43] Their formal ordination, or setting apart, occurred "by fasting, and prayer, and laying on of hands.[44] After being set apart for the work of ministry, messengers were to preach the gospel and "make out truth to the Nations in these last times."[45] In addition, Jeffrey affirmed that messengers should work to support themselves. Where the issue of authority is concerned, Jeffrey went farther than perhaps any previous source in defining the boundaries and delineating duties. Lest there be any confusion regarding the primacy of the original Apostles, Jeffrey distinguished between the "extraordinary" Apostles (a phrase Grantham will later use) and those who would follow in their footsteps by being ordained into the perpetual office of messenger.

Jeffrey concluded his discussion of the church offices with a description of the relationship between the local church as an authority unto itself and the authority granted to elders and messengers:

---

[41] Jeffrey had already signed a statement issued by Baptists in Kent and Lincolnshire, but his relationship with Baptists in Lincolnshire was again confirmed in 1661 when he was one of seven Baptist ministers from Kent, Lincolnshire, and Hertfordshire to sign a petition addressed to the king, parliament, and people of England. In this petition, which is found in *Sions Groans for her Distressed* (London, 1661), the signatories denied the magistrate's right or claim to regulate the worship of God. Joseph Wright, who had delivered a 1660 petition to Charles II, was also a signatory. Grantham quoted Jeffrey when arguing against Quakers, *Christianismus Primitivus* (London, 1687) 4.71.

[42] William Jeffrey, *The Whole Faith of Man* (London: Printed by G. Dawson, 1659) 95–96.

[43] Ibid., 96–98.

[44] Ibid., 98.

[45] Ibid.

> But although it be so, that the power lieth in every particular Body, the Church, to govern according to the word of Christ, yet understand that with consent the Elders, and Messengers are to rule in love, and are to be obeyed, by every particular member, the exhorting and commanding duty, and declaring the sense of the Church, according to the word of Christ...and also, the Body, the Church, may command the Elders, or Pastors, and Messengers, to look to their own Ministry, which they have received in the Lord, that they fulfill it...And also note, it is good and safe for a particular church, in things of high concernment, to call for, or desire help from sister Churches, and so Messengers who are to take care of all Churches, in a special manner, are to go in such cases.[46]

It is not clear that Jeffrey's polity granted any explicit inter-congregational authority to messengers or elders, nor was their authority within their own church absolute. Rather, their authority derived from the consent of the congregation, which had the authority to "command" that its messengers perform their assigned tasks. Jeffrey then went on to clarify, but not necessarily limit, the messenger's task to inter-congregational aid. This rather ambiguous wording does raise important questions regarding the extent of a messenger's relationship with other congregations when providing assistance.

What kind of aid did Jeffrey have in mind? Already in 1656, the General Assembly explicitly mentioned "poverty" as a legitimate reason to request assistance, but it may be noteworthy that Jeffrey did not specify the assistance in financial terms. Determining what might constitute "things of high concernment" is difficult, as is the ambiguous line where messengers "are to take care of all churches, in a special manner..." Can one see in statements like these a subtle evolution of the duties and responsibilities of the office of messenger in some General Baptist churches? There is simply not enough information in the church records for these years to make the case conclusively, but there is little doubt that in another ten years the role of a messenger had expanded to include more inter-congregational duties and significant work as an apologist.

---

[46] Ibid., 109.

It has been shown that the ministerial and organizational needs of many Baptist congregations in the 1650s centered on preaching the gospel, forming new churches, and dealing with sundry issues. The records indicate that messengers were chosen from within the congregation and set apart for particular purposes, and thus the need for messengers was but one aspect of early voluntary associational principles at work among the General Baptists.[47] Messengers were a means by which various cooperating and consenting congregations maintained fellowship, shared gifts, and addressed mutual concerns.

While there was no set protocol for such ordinations during the 1650s, it is clear that both Particular and General Baptists utilized messengers to address various needs.[48] To what extent messengers exercised authority and what authority they possessed remains a mystery. Still, by 1655 General Baptists in the Midlands and Kent were convinced that the office of messenger was legitimate, distinct and separate from that of elder or deacon, and as such, it possessed a unique—if undefined—authority. It was in one of these Midlands congregations that a young man by the name of Thomas Grantham was ordained as an elder

---

[47] See Winthrop S. Hudson, "The Associational Principle among Baptists," *Foundations* 1, no. 1 (January 1958): 10–23. Hudson's seminal article was published in the United States in January 1958, the same time that Nicholson's article on messengers appeared in England. Important work by the late James Luther Adams (*Voluntary Associations: Socio-Cultural Analyses and Theological Interpretation* [Chicago: Exploration Press, 1986]) and William H. Brackney (*Christian Voluntarism in Britain and North America: A Bibliography and Critical Assessment* [Westport CT: Greenwood Press, 1995]) has explored tendencies among voluntary religious bodies. Brackney described the four basic voluntary tendencies as (1) separation from the political economy; (2) ministers supported by gifts from associated members; (3) leadership and governance derive from the consent of the associated members; and (4) voluntary participation and cooperation among various member bodies (*Christian Voluntarism in Britain and North America*, 2). Sociologically speaking, religious organizations increase in complexity over time to the point that regional structures at the very least become necessary. Early Baptists were no different in this case than Lutherans, Mennonites, and other Dissenters. It may have been the organizational structure of the Baptists and Quakers that made possible their survival even as other dissenting groups of the period disappeared.

[48] Nicholson, "The Office of 'Messenger'," 210–11.

and, later, a messenger. Attention is now turned Grantham's writings on the office he occupied for twenty-five years.

Grantham and the Office of Messenger after the Restoration of 1660

The Office of Messenger in the Grantham Corpus. John Nicholson identified Grantham's life and writings as the "main source for evidence" and the "most fully justified and expounded" treatment of the office of messenger for 1660–1700, yet he provided little more than a page in the way of summary.[49] Thus, a comprehensive examination of Grantham's writings on the office of messenger is in order if one hopes to obtain a better understanding of Grantham and the office he so vigorously defended in word and deed. The analysis of Grantham's writings below confirms Nicholson's assertions but attempts to build on them by offering a thorough and predominantly chronological examination of the primary documents.[50] This section concludes with a summary of Grantham's theoretical framework for the office of messenger.

Grantham burst onto the General Baptist scene in 1660 when he, along with Joseph Wright, signed and delivered a complaint to Charles II on behalf of the baptized churches in the Kent and Lincolnshire regions.[51] While in the king's presence, Wright and Grantham also took the opportunity to present *A Brief Confession or Declaration of Faith* signed by forty "elders, deacons and brethren" and representing more than 20,000 supposed "Anabaptists." No mention is made of messengers in *A Brief Confession*, but some of the signatories held the office. Joseph Wright, for example, was a messenger from Kent who possibly met Grantham in March of 1660 when the elders, deacons, and brethren gathered in London to draw up the confession. William Jeffrey, a defender of the office of messenger, was also a signatory. Exactly why the title of messenger did not appear in the subscription line or the discussion of leadership in the fifteenth article is puzzling, but the

---

[49] Ibid., 211–12.

[50] Nicholson cited only one treatise in *Christianismus Primitivus* (book 4, treatise 5).

[51] Grantham was called upon to deliver another petition in early 1661.

absence of any reference to the office may reflect a desire to use language agreeable to all parties. Regardless, *A Brief Confession* became the "Standard Confession" among the General Baptists, and Grantham himself appears to have been comfortable with its tenets.[52]

Grantham's writings from the 1660s never addressed directly the subject of messengers, yet something of his ordination to the office in 1666 is known. In a letter to John Connould of Norwich in 1691, Grantham recalled that he was "elected by the consent of many congregations" and ordained a messenger "by those who were in the same office before me."[53] Apparently the ordination was rather humble as it took place in his house, where the church also met for worship. He described his assignment as one "ordained to oversee the churches in divers places that had need of help."[54] Since there is no reason to believe Grantham's ordination was atypical for the Lincolnshire region, it is of some importance that multiple congregations were involved in choosing Grantham. It is important to recall that Jeffrey's description suggested that a single congregation was responsible for choosing messengers. Also, Grantham's account of his own ordination reveals that it involved—and likely required—the presence and blessing of other messengers. As such, there appears to have been, at least in the Midlands, a formal process in place for identifying, electing, and ordaining someone to the office of messenger.

Grantham's initial defense of the messenger's office can be found in *A Defence of the Offices of Apostles; and of the Continuance thereof in the Church till the End* (full title), which was appended to *A Sigh for Peace* (1671). *A Sigh for Peace* is addressed to the "Church of Christ in

---

[52] Similarly, Wright and Jeffrey seem to have been comfortable with the trajectory and meaning of the *Confession*. The confession went through several revisions on its way to becoming the *Standard Confession*. An early revision in 1663 was accepted by the General Assembly, as were Grantham's revisions and explanations in 1678. See also Lumpkin, *Baptist Confessions of Faith*, 221–23.

[53] Thomas Grantham to John Connould, 21 April 1691 (and 11 June 1691). The letters passed between Grantham and Connould are housed at The Beinecke Rare Book and Manuscript Library, Yale University Library, New Haven CT.

[54] Ibid.

London, with the General Assembly of Messengers" in hopes that it might bring "brotherly concord, peace and truth" to a polarized situation.[55] The immediate context of the treatise was the controversy over the imposition of hands, but Grantham added a "vindication" of the messenger's office since it, too, was "much questioned by some."[56]

A Defence of the Offices of Apostles is Grantham's most detailed and complete extant treatment of messengers. A quick glance at the publication history suggests that Grantham was largely pleased with his work. The treatise was reprinted in 1674 under the title *The Successors of the Apostles* (short title). The entire treatise was included in the fourth book of *Christianismus Primitivus* under a similar but more nuanced title: *A Defence of the Office of Subordinate Apostles* (short title). Regardless of the changing titles, the basic structure of the work generally remained the same.[57] When writing of the office in 1687, Grantham briefly described how the primitive church "was endowed with a three-fold order of ministry," but rather than outline the office in detail Grantham referred the reader to the much fuller defense "demonstrated" in *Christianismus Primitivus*.[58]

Instead of going directly to the 1678 edition in *Christianismus Primitivus*, as Nicholson did, it seems wise to begin with an examination of Grantham's defense of the office of messenger by looking to his earliest treatment of the question in 1671, as it appeared in *A Sigh for Peace*. Edward Barber had not hesitated to use "apostle" and "messenger" interchangeably, with the result that "messenger" became the preferred term. Lack of clarity and distinction on the matter seems to have aroused great concern among some congregations by 1671, for it was unclear how the messengers differed from their apostolic forebears. It is in this context that Grantham wrote *A Defence of the Offices of Apostles*. A corrective to misunderstandings and misconceptions,

---

[55] Thomas Grantham, *A Sigh for Peace* (n.p.: 1671) Epistle Dedicatory, A2.

[56] Ibid., Epistle Dedicatory.

[57] Grantham made changes to the treatise in 1674 and 1678.

[58] Thomas Grantham, *Hear the Church: Or, An Appeal to the Mother of us All* (London, 1687) 13.

Grantham writes, is "to call old things by their old names."[59] With this comment, Grantham went behind or beyond any linguistic quibbling and critically questioned "whether God hath given to his Church ANY Apostles or Messengers to succeed the Primitive Apostles, as a constant Ministry in the Church to the end of the World."[60] Particular Baptists during this period believed not, but the typical General Baptist would probably have been inclined to believe so, for they were not as of yet clear about the office's parameters. But Grantham's published articulation of a clearly defined justification for the perpetuity of the office of messenger provided the General Baptists with a defensible position on the matter.

It was noted above that William Jeffrey used "extraordinary" to describe the premier Apostles, though he did not specify in what ways they were extraordinary. Grantham employed this same vocabulary in *A Defence of the Offices of Apostles*, which began by spelling out the differences between the "extraordinary" (i.e., temporary) roles of the original Apostles and those parts of their ministry that were "ordinary" (i.e., fixed). He tersely outlined four elements of the primitive apostolic ministry which the original Apostles alone possessed: (1) they received a unique mission to spread the gospel; (2) they learned their doctrine directly from Jesus or by direct revelation; (3) they laid a doctrinal foundation for others to build upon and this foundation was both a pattern and measuring stick for examining all other doctrines; and (4) they were endowed with the gift of tongues to illustrate that they were commissioned by God and their message was of divine origin.[61]

Grantham provided little elaboration on these points, but Nicholson's paraphrase captured the essence of the argument: "[T]here are now no apostles, in the sense that the first apostles received their mission from Christ himself by infallible revelation to lay an infallible

[59] Ibid., *A Sigh for Peace*, 138.
[60] Ibid., 139.
[61] Ibid., 139–40.

foundation, for which mission they were endowed with gifts of tongues, miracles, signs or mighty deeds."[62]

Yet Grantham concluded that the apostolic office persists in several ways that were not confined to the original Apostles. He highlighted the static elements of the apostolic ministry by first pointing to the God-given "authority to preach the gospel" at all times and in all places.[63] A second ordinary task was twofold and involved teaching and governing the churches. The third fixed aspect of the apostolic office is the requirement to defend the gospel against false apostles. The final remaining aspect of the apostolic ministry is to assist pastors in resisting "Usurpers, and such as despise the Ministers of Christ." In sum, Grantham identified four tasks of the apostolic office that remained in effect and incumbent upon all who hold the office of "apostle."

Having laid out his position with regard to the nature of the apostolic office, Grantham proceeded to support his claim that "the chief Apostles have some to succeed them in the Apostleship."[64] He began by returning to the commission in Matthew 28:19–20 and Mark 16:15, where Jesus instructed the disciples to preach the gospel to all people. Grantham proposed three ways of interpreting the command: (1) some people in particular are to preach the gospel to all people; (2) all Christians are bound to preach the gospel to all people; or 3) the command was no longer binding after the death of the Apostles. He dismissed the second and third options, leaving only the possibility that particular Christians must be sent to fulfill this command of preaching and baptizing.

The second proof is found in Ephesians 4:8–14, where the gifts of offices are given to the church universal. Removing some of these gifts from the church would be "a very dangerous thing," he wrote, for the Church would quickly realize its need. Grantham was quick to warn his

---

[62] Nicholson, "The Office of 'Messenger'," 212. Nicholson summarized the 1678 edition.

[63] Grantham explained these briefly on pages 140–41 of *A Sigh for Peace*.

[64] Grantham, *A Sigh for Peace*, 143.

readers that the continuation of all offices mentioned in Ephesians 4 in no way guarantees the continuation of tongues or miracles.[65]

Grantham's third piece of evidence was taken from the example of the primitive churches as described in scripture, where he found a great "many Apostles beside those that were Foundation layers and Master-builders."[66] Grantham seemed primarily intent upon illustrating how the ministries of Apostles such as Barnabas or Titus were directed toward every church and not restricted to the care of a specific congregation.[67] Under the weight of such evidence from the primitive churches, Grantham was convinced that "God hath ordained such a ministry to continue in his Church till the body of our Lord be perfected."[68]

Grantham next turned to the existing practices of his opponents to prove the necessity and usefulness of the messenger's perpetual office. Grantham rhetorically asked whether "our brethren"[69] did not already

> send out men to act Authoritatively both in preaching the Gospel to them that are without? in setting things in order In remote Congregations? to

[65] Ibid., 146–47. Grantham devoted the majority of this section to this point. He wrote: "And although we said before that the gift of Miracles and Tongues…was necessary to the Office of the chief Apostles, and yet was only temporary: and now say the gifts of Miracles may not be denied to have a being or continuance in the Church. In this there is no contradiction; for, the making those gifts temporary…as they were necessary to the Office of those which first preached the Gospel, doth not at all conclude that they are wholly abrogated, or taken away from the Church. And when we say that these gifts were necessary to the Office of the chief Apostle, our meaning not that Miracles was a part of their office, but only a necessary concomitant thereto; so that though this concomitant should not be found, it is no prejudice to the Office considered as we have defined it."

[66] Grantham, *A Sigh for Peace*, 147.

[67] Ibid., 150–53. Other examples included Luke, Mark, Silas, Silvanus, Titchicus, Troplimus, Apollos, Timothy, and James.

[68] Grantham, *A Sigh for Peace*, 154.

[69] Grantham did not specify who this might have been. It is possible that he was referring to the Particular Baptists, but this seems unlikely since there is no evidence of interaction with, or concern for, the Particular Baptists. It does not appear that Grantham directly mentioned Particular Baptists in his writings. It is probable then, given the audience and the imposition of hands controversy, that he had in mind other General Baptists.

> exercise Discipline by Excommunication of offenders? and remitting the penitent? by ordaining them Elders, and dispencing to them the holy Ordinances?...As these things cannot be denied, so we may justly enquire how it comes to pass that they do thus? if indeed the Church hath none to act in the capacity of Apostles, or messengers of the Gospel…[70]

He then questioned by what authority ordained elders involved themselves in the affairs of other congregations. Grantham emphasized that there were particular duties in the Church that elders were unable to perform by virtue of their own divinely instituted office. It followed that rather than using elders inappropriately, Grantham urged the churches to utilize the office of messenger, which, as it were, is also divinely instituted. But Grantham's concern was not simply semantic here, for he suggested that the Church functions properly only when there is "a ministry remaining in the Church which is related to all Congregations indifferently."[71]

Grantham's final reason for the necessity of the office of messenger was "the state of the world."[72] With this phrase he transitioned into a discussion of the Church's interaction with those outside the faith. There is a great need, he says, for the Church to "dispose of her Members to that needful work" of proclamation.[73] Elsewhere in this section he argued that preaching the gospel to all people is bound up with the consummation of all things. Thus, there must be an office "whose work it is to preach *To all Nations*, even to the end of the world." Yet the "world" is unlikely to "come to [the Church's] Assemblies" or "send to the Church of God for instruction," he wrote, and in the absence of any compulsion, the Church must rely on the proclamation of the gospel by those appointed to such a task.[74] In addition, the continued presence of "false apostles" required the Church's diligence in sending out those true apostles prepared to defend the true faith.

---

[70] Grantham, *A Sigh for Peace*, 154.
[71] Ibid., 155.
[72] Ibid., 158.
[73] Ibid., 159.
[74] Ibid.

Grantham concluded the treatise with a summary of the Church's ministry. He recognized fixed offices such as elder, pastor, and deacon, who were bound and committed to the welfare of particular congregations. There are, however, unfixed ministers whose job was to preach the gospel, plant churches, order new churches, and comfort established churches.[75] Grantham left it to the "sober and unprejudiced Reader to consider" whether it was better to follow human tradition and title unfixed ministers "Bishops," or listen to the scriptures and refer to them as "Apostles."

When Grantham published *Christianismus Primitivus* in 1678, he chose to include several previously published treatises in the fourth and final book. One of the treatises was entitled *A Defence of the Office of Subordinate Apostles of Christ, or Messengers of his Churches, and the perpetuity of his Ministry by Divine Institution, for the more orderly Promulgation of the Gospel, and the better settlement of Churches to the end of the World* (full title). This is basically the same document as that appended to *A Sigh for Peace* in 1671 and *The Fourth Principle* in 1674, yet there are several noteworthy differences in the 1678 edition.[76] First, Grantham introduced the treatise with a new explanatory paragraph:

> Seeing all sorts of Christians do allow of an Itinerate, or Travelling Ministry, as necessary to promulgate, publish, or preach the Gospel where it is not known, and to strengthen the Churches of God, specially where there is a Paucity, or Insufficiency of Instruments; it may there seem strange that any should give occasion to write a defence of that which themselves do allow; and yet so it falleth out at this time, through

[75] Ibid., 162–63.

[76] Grantham's changes to *A Defence of the Offices of Apostles* (1671) were republished as *A Discourse of the Successors of the Apostles* in 1674. What possible impact might the Declaration of Indulgence in 1672 have had on General Baptist messengers' ability to perform their duties? Several of Grantham's changes in the 1678 edition centered on questions related to the extent of a messenger's authority among the various churches. It is possible that Charles II's decision to allow licensed dissenting ministers to travel freely and interact more openly with like-minded believers indirectly exposed or exacerbated inter-congregational tensions among General Baptists regarding authority and local church autonomy.

> some mistake, partly about the Titles, or Appellations prefixed, and partly about the nature of the Institution of this Ministry, whether it be Divine, or of Humane Prudence only?[77]

Here Grantham affirmed the existence of an itinerate ministry among the General Baptists to preach the gospel, but he also acknowledged that there was disagreement over the title, function, and origin of that ministry.

Grantham also expanded definitions and included additional scripture references throughout the treatise. The more significant changes to the 1678 version included a number of objections to the office (followed by brief answers) and the addition of a short list of ancient Christian authors who utilized the term "apostle."

Grantham's source for the patristic citations, at least in this case, seems to have been Henry Hammond (1605–60), a Church of England clergyman and theologian. Hammond had extensive knowledge of the patristic sources, and in *Christianismus Primitivus* Grantham admitted to relying on Hammond's "Collections" when discussing the office of messenger.[78] Hammond was a prolific writer in the mid-seventeenth century and an ardent supporter of the episcopacy, so it is probably for these reasons that Grantham found Hammond's work helpful. That Grantham did not reference Hammond in *A Sigh for Peace* (1671) might suggest that Grantham encountered Hammond's work sometime after 1671 or even 1674, but it is by no means certain that Grantham was unaware of Hammond before 1671. Though Grantham did not specify which of Hammond's writings he uses, it is likely that he relied heavily *Of the Power of the Keyes* (first published in 1647).

In *Of the Power of the Keyes* Hammond defended the structure and role of church government against presbyterian arguments. Hammond's third chapter in particular identified "the Apostles successors" as those

---

[77] Grantham, *Christianismus Primitivus*, 4.152.

[78] Grantham, *Christianismus Primitivus*, 2.120 and 4.166. The ancient authors quoted in 2.120 are as follows: Clement of Alexandria, Theodoret, and Irenaeus; in 4.166 they are Eusebius of Caesarea, Theodoret, Clement of Alexandria, and Chrysostom.

who exercised a dual ministry of establishing new churches and governing them.[79] Hammond translated "apostle" as "ambassador" or "messenger," noting that "extraordinary privileges" such as tongues and miracles were necessary for the work of planting but were not necessary for the work of governing.[80] Hammond called on the witness of antiquity in support of his position, and it was from this litany of ancient writers that Grantham drew several quotations.

While it is clear that Grantham utilized the ancient sources provided by Henry Hammond, it is perhaps more noteworthy that the office of messenger, or bishop, constituted some small piece of common ground between the two thinkers. Moreover, was it mere coincidence that Hammond's language of "Apostles successors" when speaking of bishops in his own day was strikingly similar to Grantham's articulation? It is interesting to see that arguments and sources used to substantiate episcopacy could also be used to justify a third office among the baptized churches. Trends toward an elevated ministry, however, promoted fear among some General Baptists. The additions to *A Defence of the Office of Subordinate Apostles of Christ* in 1678 reveal that some of Grantham's fellow General Baptists may have been wary of a third office that planted *and* governed churches.

Seven objections were also included in the body of the treatise along with a postscript containing three questions submitted to Grantham by an unnamed "Judicious Friend in London."[81] Of the ten objections and inquiries Grantham provided for the reader, one dealt with the cessation of signs and miracles, one consisted of curiosity about the identity of the messengers, two others questioned whether the office is of divine institution, and six revolved around issues related to the extent of the office's authority.

In responding to an objection concerning signs and wonders, Grantham repeated the distinction between the chief and subordinate apostles, noting that neither Timothy nor Titus was reported to have performed

---

[79] Henry Hammond, *Of the Power of the Keyes* (London, 1647) 18.
[80] Ibid.
[81] Grantham, *Christianismus Primitivus*, 4.167.

miraculous signs.[82] He added that it was "unsafe" to assume that miracles ceased in the Church, but warned the reader to be wary of those who would prove that they were apostles by means of signs, for such signs "rather prove them Deceivers."[83]

Grantham's response to the objection related to the identity of the messengers was perhaps as odd as the objection itself. Grantham referenced Ezra 5:4 and retorted, "what would it profit you to tell you their names?"[84] The objection may reflect a bias against the "meanness," or low social standing, of those who occupied the office, for he contended that the validity of the office should stand or fall on the basis of the scriptures and not one's wealth or position.

The two critiques regarding the origin of the office basically speak to the same question: is the office of messenger of divine or human origin? In response to this query, Grantham answered that since the "Church is of Divine Institution by Christ, so are all her Officers."[85] Thus, the church sent messengers in the name of Christ alone. Grantham also argued that if the offices of elder and deacon are assumed to be of divine origin, then the office of messenger should have been deemed divine also.

The last six objections and questions all pushed for clarity regarding the extent of the messenger's authority. In Grantham's responses to these objections and questions, one is able to gain a clearer picture of the duties, limits, and ordination of messengers during the 1670s.

One objection raised the question of why messengers apparently did not "magnifie their Office" or "impose themselves upon the Churches where they come."[86] Grantham responded by clarifying that messengers were endowed by Christ with "Power and Capacity" but had no

---

[82] Ibid., 4.163.

[83] Ibid.

[84] Ibid., 4.164.

[85] Ibid., 4.159. Grantham made the same argument in the postscript (4.167–68), where he wrote, "I say, this Ministry is of Divine Institution, because the whole Ministerial Authority, which the Church hath received as such is of Divine Institution; yea, the very Church her self is of Divine Institution…"

[86] Grantham, *Christianismus Primitivus*, 4.164.

"dominion" over the faith of the churches, especially those churches that they did not plant.[87] Grantham's response suggests that messengers' authority was limited only to those churches they planted, and even then a messenger's power was not absolute.

Another objection regarding authority was the concern that such a ministry might result in the establishment of archbishops or other forms of "Anti-christian Usurpation" among the churches.[88] Grantham contended that the best way to prevent such usurpation of power was to establish firmly the office of messenger, for "it preserves all particular Churches Right to send forth such Ministers as there is occasion for them so to do, and no one Church is herein priviledged above another."[89] Grantham upheld the duty and right of individual churches to set apart Messengers for service, but he defined the elevated status of the office as a position of "Honor" instead of "Power."[90] He concluded his response to this objection by listing three chief reasons the office is necessary: (1) to plant churches; (2) to organize and order the affairs of churches that request help; and (3) to provide assistance to pastors and churches in confronting the propagation of false teaching.[91] Notice that messengers were only to assist churches that expressed a desire for their services.

A third objection raised the question of ordination: "But do you not give the sole Power of Ordination to your Messengers, or Apostles?"[92] Grantham offered a qualified "no" to this question. He briefly outlined the role of messengers in the ordination process. First, messengers were the only officers capable of ordaining elders in new churches that had no officers. Second, churches that had elders were equipped to ordain the full range of offices: deacons, elders, and messengers.

---

[87] Ibid.

[88] Ibid.

[89] Ibid.

[90] Ibid.

[91] Ibid., 4.164–65.

[92] Ibid., 4.165.

A fourth objection centered on the discipline or correction of messengers who "fall into Errors in Life or Doctrine."[93] Since it was required that every messenger belong to a particular congregation, each particular congregation was, he thought, "the most proper Judge" to decide on the judgment of erring officers. Moreover, Grantham affirmed that any local congregation, as a part of the Church, "may lawfully anathematize…an Apostle of the greatest dignity…"[94]

A fifth question demanded that Grantham reveal whether he was a messenger before anyone was obligated to obey him. Grantham's brief answer was self-deprecating and evasive: "Paul was constrained to *become a Fool*…and it is no marvel if such as are not worthy to loose the latchet of his Shoes, be constrained, by the unfriendly dealing of some of their Brethren, to come into the same predicament. And therefore…I here expose my self to your contempt….Thus *I am become a Fool, but ye have compelled me*."[95] Given that Grantham's status as a messenger was public knowledge by 1678, this indirect response is intriguing.

Reluctance to articulate a strong defense of the office's authority is evident in the sixth and concluding question, which had two elements: (1) the duty of churches to receive messengers; and (2) whether it was a sin if they refused messengers.[96] Grantham argued that since Timothy and Titus were generally received as ministers without any previous agreement with the various churches they visited, all messengers should likewise be received. He allowed that some churches might be ignorant of the office and its functions. In such cases, these churches were to be instructed regarding the "Mind of God in this particular," and once instruction has been given, "Churches which shall then reject such Servants of Christ, do sin, and are to be blamed…."[97] Grantham also recommended that letters of commendation be written to facilitate peaceful and trustworthy encounters.

---

[93] Ibid.

[94] Ibid.

[95] Ibid. Grantham cited 2 Corinthians 12:11.

[96] Grantham, *Christianismus Primitivus*, 4.169–70.

[97] Ibid., 4.170.

That so much attention is devoted to the issue of authority in these objections and questions suggests that the authority of a perpetual apostolic office was a major obstacle that prevented consensus among the General Baptists in the 1670s. Grantham was aware that granting substantial authority to messengers threatened the freedom and autonomy of each local congregation. In his writings, therefore, he not only provided a theoretical justification for the office, but he also offered biblical guidelines to govern the office's implementation in the Baptist churches.

Grantham's treatment of the office of messenger was not limited to the detailed discussion in *A Defence of the Offices of Apostles* (1671) or the later editions in 1674 and 1678. Elsewhere in *Christianismus Primitivus* Grantham described the various ministers "God hath given or appointed to Govern the Christian Church to the End of the World."[98] Grantham added little in the way of new insight in the chapter concerning messengers. Perhaps he was content to let the fuller treatment of the office at the end of *Christianismus Primitivus* suffice. He included, however, a condensed justification for subordinate apostles and notes again that "sacred scripture, great Antiquity, and later Doctors" support his position on the matter of Messengers,[99] but the eighth and final section, on the election and ordination of ministers, provided additional insights.

Grantham unequivocally claimed that proper and authentic ordination flowed out of true baptism, and the phrase "No Baptism no Ordination" boldly defied both the legitimacy and leadership of the

---

[98] Ibid., 2.117.

[99] Ibid., 2.119–20. Nothing new was added at this point, though Grantham credited Hammond once more as the source of his quotations from antiquity. In this particular passage, the authors from "great Antiquity" included Clement of Alexandria, Theodoret, and Irenaeus. Heinrich Bullinger was the lone "modern writer." See further William H. Brackney's discussion of Grantham and the early church in "Thomas Grantham, Systematic Theology, and the Baptist Tradition" in *From Biblical Criticism to Biblical Faith: Essays in Honor of Lee Martin McDonald*, eds. William H. Brackney and Craig A. Evans (Macon GA: Mercer University Press, 2007) 199–216.

Roman and Anglican churches.[100] He then moved to describe the process of ordination for messengers, elders, and deacons in the baptized churches. No one was ordained in a baptized church, he wrote, until elected by the church's consent. Consent was important, Grantham argued, for churches were to select their own pastors and leaders.[101] Following the election, an inquiry was made into the nominee's background and competence, followed by fasting, prayer, and the imposition of hands.

Grantham's thoughts on the relationship between ordination and apostolic succession were also evident in this final section. He noted that in Acts 13 Paul and Barnabas were ordained by non-ordained teachers and prophets in the absence of any other living Apostles.[102] This proved, in Grantham's mind, that apostolic succession in terms of ordination was "interrupted even in the Apostles days...."[103] In the absence of a direct link with the Apostles, Grantham asserted that the gifts of the Holy Spirit and the authority of the church were sufficient grounds to appoint and commission ministers of the gospel.

Grantham's treatment of the messenger's office in *Christianismus Primitivus* consisted of two primary movements. First, Grantham included an expanded version of the 1671 treatise, complete with numerous quotations from antiquity and responses to several critiques. Second, a shorter section explained how the churches nominate, elect, and ordain messengers, elders, and deacons. Taken together, Grantham's

---

[100] Grantham, *Christianismus Primitivus*, 2.129.

[101] In support of congregational consent, Grantham referred the reader to the Council of Nicaea, Leo the Great, and Cyprian. Writers contemporary to Grantham included Thomas Bilson and John Field. Grantham quoted Thomas Bilson (1546/7–1616), bishop of Winchester, directly: "Each Church stands free by God's Law, to admit, maintain, and obey no man as their Pastour, without their liking, and that the Peoples Election–dependeth on humane fellowship, and first principles of humane Society or Assemblies" (*The Perpetual Gouernement of Christes Church* [London: Printed by Christopher Barker, 1593] 339).

[102] Grantham, *Christianismus Primitivus*, 2.131.

[103] Ibid.

justification of the office of messenger was probably the most complete and detailed analysis of the office from 1660 to 1700.

Grantham's justification of the office of messenger as outlined in *Christianismus Primitivus* (1678) was given expression in the *Orthodox Creed,* which also appeared in 1678. This statement, probably written by farmer and messenger Thomas Monk, was put forth "in the name of many baptized Christians or congregations" in the counties of Buckinghamshire, Hertfordshire, Bedfordshire, and Oxford, specifically spoke to the office of messenger in Article XXXI[104]:

> Of Officers in the Church of Christ. The visible church of Christ…consists of officers and members; and the officers, appointed by Christ, to be chosen by his church…are these three, viz. Bishops, or Messengers; and Elders, or Pastors; and Deacons, or Overseers of the poor; and the way appointed by Christ, for the calling of any person fitted and gifted by the holy ghost, unto the office of bishop, or messenger, in the churches, is, viz, That he be chosen thereunto by the common suffrage of the church, and solemnly set apart by fasting and prayer, with imposition of hands, by the bishops of the same function, ordinarily, and those bishops so ordained, have the government of those churches, that had suffrage in their election, and no other ordinarily; as also to preach the word, or gospel, to the world, or unbelievers.[105]

Several aspects of Article XXXI stand out. First, the creed clearly reflected a tri-fold ministry of messengers, elders, and deacons. Second, the creed's description of the ordination of messengers outlines election, imposition of hands by other messengers, and the task of preaching. Finally, this creed published by congregations in four Midlands counties did not name Lincolnshire specifically as a contributing county, but it is important to remember that Lincolnshire fell in the geographical region known as the Midlands. Even though Grantham was not a signatory and there is no textual link to his work on the office of messenger in the creed, the similarities between the *Orthodox Creed* and *Christianismus Primitivus* on the subject of messengers are unmistakable. Thus, it seems

[104] See Lumpkin, *Baptist Confessions of Faith*, 297–334.
[105] Ibid., 319–20.

possible that the office of messenger had been accepted regionally as a viable and critical third office by the end of the 1670s. William T. Whitley confirmed this and pointed to the year 1678 as a key moment in the evolution of the office: "From this time forward there is no indication that any doubt was felt as to the scripturalness of the office, its permanence, and its necessity."[106]

Consensus, however, should not suggest that the office's opponents were silenced. Opposition to the office continued, as the aforementioned objections and questions show. When Grantham edited and included the text of the *Standard Confession* (1660) in *Christianismus Primitivus* (1678), "Explanatory Supplements; and the Testimony of many of the Ancient Writers of Christianity" were also added.[107] Yet the absence of even an allusion to the office of messenger when commenting on Article XV (officers of the church) is telling, especially since Grantham's aim was to explain some passages "for the better understanding of the Reader."[108] It is possible Grantham avoided the subject for the sake of unity, which could be why a third office was left out of the original confession in 1660. Regardless, Grantham's edits obviously found favor with a majority of the General Baptists, and his edits were accepted and affirmed by the General Assembly in 1691.[109]

One final document written by Grantham in 1687 provides additional details regarding the office of messenger during this period. In *Hear the Church*, Grantham reaffirmed the messenger's office and also commented on the biblical pattern of councils or assemblies "settling the Churches in peace, when troubles did arise among themselves, by means of false Teachers."[110] These assemblies consisted of "Messengers, Elders, and Brethren" who all participated in the discussions and

---

[106] Whitley, *Minutes of the General Assembly of the General Baptist Churches in England*, 1.xxix.

[107] Grantham, *Christianismus Primitivus*, 2.62.

[108] Ibid., 2.74.

[109] Whitley, *Minutes of the General Assembly of the General Baptist Churches in England*, 1.30.

[110] Grantham, *Hear the Church*, 14.

deliberations.[111] Based on their example, Grantham contended that decisions were to be reached by consensus and not by the imposition of power. In addition, he limited the authority of the general assemblies with regard to punishment and granted the local church the power to punish offenders. In the end, neither messengers nor general assemblies were granted complete authority or control, but they were to be the means of addressing disagreements and securing consensus.

When explaining how baptized churches approach the baptism of a believer, he noted that the messenger or elder preaches and presides "attired in comely Raiment, not much different from the rest of his brethren…."[112] In addition, messengers and elders led the congregation in the celebration of Communion. Such insights into the ministry of General Baptist Messengers in the second half of the seventeenth century are not surprising, but they are important reminders of the broad type of leadership these itinerant apostles provided. That so much attention was devoted to justifications for the office of messenger could obscure the fact that a messenger's most basic and common task among the General Baptists was to organize and lead congregational worship, which was an important issue for Quakers and later the Methodists.

Grantham's last and final defense of the messenger's office appeared in the form of an epistolary dialogue with John Connould, vicar of St. Stephen's in Norwich. In April 1691 Connould wrote to Grantham questioning the latter's authority to gather a church and insistence on believer's baptism.[113] A prolific and friendly correspondence ensued regarding the two questions. In the course of the discussion of Grantham's authority to gather a congregation separate from the established Church of England, Connould expressed a keen interest in Grantham's status as messenger. In response, Grantham outlined his understanding of the tri-fold ministry of deacons, presbyters, and messengers before detailing his own distinct ordinations to the offices of presbyter and

[111] Ibid., 15.

[112] Ibid., 23.

[113] Thomas Grantham to John Connould, 17 April 1691.

messenger.[114] Connould accused Grantham of bringing into the Church a "new" office. Grantham, however, adamantly denied any hint of novelty: "God forbid that I should be for a new order in the church."[115] In the end, both men ultimately agreed on the presence and importance of messengers but disagreed on whether they should form a distinct office.[116]

In summary, this survey of Grantham's writings on the office of messenger demonstrated his concern to legitimate and establish a third office in addition to those of elder and deacon. His major discussion of the office, *A Defence of the Offices of Apostles*, was first published in 1671 and appended to *A Sigh for Peace*. Grantham published *A Defence of the Offices of Apostles* with *The Fourth Principle* in 1674 but under a different title: *The Successors of the Apostles*. In 1678 Grantham edited and expanded the treatise a third time before including it in the fourth book of *Christianismus Primitivus* under the title *A Defence of the Office of Subordinate Apostles*.

The common thread in all versions of the treatise was that the office of messenger, or apostle, was biblical and therefore required of all true churches. Post-biblical apostles were not identical to the original Apostles in every way, but their office did involve three common tasks: preach the gospel in all places, establish churches, and defend the gospel. Grantham's writings suggest that in his context messengers were elected by, and served under, the authority of their own particular local congregations; however, their ordination service reflected an inter-congregational gathering of elders and other messengers. Messengers worked in conjunction with local and regional churches—especially those they planted—to preach, baptize, lead in the celebration of the Lord's Supper, ordain, arbitrate, and defend.

Thomas Grantham's Activities as a Messenger

[114] Thomas Grantham to John Connould, 21 April 1691. Grantham used "presbyter" instead of "elder" in the letters.

[115] Thomas Grantham to John Connould, 5 May 1691.

[116] Ibid. See also John Connould to Thomas Grantham, 8 May 1691.

The previous section analyzed Grantham's writings on the office of messenger that Nicholson identified as the main source for information on the office of messenger from 1660 to 1700. Grantham himself was convinced that a part of his "duty" as a messenger was to write and publish as necessary.[117] Grantham's impact upon the office he occupied should not be confined to publications alone, for to do so underestimates other contributions and leadership. Adam Taylor later emphasized Grantham's writings and also depicts him as a tireless minister who went about "preaching the gospel, founding churches, nursing them up to maturity, and setting in order the things that were wanting in London, at Norwich, at Lynn Regis, at Warboys, at Warwick, and various other distant places…."[118] Taylor's litany accurately portrayed the range of Grantham's ministry, but it also conveys the sense that his ministry reflected his writings, or vice versa. The remainder of this chapter will briefly examine Grantham's labors as a messenger recorded in local church books and General Assembly records.

Grantham's writings are the primary sources for information regarding his ministry. Almost nothing is known of Grantham's preaching since no manuscripts and few details of his sermons survive; still, it seems likely that he preached on a regular basis.[119] The little that can be gleaned from local church records and General Assembly minutes, however, suggests that he consistently labored to plant new churches, establish existing congregations by means of baptism and ordination, and support the office of messenger at the national level.

Grantham played a key role in founding several General Baptist congregations in Lincolnshire and Norfolk during his career. In the chapter "A Man and His Remains" it was shown that prior to his ministry as a messenger, Grantham was instrumental in establishing a General

---

[117] Grantham, *Hear the Church*, 20.

[118] Adam Taylor, *The History of the English General Baptists*, 1.211.

[119] The manuscript of a sermon on the promise of the Holy Spirit in 1 Corinthians 12:1 was included in *The Paedo–Baptist Apology* (n.p., 1671) 66–97. It is probably safe to assume that Grantham authored the sermon even though no information is given.

Baptist congregation in the South Marsh area of Lincolnshire during the 1650s. He expended most of his efforts and energy in and around Lincolnshire, but most of what is known of the church-planting efforts comes from his time in Norfolk. Robert Kershaw attributed Grantham's increased presence in the few extant church records after 1685 to the more tolerant regime of James II, which may have "allowed Grantham to minister fully as a messenger."[120]

Upon his move to Norfolk sometime between 1686 and 1690, Grantham worked to gather a Baptist church in Norwich. He also founded churches in Yarmouth (1686) and in King's Lynn (1689/90). At some point during these years he is also credited with starting a church at Smallburgh.[121] Almost nothing is known of his activities in Yarmouth and Smallburgh, but the available information for Norwich and King's Lynn confirms that he provided important leadership as a General Baptist messenger.[122] It seems that one of Grantham's first goals as a church planter was to secure a permanent and stable meeting space. In Norwich, he gained long-term use of White Friars' Convent for worship and burial.[123] A similar strategy is evident in his work with James Marham in King's Lynn.

---

[120] Robert Kershaw, "Baptised Believers: Lincolnshire Baptists in Times of Persecution, Revolution and Toleration, 1600–1700" (Master's thesis, University of Nottingham, 1995) 34.

[121] Taylor, *The History of the English General Baptists*, 1.224. Jewson noted that the Smallburgh church was gathered "in the country round about North Walsham where there were many Baptists who he might hope to bring to his way of thinking…" (*The Baptists in Norfolk*, 32).

[122] The text of a memorial erected in Norwich by Grantham's grandson, Grantham Killingworth, mentions that Grantham was "A learned messenger of the baptized churches, And pious founder of this church of believers baptized…." For the full text of the memorial see Appendix B. The text is found also found in Jewson, *The Baptists in Norfolk*, 29.

[123] John Kirkpatrick and Dawson Turner, eds., *History of the Religious Orders and Communities and of the Hospital and Castle of Norwich* (Yarmouth: C. Sloman, 1845) 150–95. See also, Francis Blomefield and Charles Parkin, eds., *History of Norwich*, vol. 4 of *An Essay towards a Topographical History of the County of Norfolk* (London, 1805) 416–23.

Marham, who had previously ministered in Spalding and planted churches in Holbeach and Walpole during the 1680s, made his way to King's Lynn after the death of his wife circa 1689. A deliberate drift westward marked Marham's movements in these years, and there was no discernible General Baptist presence in King's Lynn before Marham's arrival. He quickly sought Grantham's assistance. Grantham preached "frequently in the Town-hall to numerous and attentive congregations," and the nascent congregation grew in size. Grantham thought it best to secure a place for public worship by obtaining a license to meet for worship.[124]

Broadly speaking, Grantham's work to establish the congregation in King's Lynn resulted in a legitimate General Baptist presence in the three most populated areas of Norfolk: Norwich, Yarmouth, and King's Lynn. If Grantham was part of a concerted—but unrecorded—effort to establish General Baptist roots in Norfolk, the campaign seems to have been successful. In 1733 three of the four churches he took part in founding remained in direct touch with the General Assembly.[125] Thus, Grantham planted and established congregations in keeping with his self-defined role as a General Baptist messenger.

The available records for Baptist churches in Bourne and Warboys confirm that Grantham remained active and influential as a messenger in Lincolnshire even after beginning work in Norfolk. The records for the church in Bourne, Lincolnshire, indicate that Grantham participated in the ordination of Joseph Hooke as an elder on 7 September 1687.[126] Grantham, who was described as "Messenger of the Baptized Churches in Lincolnshire," ordained Hooke "by Fasting and Prayer, with Laying on of Hands."[127] Another entry, this one from 30 June 1688, includes a

---

[124] *The Lyn Persecution* (n.p., 1692/3) 7–11.

[125] Whitley, *Minutes of the General Assembly of the General Baptist Churches in England*, 1.lxiii. The original King's Lynn congregation was nearly extinct by 1773 but had been revived by 1801.

[126] The entry can be found on page 7 of the church book. The record was entered in 1720. For commentary, see F. J. Mason, "The Old Minute Book of Bourne Baptist Church," *The Baptist Quarterly* 15, no. 5 (January 1954): 226.

[127] See Mason, "The Old Minute Book of Bourne Baptist Church," 226.

lengthy list of officers and members. Grantham's name, followed by the title "Messenger," heads the list.[128]

The case of Joseph Hooke provides important insights into Grantham's long-term influence where the office of messenger was concerned. Hooke was ordained as an elder in 1687. In 1695 the General Baptist churches in Lincolnshire formed an association to foster "mutual support and cooperation."[129] At the first meeting they proposed to ordain Hooke to the office of messenger, assuming his church at Bourne, and Hackenby, the General Assembly, and Hooke himself were all amenable. All parties consented, and in September 1696 Francis Stanley, a messenger from Northamptonshire, ordained Hooke to the office of messenger.[130] This episode reveals important details regarding the ordination process, which appears to have been formalized by the end of the seventeenth century. Nicholson noted that the local association was responsible for starting the process, but everyone from the candidate to the General Assembly needed to confirm the nomination.[131]

In 1701 Hooke wrote *A Necessary Apology for the Baptized Believers* in response to attacks by William Eratt, a parish minister in Hatfield, Yorkshire.[132] One of Hooke's primary goals in the treatise was to demonstrate that the baptized churches were, in fact, true churches. Hooke, like Grantham, appealed to the "Primitive Pattern" found in the scriptures as normative.[133] Following a discussion of the primitive model of "free" and uncoerced fellowship, Hooke explained how the baptized

---

[128] Ibid.

[129] Taylor, *The History of the English General Baptists,* 1.318. See also William T. Whitley, "Associational Life till 1815," *Transactions of the Baptist Historical Society* (1916–17): 20.

[130] Taylor, *The History of the English General Baptists*, 319.

[131] Nicholson, "The Office of 'Messenger'," 215.

[132] Joseph Hooke, *A Necessary Apology for the Baptized Believers* (London: Printed by R. Tookey, 1701). William Eratt had attacked the Baptists in *Anabaptism considered Wherein the Chief Objections of that Sect against Infant-Baptism, and the Manner of Baptizing by Aspersion, or Sprinkling, are Fairly Stated and Answered....* (London: Printed by W. B., 1700).

[133] Hooke, *A Necessary Apology for the Baptized Believers*, 76.

churches "are not without a Ministry that is of Divine Authority."[134] He proceeded to describe the tri-fold nature of General Baptist polity: messengers, elders, and deacons.

Nicholson rightly noticed that Hooke's justification of the messenger's office "follows Grantham closely in claiming scriptural justification for a third order of ordained messengers."[135] Hooke, like Grantham, argued that the biblical witness required that itinerate ministers, or messengers, preach the gospel in remote locations, plant churches, set things in order, and defend the gospel.[136] Yet it seems that Grantham provided more than a methodology or model for exegesis, for when writing of the election of officers Hooke specifically cited *Christianismus Primitivus* and quoted the same passages as Grantham.[137] In fact, Hooke's justification of the office of messenger in many ways paraphrased Grantham's own work some twenty years earlier.

Hooke's dependence on Grantham illustrates well the latter's literary and personal impact on the developing office of messenger among the General Baptists. Grantham fulfilled the role of messenger when he ordained Hooke as an elder in 1687, and Grantham's justification of the office also served as a template and source for defending it against opponents in the early eighteenth century.

In 1688 Grantham was also in Warboys, Cambridgeshire, where he baptized Richard Read and Susan Homes. The church book entry curiously described Grantham as an "Elder of the church, according to the primitive practice of the apostles."[138] This appears to be a common practice in the Warboys records, but it is not clear that the records distinguished between "messengers" and "elders." John Denne and Edmund Mayle, both of whom were elders of the Fenstanton

---

[134] Ibid., 77.

[135] Nicholson, "The Office of 'Messenger'," 219.

[136] Hooke, *A Necessary Apology for the Baptized Believers*, 80.

[137] Ibid., 86–87. The same quotations are found in *Christianismus Primitivus*, 2.130.

[138] Underhill, *Records of the Churches of Christ Gathered at Fenstanton, Warboys, and Hexham, 1644–1720*, 1.282.

congregation, ordained officers at Warboys and were labeled "Elders" in 1655 and 1684 entries from the Warboys minutes.[139] Regardless of the exact meaning of "Elder" in the Warboys records, the congregation evidently valued Grantham's presence and recognized his authority to baptize.

The minutes of the General Assembly of General Baptists from 1689 and 1691 also confirm and elucidate Grantham's importance as a messenger in the second half of the seventeenth century. The 1689 proceedings of the Assembly were "Digested & written by Thomas Grantham."[140] An important issue related to the office of messenger appears in the minutes. No particular speakers were mentioned by name, but as a messenger Grantham likely participated in the discussions. First, there was some question regarding whether those who were ordained as elders of particular congregations could later be ordained as messengers. The assembly, citing precedent, agreed that it was advisable to continue to allow elders to be ordained to the office of messenger, with the caveat that each office must have its own ordination. Thus, it was decided that for an elder to be ordained to the office of messenger, a second and unique ordination was required.[141] Grantham's own ministry contributed to the pattern of distinct ordinations for distinct offices. In 1656 he was ordained "to the office of presbyter, to take the oversight of a small congregation"[142] by the South Marsh church, and then in 1666 he was "ordained to the office of a messenger by those who were in the same office before me."[143] Based on Grantham's own history with ordination, it seems plausible that he would have supported arguments in favor of unique and distinct ordinations for all three ministerial offices.

Grantham was not present for the 1691 General Assembly in London, but his name appears twice in the minutes. The first reference is

---

[139] Ibid., 280.

[140] Whitley, *Minutes of the General Assembly of the General Baptist Churches in England*, 1.28.

[141] Ibid.

[142] See Thomas Grantham to John Connould, 11 June 1691.

[143] Ibid.

the acceptance of Grantham's comments on the *Standard Confession* (1660) in *Christianismus Primitivus* (1678).[144] It is also recorded that Nathan Foxwell was sent from Canterbury to Norwich in order to "Assist Bror. Grantham in the Ministerial work of the Gospel."[145] Grantham's death in 1692 apparently left an involved and large ministry to Foxwell, for the 1693 Assembly granted Foxwell's request for assistance.[146]

Finally, the 1691 minutes also reveal that a decision had been made in 1687 to provide monetary support for traveling ministers. The Assembly affirmed the decision and agreed that "there be a Collection in all the Churches" for the support of the Messengers.[147] Thus, by the time of Grantham's death in 1692 the office of messenger was a funded and firmly established important ministry among many General Baptist congregations with a primary emphasis on planting and establishing churches.

General Baptist Messengers after Thomas Grantham

Whitley noted that the scriptural basis, necessity, and permanence of the messenger's office became widely accepted among the General Baptists during Grantham's lifetime, but the office continued to evolve and change in the decades following Grantham's death.[148] By the end of the eighteenth century, evangelism, which was perhaps the cardinal task of the office in the seventeenth century, was gradually disappearing as a task of the messengers. Instead of working to plant new churches, messengers increasingly acted as superintendents of existing

---

[144] See Whitley, *Minutes of the General Assembly of the General Baptist Churches in England*, 1.30. See *Christianismus Primitivus* 4.152–70 for Grantham's proof-texts and brief explanations. The General Assembly elected to republish the confession in 1691; Grantham's comment on the third article was included in the text.

[145] Whitley, *Minutes of the General Assembly of the General Baptist Churches in England*, 1.31.

[146] Ibid., 1.39.

[147] Ibid., 1.31.

[148] Whitley, *Minutes of the General Assembly of the General Baptist Churches in England*, 1.xxix.

congregational relationships. The causes for such a shift are not altogether clear, but several factors have been identified.

First, Nicholson suggested developments in the messengers' appointment and duties as important factors in the eighteenth century.[149] In Grantham's own ministry and writings, it is clear that local congregations and associations were ordinarily responsible for identifying and ordaining messengers. Nicholson has shown that the consent of local associations was paramount, and not all associations or congregations were necessarily willing to release capable and gifted elders to become messengers.[150] In Lincolnshire, the congregation at Monksthorpe and Burgh repeatedly refused to allow the Lincolnshire association to ordain its pastor, John Hursthouse, to the office of messenger.[151] One can only wonder how Grantham's departure for Norfolk in the 1680s may have affected the sentiments of the Lincolnshire association with regard to the appointment or release of future messengers. After all, Grantham was a well-known and nearly irreplaceable messenger in Lincolnshire is the time of his departure for Norfolk.

Rodney Ambler found that the strong ministry of the messengers in the second half of the seventeenth century was directly related to the level of inter-congregational cooperation and effort.[152] Reluctance to release elders at the local level may have played some part in an apparent dearth of messengers among the General Baptists in the 1700s. The recorded minutes of the General Assembly reveal that between 1709 and 1767 the assemblies of General Baptists issued frequent requests to the local associations for more messengers and additional money to support them.[153] The abundance of appeals may be a sign that local associations

---

[149] Nicholson, "The Office of 'Messenger'," 215–16.

[150] Ibid., 215.

[151] Taylor, *The History of the English General Baptists,* 2.106.

[152] Rodney W. Ambler, "Place and Structure: Lincolnshire General Baptists in the Seventeenth Century," in *La christianisation des campagnes*, eds. J. P. Massaut and M. E. Henneau (Rome: Brepols Publishers, 1996) 417–18.

[153] Nicholson, "The Office of 'Messenger'," 216–17. See also Rodney W. Ambler, "Church, Place and Organization: The Development of the New Connexion

slowly relinquished the responsibility to appoint messengers, yet it may also have been the case that the paucity of messengers indicates that there was an absence of desire or vision or resources for evangelism on the part of local congregations and associations.

A sermon preached by William Evershed at an ordination service for messengers in Canterbury in 1783 illustrates well the move away from evangelism as a primary duty of the messenger.[154] In an appendix to the published sermon, Evershed described the messenger's "proper work and business" as regulation of existing congregations, but denied that evangelism and church planting were the "peculiar work and business" of apostles or messengers.[155] Instead, the messenger's tasks centered on visiting congregations to achieve order and ordain elders.

Messengers certainly played a valuable role in General Baptist life throughout the eighteenth century, though their specific duties evidently contracted to the point of visiting churches and ordaining elders. Nicholson concluded that waning passion for evangelism was one signal of the spiritual decline of the General Baptists in the early decades of the eighteenth century.[156] It is ironic that the New Connection of General Baptists, which formed in 1770, embodied an evangelistic energy comparable to that of the messengers of the seventeenth century, yet disagreement over the office of messenger itself was among the issues that prevented full communion among the various General Baptist factions at the end of the eighteenth century.[157]

There were two primary activities through which Thomas Grantham helped establish the office of messenger between 1660 and 1700. John

---

General Baptists in Lincolnshire, 1770–1891," *Baptist Quarterly* 37, no. 5 (January 1998): 238–39.

[154] Nicholson ("The Office of 'Messenger'," 220) pointed to Evershed's sermon and appendix as an example of development in the messenger's office in the eighteenth century.

[155] William Evershed, *The Messengers Mission* (London: Printed by J. Brown, 1783) 25–26.

[156] Nicholson, "The Office of 'Messenger'," 221–22.

[157] See Whitley, *Minutes of the General Assembly of the General Baptist Churches in England*, 2.183; and Nicholson, "The Office of 'Messenger'," 221.

Nicholson was right to identify Grantham's writings as a key source for information on the office of messenger from 1660 to 1692. During the 1670s Grantham published articulate and biblically supported defenses of the office of messenger, and his justifications remained important into the eighteenth century. In his writings, Grantham outlined a three-fold task for the messenger: (1) preach the gospel; (2) teach and strengthen churches; and (3) defend the gospel against attacks. His contributions were not merely literary; in many ways his ministry as a messenger reflected the essence of the office he defended. In continuity with the first two tasks, he preached, baptized, planted churches, and ordained ministers. Thus, Grantham's writings and ministry provided important leadership as he personally legitimized the office of messenger among the General Baptists.

But Grantham also expended considerable energy fulfilling the third task of the messenger: defending the gospel against attacks. The context of many of Grantham's publications confirms that General Baptists in Lincolnshire and Norfolk saw in Grantham a capable defender of the baptized churches' theology and ecclesiology. The analysis now turns to examine how Grantham's ecumenical and apologetic interactions with Quakers, Presbyterians, Roman Catholics, and Anglicans were an outgrowth of the office he tirelessly labored to establish and a defense of the vision proclaimed by the General Baptists.

Chapter 4

The Great Debaters:
Grantham's Ecumenical Exchanges

The historian of dissent Christopher Hill noted that in seventeenth-century England the lines separating one religious group from another were "much more blurred" than we might imagine.[1] Hill had in mind the intersections of the various sectarian groups that emerged in the 1640s and 1650s. The theological journey of Clement Writer (d. circa 1662) exemplified the inevitable dangers of sectarianism and its fluid membership. The clergyman and controversialist Thomas Edwards (d. 1648) wrote that after Writer "fell off" the Church of England, he sojourned for a time among Independents, Brownists, Anabaptists, Arminians, and Seekers before ending up an "atheist."[2] Not every sectarian individual or group followed Writer's path, but many religious adherents did migrate from one affiliation to another in pursuit of truth. Still, even in such theologically mobile circumstances clear lines of demarcation were already forming.

Then, as now, it took a great deal of courage to commit one's self to a new group and uphold different doctrines. Therefore, it is important to pay attention to the means and methods by which adherents of one religious group were urged to change allegiances. Debates were thought

---

[1] Christopher Hill, *The World Turned Upside Down* (New York: Penguin Books, 1991) 14.

[2] Thomas Edwards, *Gangraena, OR A Catalogue and Discovery of many of the Errours, Heresies, Blasphemies and Pernicious Practices of the Sectaries of this Time* (London, 1646) 82. Edwards went on to report that Writer settled, finally, as an "Anti-Scripturalist, a Questionist, and Sceptick, and I fear an Atheist," *Gangraena*, 82.

to be a critical component of gaining converts, but they could just as easily result in the loss of adherents. Thus, the reputations of the debaters and the movements they represented hung in the balance. There was much at stake in the parish when the great debaters arrived.

For example, following his baptism as a teenager in the late 1650s, Thomas Grantham sought to join a congregation that adhered to the six "foundation principles" listed in Hebrews 6:1–2.[3] Grantham's fidelity to those principles never wavered as he worked among the General Baptists until his death in 1692. For Grantham, the General Baptists proclaimed and embodied a distinct and singularly authentic vision of the church. Grantham's defense of the peripatetic ministry of General Baptist messengers, whose four-fold task included preaching the gospel in all places, teaching and governing the churches, also included defending the gospel against attacks, and assisting pastors in resisting those who would usurp authority. As a messenger, Grantham not only planted churches in Lincolnshire and Norfolk; he was also called upon to defend the baptized believers against what were considered to be false teachings. Grantham publicly, vocally, and capably challenged key theological and ecclesiological tenets of Anglicans, Catholics, Quakers, Presbyterians, and Congregationalists.

Grantham's work as an apologist and debater fostered a sense of unity and legitimacy among some General Baptist congregations vying for legitimacy and peace in the seventeenth century. His reputation as a skilled and informed spokesperson often resulted in invitations to speak on behalf of Baptist congregations in local debates and disputes. A survey of select public disputes and correspondence highlights the significance of Grantham's labors as an apologist for the baptized believers in Lincolnshire and Norfolk. The following examination, therefore, focuses on four of Grantham's disputes with religious opponents: (1) Grantham vs. William Fort of the Church of England (public debate); (2) Grantham vs. an unnamed Roman Catholic

---

[3] Thomas Grantham to John Connould, 21 April 1691. The letters passed between Grantham and Connould are housed at The Beinecke Rare Book and Manuscript Library, Yale University Library, New Haven CT.

(published correspondence); (3) Grantham vs. John Whitehead the Quaker (public debate); and 94) Grantham vs. John Collinges the Presbyterian (published correspondence).

Before moving on, it is necessary to say a word regarding the nature of public disputes and debates in seventeenth-century England. Beyond the entertainment public debates provided during this period, they were also popular forums for expressing religious differences and demonstrating the truth of one's position to potential converts. The pattern typically consisted of an invitation to debate publicly, to which the named opponent was expected to respond with acceptance or refusal.[4] Baptists were involved in more than a hundred such debates in a numerous locations between 1641 and 1698.[5] At least three such public debates occurred in Lincolnshire during this period, all of which involved Grantham.[6]

---

[4] One could obviously ignore an invitation. Robert Wright and William Silverton apparently ignored Grantham's invitation to a public debate in 1670. See Thomas Crosby, *The History of the English Baptists* (London, 1739) 2.242–43.

[5] Arthur S. Langley found evidence for at least 109 debates involving Baptists from 1641–1698, "Baptist Disputations of the Seventeenth Century," *Transactions of the Baptist Historical Society* 6 (July 1919): 216–43. The vast majority of the debates known to Langley occurred during the Commonwealth-Protectorate period.Baptists were also actively debating in New England. In 1673 a pamphlet titled *Mr. Baxter Baptized in Blood* was published in England. It alleged that Baptists in Boston, New England, had killed the Anglican minister Josiah Baxter because he had triumphed in a debate. Baptists in England soon arrived and denied the charges: *Forgery detected and innocency vindicated being a faithful account of the seasonable discovery of an horrid and detectible slander raised on the Anabaptists of New-England, in the diabolical pamphlet entituled, Mr. Baxter baptized in blood, designing so maliciously the reproach and exposure of all under that denomination* (London: Printed by J. D., 1673).

[6] Langley found only two debates held in Lincolnshire (i.e., Grantham's debates with a Roman Catholic in 1662 and the Anglican William Fort in 1673), "Baptist Disputations of the Seventeenth Century," 235–6. Jesse Plumb, "Early Nonconformity in Lincolnshire" (Master's thesis, University of Sheffield, 1940) 170, also noted two debates. It is clear, however, that Grantham had several debates with the Quaker John Whitehead in Lincolnshire in the 1670s.

Grantham and Anglicans

Background of the Debate. A considerable portion of Grantham's writings addressed differences with the established Church of England.[7] Grantham wrote of the necessity for baptized believers to separate from the established church in the Epistle Dedicatory for *Christianismus Primitivus* (1678), giving two main reasons for the separation: (1) the church "requires of us, as a condition of her Communion, an acknowledgment and profession of that for a Truth, which we know to be an Errour"; and (2) "she requires of us, as a condition of her Communion, the joining with her of some Practices, which we know to be against the Law of God."[8] In light of these disagreements, Grantham claimed it was the "duty" of dissenting believers to withdraw obedience from the Church of England.[9] Such strong sentiments did not equate to an outright rejection of all things Anglican, for as late as 1691 Grantham wrote of his "love" for the Church of England and its articles of faith.[10] Such language could imply that a gradual *rapprochement* with the Church of England was evident in Grantham's ministry.

It has been argued that Grantham did, in fact, reach an "accommodation" with some clergymen in the Church of England, and George Southcombe identifies the publication of *A Friendly Epistle to the Bishops* in 1680 and the friendship with John Connould of Norwich in 1691 as evidence of a gradual transformation.[11] In addition, the process

---

[7] No fewer than eight of Grantham's more than twenty published manuscripts specifically address differences with the Church of England: *The Prisoner Against the Prelate* (n.p., 1662); *The Paedo-Baptists Apology* (n.p., 1671); *A Religious Contest* (n.p., 1674); *Christianismus Primitivus* (London, 1678); *A Friendly Epistle* (London, 1680); *The Second Part of the Apology* (London, 1684); *The Baptists Complaint against the Persecuting Priests* (no longer extant, 1685); and *Truth and Peace* (London, 1689). There is also the collection of unpublished letters written to John Connould in 1691.

[8] Thomas Grantham, *Christianismus Primitivus*, The Epistle Dedicatory.

[9] Ibid.

[10] Thomas Grantham to John Connould, 17 April 1691.

[11] George Southcombe, "The Responses of Nonconformists to the Restoration in England" (DPhil thesis, University of Oxford, 2005) vi–viii.

of accommodation began in the early 1670s when Grantham began to exhibit signs of a growing "irenic temperament."[12] Absent from this helpful analysis was a discussion of an episode that actually supports the thesis: Grantham's debate with William Fort at Blyton in 1673 (see map 6). As will be seen, the circumstances and content of this debate reveal that Grantham and those Baptists he represented in the debate were communicative with members of the Church of England.

The small village of Blyton, in Lincolnshire, lies just a few miles from Gainsborough, that city where the famous John Smyth ministered in his pre-Baptist days. Knowledge of the debate and its context come by way of Grantham's own account of the events, which he published as *A Religious Contest* in 1674. Grantham wrote that prior to 18 September 1673, William Fort, a parish minister in Blyton, repeatedly appeared at the meetings of "a small remnant of baptized Christians" and attempted to "hinder their proceedings."[13] Fort's actions impeded the ability of the baptized believers to "edify one another," as was their custom, and he insisted that they disperse and cease gathering in Blyton for the purpose of worship.[14] No information is given as to where the Baptists met for worship. Blyton's parish church, dating to eleventh century and named after St. Martin of Tours, still stands, but nothing is known of the building or structure where the debate took place.

The small group of Baptists resisted pressures to disband, but their attempts to maintain their innocence and articulate their beliefs failed. Fort "slighted" their arguments and asked that they find someone suitable for debate, someone who "understood the Languages, and knew Logick…"[15] They replied that there were few among them capable of conversing about such matters. Fort continued to press the congregation

---

[12] Ibid., vi–vii.

[13] Thomas Grantham, *A Religious Contest*, Epistle to the Reader. The *ODNB* mistakenly claimed that Fort was a Quaker (Oscar C. Burdick, "Grantham, Thomas [1633/4–1692]," *ODNB*, http://www.oxforddnb.com/view/article/11298?docPos=2 [accessed 3 September 2008].

[14] Grantham, *A Religious Contest*, Epistle to the Reader.

[15] Ibid.

for a public debate until the people consented. Fort himself organized the meeting and secured the meeting space since the Baptists had no adequate location for a public discourse.[16]

It is unclear how Grantham came to be involved in the Blyton affair, though it seems likely that the small congregation sought his help in the matter. This would have been natural given Grantham's activities in the early 1670s. The appearance of *The Paedo-Baptist Apology* in 1671 exhibited Grantham's willingness to challenge the established church's treatment of the Baptists and infant baptism. In *The Paedo-Baptist Apology* Grantham described the "unkind usages which the Baptized Churches have received from the Paedo-Baptists, by violently dispersing their Assemblies, by defacing and taking away their meeting places, by imprisoning their persons seizing and wasting their estates, by injuring them in their trade by means of excommunications… and penal proceedings…"[17] Grantham never specified where this unrest occurred, but the context was not unlike that of Blyton in 1673. Grantham's debating skills were also on display against the Quaker John Whitehead in Sleaford in 1672. Grantham's reputation may also have been enhanced when he was granted a government license as a Baptist preacher in February 1673.[18] Based on these factors it seems plausible that the Blyton congregation would have had good reason to seek Grantham's assistance when confronted with a knowledgeable and educated opponent such as William Fort.

The Debate. On 18 September 1673 in Blyton, Lincolnshire, William Fort, a Mr. Wright, another unnamed Anglican minister from Blyton, and a number of local townspeople congregated in the designated meeting place for the debate with Thomas Grantham. Grantham's account of the proceedings was based upon his own recollection, and he assures the reader that he has reproduced the "substance" of the

[16] Ibid.

[17] Thomas Grantham, *The Paedo-Baptist Apology*, The Epistle to the Reader.

[18] See George L. Turner's *Original Records of Early Nonconformity under Persecution and Indulgence*, 3 vols. (London: T. F. Unwin, 1911–14) 3.58.

arguments.[19] Grantham claimed that he has "rendred rather more advantageous" Fort's own arguments in the published document, though exactly how he did so is unclear.[20] Thus, one must approach Grantham's presentation of Fort's positions with a healthy suspicion, yet there is little reason to doubt that Grantham accurately represented the general contours of the dispute.[21]

There was apparently some confusion at the outset regarding the agenda and topics for debate. Fort assumed Grantham intended to defend the Baptists against charges that "their meetings are unlawful…their way of Anabaptism is sinful, And…that our way of baptizing Infants is lawful."[22] Grantham, however, had not been informed that the lawfulness of "our Meetings" was to be the subject of the debate.[23] In light of the oversight, Fort graciously limited the scope of the debate to two principal issues: (1) the mode of baptizing in the Church of England and (2) the baptism of infants.

Grantham began by presenting seven arguments against the Anglican baptismal mode and seven arguments against baptizing infants. Grantham's critiques of the prevailing baptismal mode in the Church of England can be outlined as follows:[24]

1. Scripture does not support sprinkling or making the sign of the cross as legitimate forms of baptism.

2. The Anglican mode of baptism ridicules the example of the Jesus and the apostles.

---

[19] Grantham, *The Paedo-Baptist Apology*, The Epistle to the Reader.

[20] Ibid.

[21] There seems to be no extant published rebuttal contesting the accuracy of Grantham's representation of the debate.

[22] Grantham, *A Religious Contest*, 1.

[23] Ibid., 2.

[24] The arguments summarized below are found on pages 2–10 of *A Religious Contest*.

3. The Anglican mode of baptism "brings unavoidable confusion into the Church" because there is no reason to sprinkle water on the head as opposed to the foot, chest, or back.[25]

4. Similar to argument three, baptizing only one part of the body leads the new convert to question whether he or she has done the will of God.[26]

5. Anglican baptism does not adequately signify that which it represents: complete burial with Christ.

6. Anglican baptismal practices do not conform sufficiently to the meaning of the Greek word βαπtiζω (*baptizmo*).

7. The Anglican mode of baptism "was innovated long after the institution of baptism."[27]

At least two important themes emerged in this initial round of the debate. First, Grantham made the case that the Anglican practices of sprinkling and making the sign of the cross were illegitimate. In the course of responding to Grantham's first point, Fort voluntarily confessed that sprinkling did not constitute true baptism. It is unclear why Fort would admit this opinion in public, but the ensuing dialogue showed that he was forthcoming about his beliefs and practices. For example, he claimed that not once "did I ever sprinkle any in all my life."[28] At this point Grantham called attention to *The Book of Common Prayer*, where there were instructions "to sprinkle and cross the infant."[29] Fort granted that the "old" edition did include the word "sprinkle," but pointed out that the disputed word was removed when the "new" edition was published.[30] Grantham and Fort agreed in principle that the practices

---

[25] Grantham, *A Religious Contest*, 6.

[26] Grantham's point here was that since scripture did not identify a particular body part to be baptized, a baptismal candidate could seriously doubt that it was God's will to sprinkle the head as opposed to any other body part. Therefore, sprinkling could not be considered a legitimate mode of baptism.

[27] Grantham, *A Religious Contest*, 9.

[28] Ibid., 3.

[29] Ibid.

[30] This is a curious exchange. One looks in vain for any baptismal reference to "sprinkle" in the 1549, 1552, 1559, and 1662 versions of *The Book of Common*

of sprinkling and making the sign of the cross had no place in baptism. Having secured the point, Grantham proceeded to point out that sprinkling is a common practice in other parishes. Grantham's aim, then, was to demonstrate that the Church of England included large numbers of people who, by virtue of being sprinkled, could claim no authentic baptism.

Second, Fort had asked the small Baptist congregation to find a capable debater. Grantham did not disappoint. It is clear from his opening arguments that he had acquired considerable debate skills. Grantham capably crafted his arguments according to the popular syllogistic model: a major premise, a minor premise, and a conclusion.[31] The second argument provides a good example for analysis[32]:

1. Major Premise: "That which renders the practice of Christ and his Apostles superfluous and ridiculous is not the right way of baptizing…"

2. Minor Premise: "…But your pretended way of Baptising renders the practice of Christ and his Disciples superfluous, or ridiculous…"

3. Conclusion: "…Ergo. Your way of Baptising is not the right way of Baptising."

Each of Grantham's fourteen arguments conforms to this model.

It is important to point out that the assumption behind syllogistic disputes is that the major premise is correct, which means the opponent must confirm or deny the minor premise. Grantham understood that the weight of the argument rested on the minor premise. So, when Fort denied the minor premise in the syllogism above, Grantham was aware of his own responsibility to "evince" the premise with a "demonstration."[33] Grantham demonstrated his point by appealing to the example of Jesus and John the Baptist, who baptized with "much water,"

Prayer. All four editions allowed for dipping or pouring, depending on the health of the infant.

[31] For a discussion of syllogisms in logic and disputes, see Alexander Broadie, *Introduction to Medieval Logic* (New York: Clarendon Press, 1987) 124ff.

[32] Grantham, *A Religious Contest*, 4–5.

[33] Ibid., 5.

while the Church of England simply dips the fingers or hand in a little water.[34] Grantham's understanding of the debate method was even more apparent in his second set of arguments.

In the second stage of the debate Grantham offered seven reasons that infants should not be baptized. They are as follows:[35]

1. The scriptures do not show that infants should be baptized.

2. Only those who claim to be disciples of Jesus are to be baptized.

3. Infants are not among those whose duty it is to be "born again of water and of the Spirit," and therefore should not be baptized.[36]

4. Faith and repentance are not required of infants; therefore, they should not be baptized.

5. "All that ought to be buried with Christ in Baptism, ought first to be dead with him from the rudiments of the world. Infants ought not to be dead with Christ from the rudiments of the world. Ergo, Infants ought not to be baptized."[37]

6. Neither Jesus nor the apostles baptized infants.

7. Infants are unable to worship God in spirit and truth; therefore, they should not be baptized.[38]

Grantham's arguments against infant baptism in this debate appeared to be standard seventeenth-century Baptist boilerplate. It is beyond the

---

[34] Ibid.

[35] The arguments summarized below are found on pages 10–16 of *A Religious Contest.*

[36] Grantham, *A Religious Contest*, 12.

[37] Ibid., 14.

[38] Baptists may have rejected infant baptism, but they were not necessarily opposed to dedicating young children. Michael J. Walker of Cardiff argued that Grantham's comment in *Christianismus Primitivus* (2.6) could be taken as an allusion to a distinct child dedication service based on the example of Jesus ("Baptist Theology of Infancy in the 17th Century," *Baptist Quarterly* 21, no. 6 [April 1966]: 250). See also Richard A. Underwood, "Child Dedication Services among British Baptists in the Seventeenth Century," *Baptist Quarterly* 23, no. 4 (October 1969): 164–69.

scope of this study to probe every facet of Grantham's baptismal theology, but by 1671 his own thoughts had been shaped by Baptist authors representing differing perspectives, Henry Denne (d. 1666) and John Tombes (d. 1676), whom Grantham described as producers of the "learned works of those of our way."[39] Grantham pointed the interested reader specifically to Denne's *ANTICHRIST Unmasked* (1645) and Tombes's three-volume tome, *Antipaedobaptism* (1652–57), as valuable sources in the struggle against infant baptism. Grantham's commendation of Denne and Tombes suggests that the authors' writings and arguments were held in high esteem among Baptists during the reign of Charles II.

A comparison of Grantham's arguments with those provided by Denne and Tombes reveals that the former's approach to questions regarding the legitimacy of infant baptism was shaped by the latter. One example of this influence is found in Grantham's argument that the "water and spirit" baptism did not apply to infants. Grantham insisted that baptismal candidates must be able to provide a "demonstration" that they have been reborn of the Spirit.[40] Henry Denne had argued similarly in a 1645 debate with the Anglican minister Dr. Daniel Featley that "faith (whose object is remission of sin in Jesus Christ) is required in persons to be baptized."[41] Tombes also contended that "the person baptized is supposed to be born again, to be a repenting and believing person afore he is baptized."[42]

Emphasis on being "buried with Christ in baptism" was another common image employed by seventeenth-century Baptists (especially

---

[39] Grantham, *The Paedo-Baptist Apology*, The Epistle to the Reader. Tombes was especially influential for many early paedo-baptist opponents. For a discussion of Tombes's positions on infant baptism, see Michael T. Renihan, *Antipaedobaptism in the Thought of John Tombes* (Auburn MA: B&R Press, 2001). As Renihan noted on page 70ff., Tombes also used syllogisms when arguing against infant baptism.

[40] Grantham, *A Religious Contest*, 13.

[41] Henry Denne, *ANTICHRIST Unmasked* (n.p., 1645) 16.

[42] John Tombes, *Anti-Paedobaptism, or, The Second Part of the Full Review of the Dispute Concerning Infant-Baptism in which the Invalidity of Arguments* (London: Printed by Henry Hills, 1654) 214–21.

the Seventh-Day Baptists). In 1652 Tombes rhetorically asked, "What resemblance of our burial or resurrection with Christ is there in sprinkling?"[43] The complete and total nature of burial, Tombes suggested, demands an equally all-consuming mode of baptism. Grantham built on the burial imagery when he argued that since infants are not spiritually dead they should not be buried spiritually in baptism. Illustrating Grantham's reliance on established Baptist arguments for believer's baptism by immersion is important for the purposes of this study because it provides valuable insight into the nature of his leadership. That Grantham articulated standard arguments against infant baptism underscores the way in which he incorporated established Baptist arguments into his own apologetic disputes. In so doing, Grantham was perhaps indirectly legitimating and solidifying Baptist baptismal theology in the public sphere.

Grantham's knowledge of the laws of debate was also on full display in this second stage of the debate. On at least three occasions Grantham accused Fort of violating the accepted rules of debate. The first instance involved Fort's objection to the premise that the scriptures do not show that infants should be baptized. The claim in question was Grantham's minor premise in the following syllogism: "Holy Scripture doth shew who are to be baptised, Holy Scripture doth not shew that Infants ought to be baptised. Ergo, Infants ought not to be baptised."[44] In reaction to this syllogism Fort proclaimed that he could prove "that Infants ought to be baptised, from Mat. 28.19."[45] Understanding that Fort was technically prohibited from arguing a point, Grantham complained, "Sir, you mistake your place, for you are not now to prove, but to answer me…You do violate the Law of disputing for being my respondent you ought not to argue…"[46] Grantham's account of the debate did not include Fort's reaction to the correction.

---

[43] John Tombes, *An Addition to the Apology* (London: Printed by Henry Hills, 1652) 36.

[44] Grantham, *A Religious Contest*, 10.

[45] Ibid.

[46] Ibid.

The second violation of protocol also occurred in the argument over whether the scriptures taught that infants should be baptized. Fort again stated his intention to "prove that infants ought to be baptised as being disciples from Acts 15."[47] At this, Grantham again noted the mistake: "Sir, I marvel you should no better observe the Law of disputing which must hold you to, and the rather because you were pleased to glory so much over your poor Neighbours because of your skill in Logick..."[48] Was there a hint of sarcasm in this rebuttal? Perhaps, but Grantham certainly reminded those in attendance that Fort initiated the debate and requested a capable opponent.

Fort's third and final misstep once more highlighted Grantham's skill in syllogistic debate. The disagreement occurred after Grantham put forth the following syllogism (argument five above): "All that ought to be buried with Christ in Baptism, ought first to be dead with him from the rudiments of the world. Infants ought not to be dead with Christ from the rudiments of the world. Ergo, Infants ought not to be baptized."[49] Fort's denial of the conclusion prompted a rather blunt reply from Grantham: "No Sir, you cannot deny the consequence in a Categoricall syllogism, so that you must either distinguish, or deny one of the propositions."[50] Here again Grantham proved his mettle as a disputant. That Fort chose to deny the major premise is perhaps less important than his acquiescence to Grantham's correction. It is noteworthy that Grantham, a Baptist minister with no formal or classic education, was familiar enough with the laws of debate to oppose and correct an Anglican clergyman in a formal debate.

In the final stage of the debate Fort presented two syllogistic arguments in support of his claim that "our way of baptizing [is] the right

---

[47] Ibid., 11.

[48] Ibid.

[49] Ibid., 14.

[50] Ibid.

way of baptizing, and that Infants ought to be baptised."[51] His first argument addressed the Anglican mode of baptism:[52]

1. Main Premise: If the Anglican mode of baptism signified that which should be signified, then it is correct.

2. Minor Premise: The Anglican mode of baptism signified all that should be signified in baptism.

3. Conclusion: The Anglican mode of baptism was correct.

Debate on this argument was fairly brief. Fort held that the Greek word βαπτίζω (*baptizo*) meant to wash something or someone, and so the Anglican form of baptism signified the washing away of sins. Grantham denied Fort's minor point and contended that there was no scriptural evidence that Greek word βαπτίζω (*baptizo*) when used in the context of baptism, implied washing the forehead. It is with Fort's second argument, however, that Grantham took particular offense.

The dialogue that ensued as a result of the second argument may, more than any other dialogue, underscores the distance between the disputants. Fort argued,[53]

1. Main Premise: If infants were to be included in the covenant of grace, then it followed they were to be sealed with the appropriate seal of that covenant: baptism.

2. Minor Premise: Infants were included in the covenant of grace and therefore were to be sealed.

3. Conclusion: Infants were to be baptized.

Grantham's initial response was to seek clarification on the number and nature of the seals of the covenant of grace. Fort identified two seals: baptism and the Lord's Supper. Upon hearing this, Grantham denied the minor premise by pointing to what he considered to be an Anglican inconsistency: allowing infants access to one seal (i.e., baptism) while

---

[51] Ibid., 16.
[52] Ibid., 17.
[53] Ibid., 18.

denying them access to the other (the Lord's Supper). Fort defended the restriction by pointing Grantham to the requirement that Christians examine themselves before partaking of the elements.[54] Grantham conceded that self-examination is a requirement but also spoke of repentance as a requirement for baptism in Acts 2:38.[55] According to Grantham's logic, both requirements were binding on infants or neither requirement was binding; he could not understand how infants were capable of one and not the other. For Grantham, it appears to have been a matter of ability and responsibility. Interestingly, by 1678 Grantham could affirm that the children of members of the visible church were "related to the visible church," but he in no way suggested infants should be "brought to particular duties of the New Covenant."[56] Again, infants were incapable and unable to bear the weight of responsibility that is expected of adults.

The debate concluded on a rather friendly note. Grantham called for both sides to "maintain the great duty of Charitie towards each other, till God shall rectifie our judgements in these things."[57] Mr. Wright, who earlier in the debate expressed anger at Grantham's lengthy arguments, expressed similar sentiments and urged all "to walk in love one towards another."[58] So the meeting dissolved with neither side convinced by the other's arguments, but all "went away in peace."[59]

The Day after the Debate. The debate on 18 September evidently left Fort and Wright with additional questions for the Baptists. The next day the two clergymen appeared again at the Baptist meeting and "in a very civil manner" questioned the authority by which the Baptists preached. Fort and Wright assumed that Baptists had no ordination or

---

[54] 1 Corinthians 11:28.

[55] Grantham, *A Religious Contest*, 18.

[56] Grantham, *Christianismus Primitivus*, 2.6. Michael Walker described the difference in terms of "status" versus "service" ("Baptist Theology of Infancy in the 17th Century," 248).

[57] Grantham, *A Religious Contest*, 20.

[58] Ibid.

[59] Ibid.

formal call to preach, but the Baptists reported that they only recognized ministers who had been elected, ordained, and had received the imposition of hands "by the Presbiterie, Bishops, and overseers of the Church."[60] Grantham writes that they debated for some thirty minutes "in friendly discourse...but not agreeing in our expositions ..." before "...Mr. Fort took his leave and we proceeded in our work."[61]

A close examination of Grantham's debate with William Fort at Blyton in 1673 reveals that Grantham's leadership averted an impending crisis in the life of the small Baptist congregation. Furthermore, it is a reminder that Baptists were often subjected to the whims of local leaders. Prior to Grantham's arrival, the small Baptist congregation was being harassed by local ministers of the established church and was on the verge of being suppressed. This situation implies that the congregation did not meet secretly and that the place of worship was not hidden. There is no suggestion that Fort threatened legal action beyond suppressing Baptist meetings. Thus, Grantham's presence and participation in the debate secured for the congregation the opportunity to continue the work of edification and worship. Moreover, it seems that Grantham's theological arguments, which he capably expressed in syllogistic terms, persuaded clergymen of the established church that the Baptists should not be harassed or suppressed further. Understanding and tolerance, if not agreement, prevailed in Blyton.[62]

When Grantham published his account of the Blyton debate in 1674, he directed the Epistle Dedicatory at William Fort and the other Anglicans who attended the debate. There was an overriding conciliatory tone to the dedicatory that was expressed in three recommendations for

---

[60] Ibid.

[61] Ibid.

[62] This was not always the case when Dissenters agreed to participate in parish debates with ministers of the established church. In 1648 Edward Barber recounted how he had recently been invited to debate the acclaimed Edmund Calamy in the parish of St. Benet Fink, Barber's home parish. Those present responded angrily when it was Barber's turn to respond, and Barber's safe removal from the situation required the assistance of a local constable. For Barber's full account, see *A Declaration and Vindication of the Carriage of Edward Barber* (London, 1648).

ecclesial reconciliation. First, Grantham lamented that "we who differ not about the Godhead, should at all differ about things which pertain to his blessed Service."[63] He then commended the Church of England for its reformation of the Eucharist and encouraged it to look with more "diligence" at the institution of baptism. Second, Grantham drew attention to the significant common ground that existed between the two parties where the "Thirty-Nine Articles" were concerned, but he suggested that the three or four articles over which they disagreed be removed. Finally, he called for a conference between Anglican bishops and Baptist bishops and pastors for the purpose of achieving "brotherly concord."[64] That Grantham's proposals for union in 1674 were strikingly similar to those outlined six years later in *A Friendly Epistle* lends additional support to the accommodation thesis mentioned previously. While there is certainly evidence of an irenic position in 1680, *A Religious Contest* suggests that Grantham's irenic trajectory was apparent and established as early as 1674.[65]

Grantham and Roman Catholics

Background of the Correspondence. In late 1662, Charles II issued a Declaration of Indulgence in order to secure religious tolerance for all Dissenters, even Roman Catholics. Roman Catholics, however, were among the most feared and loathed of any dissenting Christians in seventeenth-century England.[66] Charles II underestimated the anti-Roman Catholic sentiments in the country and his effort was rejected by Parliament in 1663.[67] In reality, to be labeled a "papist" was perhaps

---

[63] Ibid., The Epistle Dedicatory.

[64] Ibid.

[65] See Southcombe, "The Responses of Nonconformists to the Restoration in England," 194–98.

[66] For a discussion of the development of anti-Catholic sentiments, see John Miller's *Popery and Politics in England 1660–1688* (New York: Cambridge University Press, 1973) 67–90.

[67] A similar series of events transpired in 1672–73 when Charles II again enacted a Declaration of Indulgence.

worse than being branded an "Anabaptist."[68] Some in England played on common fears of Roman Catholicism to further their own interests; thus, painting one's opponent in a "papist" light was not an uncommon strategy in local disputes. In 1659 the Quaker George Whitehead was accused of being a papist for refusing to take oaths. The Baptist Henry Denne, though not opposed to oaths himself, defended Whitehead and claimed that refusal of oath-taking was not a clear sign of papist sympathies.[69] Just a few years later, in 1662, Thomas Grantham was accused of being a Jesuit while imprisoned in the Lincoln jail. The accusation was apparently an "ordinary aspersion" thrown at Baptists.[70]

The conversion of a dissenter like Robert Everard to the Roman Church, however, is a reminder that alleged "papism" was not always fabricated as a smear tactic. Everard, who had achieved the rank of Captain in the New Model Army and was a well-known General Baptist author in the 1650s, underwent a conversion to the Roman Catholic faith sometime in the early 1660s.[71] Everard published An Epistle to the Several Congregations of the Non-Conformists in 1664 as an account of his conversion. Its appearance drew the ire of a number of different Dissenters.[72] Jeremiah Ives, a General Baptist, published *Rome Is No Rule* in 1664.[73] Francis Howgill, a Quaker, responded with *The True*

---

[68] See Robin Clifton, "The Popular Fear of Catholics during the English Revolution," *Past and Present* 52 (August 1971): 23–55.

[69] Henry Denne, *The Quaker no Papist* (London, 1659) 6. M. G. F. Bitterman has examined the nature of Quaker responses to such accusations in "The Early Quaker Literature of Defense," *Church History* 42, no. 2 (June 1973): 203–28.

[70] Thomas Grantham, *The Baptist against the Papist*, The Author to the Reader.

[71] The exact date of his conversion is unknown. For biographical information on Everard, see George Southcombe, "Everard, Robert (fl. 1647–64)," *Oxford Dictionary of National Biography*, http://www.oxforddnb.com.ezproxy.baylor.edu/view/article/9000?docPos=10 (accessed 15 September 2008). See also Southcombe, "The Responses of Nonconformists to the Restoration in England," 224–58.

[72] Robert Everard, *An Epistle to the Several Congregations of the Non-Conformists* (Paris, 1664).

[73] Jeremiah Ives, *Rome is No Rule* (London: Printed by T. M., 1664).

Rule, Judge and Guide in 1665.[74] Matthew Poole, a Presbyterian, also addressed Everard's conversion in the appendix of The Nullity of the Romish Faith (1666).[75] Joseph Harrison's The Popish Proselyte was also critical of Everard's conversion some twenty years after the fact. Harrison's treatment of Everard's account was biting and approached the status of an *ad hominem* attack. He accused Everard of ignorance, inadvertency, and self-interest.[76] That Everard's conversion evoked such heated reaction years later says something of the event's profound significance. At least one scholar has wondered whether Everard's conversion was the result of a concerted effort by Catholics to "proselytize among the General Baptists congregations in Lincolnshire" in the early 1660s.[77] While there is no clear to evidence to support such intentional Catholic efforts in Lincolnshire, it is possible that Grantham had Everard in mind when he published *Hear the Church* in 1687 as an effort "to prevent others from being deceived by [Catholics]."[78]

Grantham's first known engagement with a Roman Catholic opponent occurred in 1662. Grantham, who was almost certainly sitting in the Lincoln jail at the time, wrote that an anonymous Roman Catholic (a Jesuit?) had posed seven questions to the local baptized believers regarding the authenticity and authority of the scriptures. Grantham crafted a response to the queries at the "importunity of some Friends."[79] It appears that Grantham and the unnamed Roman Catholic carried on an

---

[74] Francis Howgill, *The True Rule, Judge, and Guide of the True Church of God Discovered* (n.p., 1665).

[75] Matthew Poole, The nullity of the Romish faith (London: Printed by H. Hall, 1666).

[76] Joseph Harrison, *The Popish Proselyte the Grand Fanatick* (London,1684) 1.

[77] Southcombe, "The Responses of Nonconformists to the Restoration in England," 190, fn. 62. The possibility of an organized effort to draw General Baptists into the Catholic ranks is strengthened by the similarities between the pro-Catholic arguments referenced in Everard's account and those evident in Grantham's correspondence with an unnamed Catholic.

[78] Grantham, *Hear the Church: Or, An Appeal to the Mother of us All* (London, 1687), The Epistle to the Reader.

[79] Grantham, *The Baptist against the Papist*, The Author to the Reader. The note to the reader bears the date 10 January 1663.

extended correspondence, though the exact duration and nature of the exchanges are unknown.[80] The discourse apparently terminated when Grantham's opponent was reported to have "gone out of this nation." When Grantham was later accused of being a Jesuit while in prison, he saw fit to publish a portion of the correspondence in order to disprove the allegation and "blunt the edge" of Catholic arguments.[81]

The Epistolary Correspondence. Grantham organized *The Baptist against the Papist* into three sections. The first included a letter to the reader, seven queries sent to the baptized believers, and Grantham's seven anti-queries.[82] The second section consisted of a lengthy discourse concerning the first query posed by the Catholic: "Whether we are to resolve all differences in point of Religion, only out of the written Word of God?"[83] The third section was a discussion of ten reasons why "the present Papal Church of Rome…is not the Church of Christ."[84]

In the first section Grantham simply lists the Roman Catholic queries and his own anti-queries to provide the reader with background for the lengthy correspondence that comprises the second section of the treatise. The queries can be summarized as follows:

Query 1: Were all religious differences to be decided only out of the written Word of God?

Anti-query: What differences could be resolved in religion without the written word of God?

---

[80] The correspondence probably consisted of handwritten letters, which could be returned with marginal notes and comments. In 1687, when Grantham included the seven queries at the end of *Hear the Church*, he described in the Epistle to the Reader that his opponent never responded in print but "only sent me a few Notes in Manuscript."

[81] Grantham, *The Baptist against the Papist*, The Author to the Reader.

[82] For the queries and anti-queries, see *The Baptist against the Papist*, The Author to the Reader.

[83] Grantham, *The Baptist against the Papist*, 5.

[84] Ibid., 34. It is not clear whether the third section was written as a part of the correspondence or written solely for the purposes of publication. Since this section reads more like a treatise and no response from the Roman Catholic is included, it seems likely Grantham composed it with publication in mind.

Query 2: How did one know precisely what is the true Word of God?

Anti-query: Did not the Bible deserve the privilege to speak for itself?

Query 3: Since there were no original manuscripts, how did one know that the copies and translations were correct?

Anti-query: Since Christians had no original manuscripts, how could the copies and translations of Roman Catholics better than those of the baptized believers? Where were the original manuscripts of the prophets and apostles?

Query 4: Since the "dead Letter" of the text was unable to explain itself, who was to judge between the Roman Catholics and the Baptists when they differed about the meaning of a text?

Anti-query: Was it not the case that the scriptures, when compared together, explain themselves? Was it right to call the scriptures a "dead Letter"?

Query 5: What scriptural texts did Roman Catholics have for the following: the procession of the Holy Spirit from the Father and Son, changing the Sabbath from Saturday to Sunday, and prohibiting polygamy and infant baptism? Are there not clear texts to prove the unwritten traditions of purgatory and real presence?

Anti-query: Did Papists not confess that infant-baptism is not found in scripture? Did not John 14:26; 15:26; and 16:27 show that the Spirit proceeds from the Father and the Son? Did not 1 Corinthians 7:1–3 prohibit a husband from having more than one wife? Were there any among them who believe Sunday to be the Sabbath? Was it not absurd for Roman Catholics to ask for scriptural proof from the Baptists while they affirmed belief in purgatory and real presence, neither of which could be found in scripture?

Query 6: Was not the universality of both time and place the mark of the true church?

Anti-query: What church could Roman Catholics name that had that mark? Was not the woman that John saw none other than Rome?

Query 7:If Roman Catholics really had the mark of universality, should they not have been able to identify out of all ages and nations those who held to their religion?

Anti-query:Who could show this without the help of human history, and was history a good rule for divine faith? Were not the earliest histories destroyed and those that do remain contradict each other? Was it not true that a church whose gathering, constitution, and government conform to the scriptures was the true church? And in this sense, did not the baptized churches exceed all others?

These queries provide important insights into how General Baptists thought of the Roman Catholic positions on baptism and the nature of the true church. The Roman Catholic's unsolicited queries called attention to two central differences with the baptized believers: (1) the sole authority of scripture in matters pertaining to religion and (2) the marks of the true church. The queries sought clarification on the proper role of scripture in religious discourse, and they also pressed the baptized believers to justify the legitimacy of scripture as an authority in light of the absence of original manuscripts. The papist interlocutor also drew attention to certain practices and beliefs among the Baptists that were seemingly discordant with scripture (e.g., not keeping the Sabbath and prohibiting polygamy). The last two queries forced the Baptists to define the universal nature of the church and demonstrate how they had been a part of it from the beginning. These were all serious and pointed questions, and there is little wonder that Grantham believed Roman Catholic adversaries "to be the most subtil, as well as coherent with their Principles…" of all his adversaries.[85] It is significant, then, that at such a

[85] Grantham, *Hear the Church*, 47.

young age (not even thirty years old) Grantham's fellow General Baptists urged him to respond to such serious questions.

The second section of *The Baptist against the Papist* was the heart of the treatise and contains the dialogue between the two writers. As we noted earlier, Grantham did not publish the entire correspondence, but opted instead to save portions for possible future publication. The portion included in the treatise addresses what Grantham considered to be the chief question between himself and his Catholic counterpart: "What is the authoritative Judge of Controversies?"[86] Grantham dismissed the Quaker conception of the light within as inadequate since it led to as many judges as there are people. He also rejected the notion that the "Papal Church of Rome is the Supream Judge and Catholick Moderatrix of all Disputes in matters of faith…"[87]

What then was left? Grantham offered the scriptures coupled with "right reason" as the "only infallible and authoritative Judge" in religious controversy.[88] Yet he did allow that pastors had been of "great importance" in settling disputes in ages past, as have the "Records of Antiquity."[89] In addition, he wrote that "there is a Judgement of Science to be allowed every man, as touching all things which he chuseth or refuseth in matters of religion, to be used with moderation and discreet subjection."[90] Grantham outlined an approach to understanding the

---

[86] Grantham, *The Baptist against the Papist*, 3.

[87] Ibid., 4.

[88] Ibid.

[89] Ibid.

[90] Ibid. Grantham took up this idea again on pages 16ff., where he distinguished between a "Judgement of Science" and a "Judgement Authoritative." Grantham understood the "Judgement Authoritative" to be an authority only present "in the Church as embodied together," whereas the "Judgement of Science" is localized in each individual member of the church. Grantham did not provide an example of a "Judgement Authoritative," but as an example of a "Judgement of Science" he pointed to 1 Corinthians 10:15: "I speak as to wise men; judge ye what I say" (Authorized Version of 1611). Grantham concluded that "each particular ought to have the free exercise of his judgement in what he chuseth or refuseth, since without this he cannot chuse or refuse any thing with confidence, nor to his comfort," 17. In some sense Grantham's appeal to the "Judgement of Science" could have fallen prey

scriptures that stayed clear of excessive emphasis on the individual, the congregation, or the tradition. At the same time, he granted that all three had some role to play in settling religious disputes.

Several other notable differences emerged in the course of the dialogue. Grantham and the Catholic disagreed on how to conceive of the "living voice of the church." The Catholic understands the "living voice" to include the "Holy Fathers and General Councils," while Grantham took the designation to mean "the present Church and her Pastours."[91] Grantham castigated the Roman Catholics on this point and claimed that the errors of both the fathers and the councils were "undeniable."[92]

The admission of errors, however, did not negate tradition's importance in religious disputes. The difficulty was that both Grantham and his opponent understood that the other side claimed to possess the support of scripture and tradition. Grantham wrote that, "because you do cry up the Fathers…I will therefore shew you, that they do clearly avouch the Answer which I have given to this your first inquiry."[93] This apparent impasse is probably why Grantham identified the Catholic's fourth query as the "most difficult."[94] The difficulty was that neither side could agree on the past in such a way that it could become usable.

---

to the detested individualism of the Quakers. The phrase "judgement of science" was not unique to Grantham in this period, but his use of it seems to have been. Both Samuel Fisher (*Baby-baptism meer babism*, 76) and John Tombes (*Anti-paedobaptism, or, The Third Part Being a Full Review of the Dispute Concerning Infant Baptism* [London: Printed by E. Alsop, 1657] 552) employed the phrase in an anti-paedobaptist context. In both cases, the phrase "judgement of science" referred to the need to wait until infants are old enough to show observable signs of faith. Grantham, on the other hand, used the phrase as a means by which individuals were responsible to draw their own conclusions regarding religion.

[91] Grantham, *The Baptist against the Papist*, 9

[92] Ibid., 11. Grantham included a litany of supposed mistakes and contradict-ions on pages 11–14.

[93] Ibid., 29.

[94] Grantham, *Hear the Church*, 42. The fourth query reads: "Where we differ about the Sense of the Word, by whom must we be tried? The dead Letter cannot explain it self."

Therefore, for Grantham, tradition and history were equally disqualified from judging all matters religious.

The employment of miracles as support for one's position also became a problematic approach. Both writers accepted the occurrence of miracles. The problem again was that both sides claimed miracles in support of their own position. The Roman Catholic appealed to the signs and wonders experienced at Loreto, a popular pilgrimage destination in Italy. Grantham allowed that miracles may have occurred at Loreto, but also pointed out that it was reported to be a "place of most gross Idolatry, blind devotion, and deceit."[95] Grantham even referenced a story of a Roman Catholic who traveled to Loreto to inquire about the truthfulness of the faith before separating from the church.[96] In this way Grantham responded to particular miraculous events and attacked the larger question of miracles by appealing to the plague narratives in Exodus. The narratives in Exodus where Moses and the magicians perform miracles gave rise to the dilemma of opposing miracles, Grantham noted, and he expressed this dilemma succinctly: "You say, you are the Church. We say, we are the Church. Here is Testimony against Testimony, as there was Miracle against Miracle."[97] Elsewhere he noted that even the Turks and Quakers claim miracles.[98] Thus, Grantham argued that appealing to miracles was no sure way to settle religious disputes or identify the true church.

Grantham concluded *The Baptist against the Papist* with several reasons why the Church of Rome was not a true church. This final section does not appear to have been part of the original correspondence, though Grantham must have felt his readers would benefit from a delineation of the marks of the true church. For Grantham, the Roman Catholic Church is no true church because it lacks true baptism, which

---

[95] Grantham, *The Baptist against the Papist*, 23.

[96] Ibid.

[97] Ibid., 22.

[98] Ibid., 54.

results in the gathering of unregenerate persons.[99] In addition, Grantham made an Anabaptist-like critique that the Roman Church was no true church because it was a "national church" that increased its influence and followers by means of the "carnal sword."[100] Grantham also took issue with the Roman Catholic practice of forbidding the common person access to the scriptures in his or her own language. Similarly, insistence upon clerical celibacy and abstaining from eating certain meats "under pain of cursing and death" was tantamount to averring a "doctrine of Devils."[101] Grantham went on to specify the marks of the true church as antiquity, succession, universality of time and place, visibility, sanctity, unity, and miracles. In so doing, Grantham basically undermined all Roman Catholic claims of exclusivity where these marks were concerned and instead declared that the "present Assemblies of Baptized Believers…are the true visible Church of Jesus Christ."[102] For Grantham, the Roman Catholic Church could not have been the Church of Christ because that was a position occupied by the Baptists. In essence, then, Grantham's Baptists possessed the birthright of the true church.

The End of the Affair. The immediate results of Grantham's correspondence with the unnamed Roman Catholic are not recorded. What is clear is that in 1662 a Roman Catholic sent unsolicited queries to the baptized believers in Lincolnshire, queries that Grantham was encouraged to answer. Grantham responded with seven anti-queries and several letters. The impetus to publish the correspondence came in early 1663 when Grantham was accused of being a Jesuit in disguise. Grantham published the correspondence under the title *The Baptist against the Papist* to dispel the circulating rumors. He affirmed his

[99] See *The Baptist against the Papist*, 37–40, 56–47. The lack of true baptism was Grantham's second reason, while the gathering of unregenerate persons was reason six.

[100] Grantham, *The Baptist against the Papist*, 41–43.

[101] Ibid., 47.

[102] Ibid., 58. See also Southcombe, "The Responses of Nonconformists to the Restoration in England," 190–91.

identity as a Baptist by publicizing the disagreements between himself and an unnamed Roman Catholic.

When Grantham's magnum opus, *Christianismus Primitivus*, appeared in 1678, he judged it beneficial to include *The Baptist against the Papist*. In addition, Grantham attached the seven queries and seven anti-queries to the end of *Hear the Church* in 1687.[103] Knowledge of Grantham's interaction with Roman Catholics is limited to the epistolary correspondence of 1662, but the publication history of the correspondence is also informative.

The circumstances surrounding the correspondence and subsequent publications of *The Baptist against the Papist* draw attention to several aspects of Grantham's leadership among the General Baptists during the Restoration. First, the specific content of the dialogue suggests that the theological distance between the Roman Catholics and the Baptists was great. This may seem obvious, but in the previous section it was clear that Grantham held out some small hope of reconciliation with the Anglican establishment. This was certainly not the case with the Roman Church. The central issue of disagreement was not simply the place of scripture in the life of the church, but rather the place of scripture in defining, constituting, and governing the true church. By engaging the "papist" in epistolary correspondence and then publishing that correspondence, Grantham provided his fellow Baptists in Lincolnshire with legitimate responses to questions concerning the authority of scripture and the place of Christian tradition in contemporary disputes. Moreover, Grantham felt that he demonstrated how the nomenclature of "true church" belongs to the "Assemblies of Baptized Believers."

Second, a recurring question is how the assemblies of baptized believers could have been mistaken for Roman Catholic enclaves? How could Grantham have been confused for a Jesuit? Moreover, this was not an allegation that disappeared with time, for in 1691 he wrote of

[103] In 1687 Grantham added a few additional explanatory comments to his anti-queries. This is the only difference between the queries and anti-queries as they appear in the 1662/1678 version and in the 1687 publication.

continued accusations of papist sympathies while living in Norfolk.[104] At first glance one answer may be that, regardless of reality, accusing someone of "papism" was the quickest and easiest way to discredit and dismiss an opponent. Perhaps his debate skills caused some opponents to see in him "Jesuitical" tendencies, a propensity for closely argued points. It is also possible that Grantham's irenic tendencies rendered him susceptible to unfavorable association with Roman Catholics. Looking deeper, however, it is quite possible that Dissenters and Roman Catholics were thought to have similar aims. This assumption is evident in another anonymous author from the period: "The Papists would destroy our Church and State; so would the Common-Wealthsmen: The Papists would set up Popery and absolute Monarchy; the other an Amsterdam Religion, and Arbitrary Government in the hands of the many…"[105] The anonymous author went on to point out that whereas the Catholics had plotted against the king in the 1640s, only the "Common-Wealthsmen" had succeeded in killing him.[106] Because of this, the king had equal reason to be jealous of the Dissenters as he did of the papists.[107] Thus, at least from a political perspective, there was good reason for some in England to believe that Baptists were merely masquerading papists.

Finally, the circumstances of the 1663 and 1687 publications of the correspondence may provide important insights regarding the situation facing Dissenters in the early 1660s and late 1680s. Grantham chose to publish the correspondence at times when anti-Roman Catholic sentiment swelled and accusations of being a papist in disguise were serious allegations. In 1662 Charles II unsuccessfully attempted to extend some level of toleration to some Catholics and other Dissenters with a Declaration of Indulgence. James II did so again, with the same result, in 1687. Tim Harris has noted that the pro-monarchial Tories often sought

---

[104] Grantham, *The Grand Imposter* (n.p., 1691) 10.

[105] *Advice to the Men of Shaftesbury* (n.p., 1681?) 1. For a more detailed discussion, see Tim Harris, *Politics under the Later Stuarts* (New York: Longman, 1993) 99–101.

[106] *Advice to the Men of Shaftesbury*, 1–2.

[107] Ibid., 2.

to paint Whigs and Roman Catholics with similar strokes; that is, that both groups had a vested interest in an authoritarian regime.[108] If so, then it follows that dissenting Baptists would have been more susceptible to "papist" allegations in times when the possibility for religious tolerance was at the fore of national and local politics, for fears of "papism" would have been most acute at these times. The years 1662–63 and 1687 certainly qualify as periods when questions of religious tolerance were on the minds of many in England. Perhaps it was not mere coincidence that Grantham chose to publish his correspondence on the nature of the true church in 1663 and then republish those same exchanges outlining clear differences with the "papists" in 1687.

Grantham and the Quakers

Momentary lapses in persecution by authorities from 1660 to 1689 allowed the various religious sects to turn their attention toward each other.[109] This seems especially true of the often-bitter relations between Baptists and Quakers in Lincolnshire following the Declaration of Indulgence in 1672.[110] In 1672 an anonymous tract was published

[108] Tim Harris, *Politics under the Later Stuarts* (New York: Longman, 1993) 99–101.

[109] Clive Holmes, *Seventeenth-Century Lincolnshire* (Lincoln UK: Society for Lincolnshire History and Archaeology, 1980) 231.

[110] See Ted L. Underwood, *Primitivism, Radicalism, and the Lamb's War* (New York: Oxford University Press, 1997), who has argued that the idea of "primitivism," the emphasis on contemporary recovery of the faith and practice of the original New Testament church, was insisted upon by both Baptists and Quakers in the seventeenth century. Such primitivistic common ground drew them toward one another but also prompted significant debate between them. The relationship between the Baptists and the Quakers in the seventeenth century requires more scholarly attention and research. There is Reuben E. E. Harkness's now dated study of the initial contacts between the two groups in "Early Relations of Baptists and Quakers" (*Church History* 2, no. 4 [December 1933]: 227–42). In addition to his monograph, Underwood also examined the Baptist-Quaker conflict from the perspective of the Baptist Henry Denne in "Baptist Henry Denne and the Quaker Doctrine of the Inner Light" (*Quaker History* 56, no. 1 [Spring 1967]: 34–40). For an introduction to Baptist-Quaker interactions during the Interregnum, see Craig Horle, "Quakers and Baptists 1647–1660," *Baptist Quarterly* 26, no. 8 (October

alleging that circa 1663 the Quaker Richard Anderson, of Panton, Lincolnshire, was commanded by God to smite Ralph James, a Baptist minister at North Willingham, with leprosy.[111] Anderson's own family was instead struck with "restless pain in their bodies."[112] The illness was only cured when, at Anderson's request, James's own congregation prayed for the family's restored health.

The report of such an incident sparked a flurry of tracts from both Quakers and Baptists in Lincolnshire that only exacerbated the existing tension between the two groups. The Quaker Thomas Rudyard quickly countered with *The Anabaptists Lying Wonder*, which denied the events and accused James of dishonesty.[113] John Whitehead, another Quaker leader, added a postscript to Rudyard's short treatise denying that Anderson had ever been a Quaker.[114] Ralph James responded in turn with his own narration of the events, *The Quakers Subterfuge*, essentially denouncing Rudyard and Whitehead.[115] James concluded his controversial treatise with a short and anonymous postscript on the "Light within."[116] That the unnamed author of the postscript was Thomas Grantham suggests that he played no small part in the tract warfare

---

1976): 344–62. See also Donald F. Durnbaugh, "Baptists and Quakers—Left Wing Puritans?" *Quaker History* 62, no. 2 (Autumn 1973): 67–82; and Ronald L. Cobb, "George Fox and the Quaker–Baptist Controversy," *Foundations* 14, no. 3 (July–September 1971): 236–39.

[111] *A True and Impartial Narrative of the Eminent Hand of God that Befell a Quaker and his Family* (London, 1672). James had registered his home in North Willingham as a Baptist meeting place under the terms of the 1672 Declaration of Indulgence. It is quite possible that James published the tract himself, for it consists of a series of letters in which he and John Green discuss the details of the incident. Underwood assumes that James was responsible for publication, *Primitivism, Radicalism, and the Lamb's War*, 116.

[112] *A True and Impartial Narrative of the Eminent Hand of God that Befell a Quaker and his Family*, 10–11.

[113] Thomas Rudyard, *The Anabaptists Lying Wonder* (n.p., 1672).

[114] Ibid., 11.

[115] Ralph James, *The Quakers Subterfuge* (London, 1672).

[116] Ibid., 23–24.

between Baptists and Quakers in 1672.[117] Possible reasons for Grantham's anonymity will be discussed in the "Results and Conclusions" section below. As news of the Anderson-James episode spread, supporters on both sides labored to obtain the facts in order to explain the alleged incident in the best possible light. This contentious atmosphere is the context in which Grantham's conflicts with Quakers are best understood. Grantham's leadership among the Baptists was not confined to tract warfare, however, for he also engaged the Quaker John Whitehead in several public debates throughout Lincolnshire.

The Debates. Thomas Grantham and John Whitehead were not strangers when they agreed to debate in the early 1670s, for they had both been confined in Lincoln Castle in 1662.[118] While nothing resembling transcripts of Grantham's multiple debates with Whitehead is unavailable, it is possible to reconstruct with some certainty the nature of those debates.[119] Some time before November 1672 Grantham and Whitehead engaged one other in several public disputes. At least two of these disputes took place in Spilsby, while another occurred to the

[117] It seems to be a little-known fact that Grantham authored the postscript. In chapter five of *The Baptist against the Quaker* (found in *Christianismus Primitivus*, 4.70–72) Grantham inserted "what I have published before in this behalf." The text that follows is identical to that found in James's postscript of 1672.

[118] Grantham's *The Prisoner against the Prelate* was composed while he was confined in Lincoln Castle in 1662. A collection of Whitehead's letters published posthumously includes several written from the same location in the same year (*The Written Gospel-Labours* [London: Printed by T. Sowle, 1704] 73–79, 149–60, 214–28).

[119] All information on the debates is found in Grantham's, *The Baptist against the Quaker* (1678) and Robert Ruckhill's *The Quakers Refuge* (n.p., 1673). Appended to *The Quakers Refuge* is a postscript by John Whitehead, which, among other things, detailed his interactions with Grantham. Grantham's *The Baptist against the Quaker* only appealed in *Christianismus Primitivus* (4.57–74), which was published in 1678. See also Southcombe, "The Responses of Nonconformists to the Restoration in England," 191–94.

southwest in the town Sleaford (see map 6).[120] Given the contentious relationship between Quakers and Baptists in Lincolnshire, it is not surprising that the debates drew "hundreds" of observers.[121]

The chief subject of the debates seems to have been the nature of Christ's earthly body.[122] The Sleaford debate saw the two men argue over the question of "Whether Christ hath now any Body of Flesh, beside his Church?"[123] At one of the Spilsby debates, Whitehead sought Grantham's answer to the question of "What kind of Flesh Christ's body was?"[124] Whitehead would later complain that those "opposite him" asserted that he believed "nothing which was mortal was called Christ."[125]

Determining what was actually said and what was intended is a complex puzzle, however, for both men commented on the debate in a polemical context. Whitehead later insisted that his comments regarding the physical body of Christ were twisted and manipulated by Grantham in the aftermath of the debates for the purpose of turning others against the truth.[126] Likewise, Grantham accused the Quakers, and Whitehead in particular, of cheating because they employed "Wiles and Equivocations" in their conversations and disputes.[127]

---

[120] Grantham, *The Baptist against the Quaker*, 61; and John Whitehead, "Another Postscript to Ralph James," in *The Quakers Refuge*, 40.

[121] John Whitehead, "Another Postscript to Ralph James," in *The Quakers Refuge*, 40. Horle pointed out that from 1647–60 it was the common practice of Friends to publicize their meeting places and times in order to garner a wider hearing ("Quakers and Baptists 1647–1660," 348). Baptists did occasionally interrupt Quaker meetings, Horle wrote, but Baptists were less willing to suffer Quaker interruptions. Perhaps the Quaker practice was still common enough in the early 1670s that the Grantham-Whitehead debates could have drawn significant numbers.

[122] See Underwood, *Primitivism, Radicalism, and the Lamb's War*, 34–50, for a helpful discussion of Baptist-Quaker disagreements on the person of Christ.

[123] Grantham, *The Baptist against the Quaker*, 61.

[124] Ibid., 60.

[125] John Whitehead, "Another Postscript to Ralph James," *The Quakers Refuge*, 37.

[126] Ibid.

[127] Grantham, *The Baptist against the Quaker*, 59.

It is also instructive to note that each man later portrayed his opponent's actions in the debates as intolerant and unyielding. Grantham supposedly condemned Whitehead's words as "grevious Heresie" during the debates.[128] Whitehead traced the nature of the misunderstanding to Grantham's rashness and rush to judgment, noting that Grantham interrupted him and did not permit him to explain himself adequately.[129] In Whitehead's account, then, it was Grantham's intransigence that prohibited any peaceable outcome.

Grantham, on the other hand, remembered that Whitehead became so enraged that he shook his hands and head before cursing his opponent with words similar to those uttered by Richard Anderson: "Thou whited Wall, God shall smite thee; the Plagues, and Curses, and Vengeance of God is thy portion."[130] Grantham then informed Whitehead that God instructs Christians not to "render Railing for Railing, Cursing for Cursing, but contrariwise Blessing," to which Whitehead consented and replied curiously with the words "Fainer, Fainer, Fainer..."[131]

The debates themselves seem to have accomplished little in the way of resolution or mutual understanding. The verbal sparring between Grantham and Whitehead spilled over onto the printed page in 1673, with Whitehead drawing first blood. Robert Ruckhill published *The Quakers Refuge* in early 1673 as an answer to James's *The Quakers Subterfuge. The Quakers Refuge* was in many ways an attempt at damage control in the wake of the Richard Anderson-Ralph James episode and James's *The Quakers Subterfuge. The Quakers Refuge* seems preoccupied with disowning Richard Anderson and denouncing Ralph James. Ruckhill went to great lengths to absolve the Quakers and highlight their superiority to the Baptists. Toward that end, Ruckhill called attention to

---

[128] John Whitehead, "Another Postscript to Ralph James," *The Quakers Refuge*, 39.

[129] Ibid, 37–41.

[130] Grantham, *The Baptist against the Quaker*, 61. The scriptural example of this language of righteous indignation is found Acts 23:3.

[131] Grantham, *The Baptist against the Quaker*, 61. The exact meaning of Whitehead's reply is unclear.

one William Smith of Eltham, who though formerly "a Brother of the Baptists," had become "a faithful Follower of the Light of Christ" and had actually written against the Baptists in 1669.[132] Ruckhill also posed several queries for James to answer. John Whitehead's contribution to *The Quakers Refuge* was a postscript in which he decried James and Grantham.

Shortly after the appearance of Ruckhill's *The Quakers Refuge*, a "paper" was sent to Grantham that he "might answer it."[133] The "paper" was undoubtedly a copy of Ruckhill's recently released pamphlet, for Grantham wrote *The Baptist against the Quaker* in direct response to the queries and accusations in *The Quakers Refuge.*[134] Whereas *The Quakers Refuge* is almost preoccupied with disowning Richard Anderson and denouncing Ralph James, Grantham virtually ignores the controversy in *The Baptist against the Quaker*. Why? Perhaps he was uninterested in continuing the discussion. It is also possible, however, that he considered excessive focus on Anderson and James to be a distraction from the more important question of underlying fundamental differences between the Baptists and Quakers. This may also shed light on the reason his name was not attached to the postscript in James's *The Quakers Subterfuge*.

Grantham may have chosen to avoid being drawn into specific discussions of the Anderson-James controversy, but his reply to Ruckhill (and Whitehead) via *The Baptist against the Quaker* indicates his willingness to counter Quaker understandings of the scriptures, the nature of Jesus' earthly body, the nature of Jesus' resurrected body, the necessity of observing the ordinances of baptism and the Lord's Supper, and the relationship between the Holy Spirit and the scriptures.[135]

---

[132] Ruckhill, *The Quakers Refuge*, 4.

[133] Grantham, *Christianismus Primitivus*, 4.51.

[134] In the *ODNB* entry for John Whitehead, Richard Greaves claims that Grantham published *The Baptist against the Quaker* in 1673 before recounting the debate again in 1678 ("Whitehead, John [*c.*1630–1696]," *Oxford Dictionary of National Biography*, http://www.oxforddnb.com/view/article/29290?docPos=1 [accessed 19 September 2008]).

[135] Grantham devoted an entire section (which only amounted to a few pages) to each of these issues in *The Baptist against the Quaker*.

Grantham, by means of his disputes and publications, focused attention on theological differences with the Quakers.

Grantham's propensity to publish his disputes with Anglicans and Roman Catholics has already been noted, and the next section will show that Grantham also published his correspondence with the Presbyterian John Collinges. Grantham admits in *The Baptist against the Quaker* that there was much more he could have written "respecting the several Debates" with Whitehead.[136] Why, then, did he not publish a more detailed account of his debates with Whitehead?

Grantham published *A Religious Contest* without access to detailed transcripts, so it is unlikely that the lack of transcripts from his debates with Whitehead would have kept him from doing the same in this case. If anything, the Baptist-Quaker animosity in Lincolnshire, which may have been amplified in the late 1660s and early 1670s, would almost certainly been ideal atmosphere in which to recount how a Baptist had successfully debated a Quaker on several occasions. It is quite possible that Grantham had not fared well in the debates. It may also have been the case that since Baptists and Quakers lacked access to public meeting places and may have had no large meeting places of their own, debates between them tended toward informality. Whatever the reason, Grantham's decision to refrain from publishing an account of his disputes with Whitehead was surprising given the gravity of the situation in Lincolnshire.

Baptist-Quaker interaction during the early 1670s was contentious. The Grantham-Whitehead debates, and their portrayal in print, provide insight into the nature of dissent when official persecution was less common. This short examination of the debates has shown that Baptists actively confronted and resisted Quakerism in Lincolnshire during this period. It is evident that the baptized believers in Lincolnshire looked to Grantham to defend them and their assemblies in the face of Quaker accusations and expansion.[137]

---

[136] Grantham, *The Baptist against the Quaker*, 61.

[137] The *ODNB* (Oscar C. Burdick, "Grantham, Thomas [1633/4–1692]," *Oxford Dictionary of National Biography*, http://www.oxforddnb.com/view/article/

Grantham and the Presbyterians

Whereas James II's attempts to provide toleration in 1687 and 1688 ultimately failed, William III (William of Orange) and Parliament succeeded with the Toleration Act in 1689. The act removed many of the impediments to open communication among the various religious sects, which resulted in a spate of quarrels similar to those in 1672 and 1673.[138] Most of what is known of Grantham's church-planting activities pertains to his time in Norfolk, and it appears that his contentious interaction with Presbyterians and Congregationalists was primarily limited to his ministry in that county. He published at least eight treatises in support of his anti-predestinarian positions.[139] Of particular concern to Grantham were questions of the eternal status of dying infants and the nature of God's sovereignty.[140]

11298?docPos=2 [accessed 3 September 2008];) and *DNB* (Alexander Gordon, "Grantham, Thomas [1634–1692]," *Dictionary of National Biography*, ed. Leslie Stephen and Sidney Lee, 63 vols. [London: Smith, Elder, & Co., 1890] 22:410–12) both asserted that later in life Grantham was drawn to the Quaker concept of the "inner light," but there is no evidence to substantiate this claim. Burdick, who authored the *ODNB* entry for Grantham, stated that the comment suggesting Grantham gravitated toward the "inner light" later in life was not in his original draft, but must have been inserted by the *ODNB* editors (Oscar Burdick, e-mail message to author, 1 July 2008).

[138] The quarrels were not only internal feuds among the Dissenters. Harris noted that the supposed fresh air of toleration also exposed the bitterness and festering resentment that Anglicans had for Dissenters and vice versa (*Politics under the Later Stuarts*, 179–80).

[139] It is probably inaccurate to refer to the General Baptists of the seventeenth century as "Arminians." Based on the sources, they do not seem to have referred to themselves using such language. Patrick Collinson referred to the popular theology of many during the period that redemption was open to all as "rustic Pelagianism" (*The Elizabethan Puritan Settlement* [Berkley: University of California Press, 1967] 37). Murray Tolmie noted that the anti-predestinarian General Baptist sect was built upon a "rural base" that differed from its "urban Pelagian" counterpart (*The Triumph of the Saints: The Separate Churches of London 1616–1649* [New York: Cambridge University Press, 1977] 73).

[140] Grantham's *The Quaeries Examined* (London, 1676) and *The Controversie about Infants* (London, 1680) were written while he was still living in Lincolnshire;

By the time Grantham moved to Norfolk circa 1690, he had earned a reputation as a capable and formidable General Baptist apologist. In fact, word of Grantham's skill as a defender of the baptized believers may have reached Norfolk before he did. In January 1687, the Norwich minister Giles Firmin wrote that he had been informed by a "young furious Zealot [from London] against Infant Baptism" that a "great" and "learned" writer by the name of Thomas Grantham would undoubtedly prove to be a "formidable" adversary in a dispute concerning the eternal fate of dying infants.[141] Firmin also wrote that a friend encountered one of Grantham's "tribe" in London who warned that the Baptists were sending "a Taylor to dispute" with Firmin.[142] Moreover, Firmin included that this "Taylor" was held in high regard among his own people.

One of the messenger's tasks was to defend the gospel against false teachers and false teachings, which was probably an important part of the reason Grantham was involved in so many debates. In 1691 Grantham wrote specifically of his ministry in Norwich and his many disagreements with Calvinistic-minded Christians in the city:

> God's Providence having ordered my Residence in this city, and my Business being to Preach the Gospel, I have endeavoured to perform my Office amongst you; for which I have met with many unkind and undue Reflections, and more especially from that sort of Professors who have espoused the Principles and Doctrine of Mr. John Calvin, concerning his imaginary Decree of absolute and irrespective Reprobation.[143]

Grantham clearly understood his ministry in Norfolk as a fulfillment of his role as a messenger. While preaching may have been his primary

---

the latter was directed at the Presbyterian John Barret. The treatises published while he was in Norfolk include the following: *Presumption No Proof* (London, 1687); *The Infants Advocate* (London: Printed by J. D., 1688); *The Infants Advocate: the Second Part* (London, 1690); *A Dialogue between the Baptist and the Presbyterian* (London, 1691); and *The Forerunner to a Further Answer* (n.p., 1691).

[141] Giles Firmin, *Scripture-Warrant Sufficient Proof for Infant-Baptism* (London, 1688) To The Reader, A2–A3.

[142] Giles Firmin, *The Answer of Giles Firmin* (London, 1688) 3.

[143] Grantham, *A Dialogue between the Baptist and the Presbyterian*, 3.

task, a large part of his ministry as a messenger in Norfolk included debates with other Christian coteries.

Grantham was concerned that in Norwich "many were ensnared" by the "Doctrine of Mr. John Calvin" and his followers who asserted that "God did from all Eternity unchangeably decree all things whatsoever comes to pass."[144] The implications of this belief, in Grantham's mind, led to the inevitable and "dreadful" conclusion that God eternally decreed some for salvation and some for damnation. Grantham considered Collinges to be the "greatest Assertor" of the doctrine in Norwich, so he "found an opportunity to write to him, upon the occasion of a Passage in his Book."[145]

Grantham's brief epistolary dispute with John Collinges, a Presbyterian minister in Norwich, is a fitting final case study in this examination of Grantham's interaction with other religious groups.[146] Grantham had engaged other local Norwich ministers, including Samuel Petto and Giles Firmin, on issues such as infant baptism and the state of dying infants, but Grantham initiated contact with John Collinges in order to address the nature of God's eternal decrees.

The Correspondence. In September 1690 a total of three letters passed between Grantham and Collinges. Two of the three letters were written by Grantham. Grantham first sent Collinges a few observations upon the latter's claim that "God cannot seriously act, and be finally opposed."[147] By advocating such a "dangerous Position," Grantham

---

[144] Ibid., 4.

[145] Ibid.

[146] Collinges was a vocal and public opponent of the established church in Norfolk, where in 1672 he was licensed as a Presbyterian minister. See Stephen Wright, "Collinges, John (1623/4–1691)," *The Oxford Dictionary of National Biography*, http://www.oxforddnb.com/view/article/5927 (accessed 23 September 2008). See also Southcombe, "The Responses of Nonconformists to the Restoration in England," 199ff.

[147] This particular phrase is found in Collinges's *The Intercourse of Divine Love* (London: Printed by T. Snowden, 1683) 259. Grantham referred to the document as *A Discourse of Divine Love*.

wrote, Collinges was undermining the gospel and "scandalizing" those who affirmed free will.[148]

Letter 1: Grantham to Collinges, 12 September 1690. In this first short letter Grantham claimed that the maxim "God cannot seriously act, and be finally opposed" leads to a mistaken conclusion: if the statement is true, then God is to blame for human impenitence and stubbornness. Grantham then included several examples of a serious divine act that was opposed. He appealed to God's "gracious" and "serious" discussion with Cain, who himself "opposed God finally."[149] Similarly, Grantham finds that God was long-suffering with those who ultimately resisted and died in the great flood. The Pharisees, too, resisted God's command through John the Baptist to "bring forth Fruits meet for Repentance."[150] Likewise, the prophets were sent to "turn Israel from their Iniquities," but Israel did not listen and God was opposed.[151] Grantham concluded his first letter with a request that Collinges neither "oppose God finally, by such Reflections" nor reject "the Council of God."[152]

Letter 2: Collinges to Grantham, 12 September 1690. Collinges received Grantham's letter in the evening and answered it almost immediately. He had not heard of Grantham until the letter arrived at his home, and the tone of his reply suggests that Collinges gave little thought to Grantham afterward. Collinges's letter was dismissive and disparaging, going so far as to describe Grantham as one who either "knoweth God so little" or had "so little sense."[153] Collinges accused Grantham of ignorance concerning God's omnipotence and pointed out that the Apostle Paul himself in Romans wrote that no one has resisted the will of God.[154] Collinges also challenged Grantham to prove that God, by an inward act of the divine will, willed the repentance of those

---

[148] Grantham, *A Dialogue between the Baptist and the Presbyterian*, 4.

[149] Ibid., 5.

[150] Ibid. The biblical reference is Matthew 3:8.

[151] Grantham, *A Dialogue between the Baptist and the Presbyterian*, 5.

[152] Ibid.

[153] Ibid., 6.

[154] Romans 9:19.

who died in the flood or the Pharisees. Collinges concluded his letter by letting the reader know that he had "too much business further to regard such Impertinences."[155]

Letter 3: Grantham to Collinges, 1690. The final letter in this epistolary exchange was written by Grantham. In the letter he appears to be offended that Collinges would dare accuse him of ignorance regarding God's omnipotence, so Grantham retorted "And are you so sure you know therein unto Perfection?"[156] Grantham unequivocally affirmed God's omnipotence, yet he was hesitant to necessarily to equate God's "serious" acts with God's "omnipotent" acts. Said a different way, God could act seriously in a given situation without acting omnipotently. Grantham used as an example God's command to resist evil and do good to drive home the point:

> And yet you grant, God may be finally opposed in what he adviseth or commands: but seeing you explain God's resolving by his willing a thing, here seems to be a plain Contradiction, unless you can be so hardy as to say, when God Adviseth or commands Men to forsake Evil, and learn to do well, his Will is not that they should do so; and when he commands all Men everywhere to repent and obey his Voice, he inwardly never intends they shall do the one or the other, for he will not that; and if he wills not that, then he wills the contrary, that he may punish them for not doing that which he would not have them to do; or else he wills nothing at all, and so his Advice and Commands signify nothing.[157]

Grantham found such logic absurd and insisted that ministers must be able to assure their hearers that God does not will their demise and death. He concluded by saying that "God is altogether serious, even as Seriousness it self."[158] Collinges never replied to this second letter from Grantham.

---

[155] Grantham, *A Dialogue between the Baptist and the Presbyterian*, 6.
[156] Ibid., 7.
[157] Ibid., 7–8.
[158] Ibid., 9.

The results of this brief interaction between Grantham and Collinges are both interesting and informative since they help to nuance General Baptist apologetics and identity. The correspondence between Grantham and Collinges was straightforward, but the reaction to the publication of the letters draws attention to the underlying tension that existed among the various dissenting assemblies in Norwich. The lone letter from Collinges in this exchange suggests that he was uninterested in continuing any form of discourse, but his death in January 1691 precluded any further correspondence. Grantham, undeterred by the death of his opponent, proceeded to publish the letters in 1691 under the title *A Dialogue between the Baptist and the Presbyterian.* He also attached a brief poetic exchange with two nameless friends of Collinges and a short treatise dealing with the doctrine of election.

Grantham's *Dialogue between the Baptist and the Presbyterian* is the only extant document published while he resided in Norfolk that included the defining epithet "Messenger of the Baptized Churches in Lincolnshire."[159] It would be tempting to overlook this minor distinctive addition had Grantham not also alluded to his status as messenger in the preface, as noted above. Moreover, Martin Finch, a minister in Norwich and friend of Collinges, was incensed that Grantham had published "what had passed about this Controversie," especially since Collinges had died between the writing of the letters and their publication.[160] Finch, determined to vindicate his friend and refute Grantham, published *An Answer to Mr. Thomas Grantham's Book* to those ends in 1691.

In the opening pages, Finch took aim at Grantham's title page and derides the one who "stiles himself Messenger of the Baptized Churches in Lincolnshire."[161] If by "Messenger" Grantham meant those "chosen by some Churches to travel up and down to other Churches for a short space, to get Contribution and Relief for other Churches," then Finch

---

[159] Grantham, *A Dialogue between the Baptist and the Presbyterian*, title page.

[160] Martin Finch, *An Answer to Mr. Thomas Grantham's Book* (London: Printed by T. S., 1691) 6.

[161] Ibid., 1.

accepted the term "office."[162] Finch was convinced, however, that Grantham considered himself to be a messenger of another sort. "It is likely," Finch noted, that Grantham "counteth himself to have Jurisdiction and Authority over many Churches." Still, Finch questioned why, if he was "more than an ordinary Presbyter," Grantham's ministry in Norfolk was not characterized by "Mildness and Moderation."[163] Thus, it is clear that Grantham continued to face resistance in Norfolk where the office of messenger was concerned only in this situation it was not other Baptists who bristled at his office. Finch's reaction to the title suggests that inter-congregational authority was an important issue among Dissenters in the Norfolk area. Furthermore, Finch's comments confirm Grantham's importance as a leader and Baptist spokesperson in Norfolk, but they also raise serious questions regarding the nature and temperament of his ministry.

A second interesting insight gained from this study is the apparent congenial relationship that existed in Norwich between Presbyterians and Congregationalists. The friendship between Collinges and Finch highlights how the so-called "Happy Union" played out on a local and interpersonal level.[164] Collinges was especially vital to the union and spent his final days "implementing the union of Presbyterians and Congregationalists" in Norwich.[165] On a practical level, Grantham's publication of the correspondence prompted a Congregationalist minister to defend the dignity and theology of a deceased Presbyterian against the accusations of a General Baptist minister.

Finally, it is instructive to consider Grantham's *A Dialogue between the Baptist and the Presbyterian* in the context of the *rapprochement* of Presbyterians and Congregationalists in Norwich. It is likely that for

---

[162] Ibid., 2.

[163] Ibid., 3.

[164] For a discussion of the "Happy Union" between Presbyterians and Independents in the early 1690s, see R. Tudor Jones, *Congregationalism in England* (London: Independent Press, 1962) 112–18. For the text of the *Heads of Agreement* see R. Tudor Jones, ed., *Protestant Nonconformist Texts*, 4 vols. (Burlington VT: Ashgate, 2006) 1:400–04.

[165] Stephen Wright, "Collinges, John (1623/4–1691)," *ODNB*.

many in Norwich the visible union of previously divided congregations joining together demonstrated the unique veracity of Calvinistic theology. For Grantham such a union was by no means a "happy" occasion, for he was greatly concerned that "many were ensnared" by their "dreadful and blasphemous" doctrines.[166] Thus, Grantham chose to engage someone of Collinges's stature and then publish the correspondence in order to curb increasing Calvinistic momentum in Norwich.

Assessing Grantham's Debates

Grantham provided important leadership for General Baptists in Lincolnshire and Norfolk by publicly confronting an array of theological opponents: Anglicans, Roman Catholics, Quakers, and Presbyterians. He served as a spokesperson for his fellow General Baptists in a variety of contexts. In some cases, as evident in his debate with the Anglican minister William Fort, beleaguered congregations solicited Grantham's aid in responding to external critiques. At other times, as seen in his correspondence with the unnamed Roman Catholic, Grantham's friends urged him to answer a series of questions posed to the baptized believers in general.[167] A third avenue to apologetic interaction involved Grantham initiating contact for the purpose of redressing what he considered to be dangerous theological tenets. In all of these circumstances it is clear that Grantham was fulfilling one of the main tasks of his office: defending the gospel against a variety of attacks.

A second important element of Grantham's ministry as a General Baptist apologist was his pattern of publishing accounts of his polemical correspondence and debates. Grantham was more than willing to write, receive, and publish letters. The desire to publish suggests that Grantham and at least some fellow General Baptists considered his interactions with opponents worthy of circulation. It should be remembered, however, that Grantham apparently did not publish details of all his

[166] Grantham, *A Dialogue between the Baptist and the Presbyterian*, 4.

[167] Grantham, *The Baptist against the Papist*, The Author to the Reader. The epistle to the reader bears the date 10 January 1663.

interactions. There are any number of possible reasons for this, but given his habit in other cases such a gap in the history stands out all the more.

One must not assume Grantham's presentation of his disputes with various opponents to be wholly accurate, but from his own accounts he comes across as a capable, confident, and informed disputant. In the debate with Fort, Grantham's own command of debate protocol was on full display. In the debates with Whitehead, Grantham is portrayed as remaining calm while his opponent becomes angry. Where the exchanges with Collinges are concerned, Grantham chose to publish the correspondence despite the recent death of his opponent. Regardless of any redaction these documents might have undergone, they remain valuable as Baptist window through which to view the troubled and volatile world of dissenting religious dialogue in the second half of the seventeenth century.

It has been argued that on account of the "crises" of the seventeenth century and numerous disputes with other Dissenters, Grantham's religious identity gradually shifted toward better relations with the established Church of England. Grantham's irenic correspondence and personal friendship with the Anglican John Connould in Norwich is the strongest testimony of such a shift. The evidence presented in this chapter corroborates the conclusion that Grantham "could only stand closer to the Church of England by standing further away from those outside it."[168]

Much of Grantham's apologetic activity occurred during tumultuous times on a national scale. Royal attempts by Charles II to provide religious toleration in 1660s, 1670s, and 1680s provided the backdrop for all four case studies above. It is true that moments of toleration allowed the various dissenting groups to war against one another, but it was also the case that those same brief moments of freedom allowed the sects to distinguish themselves from one another by means of letters, publications, and great debates. The debaters and apologists argued incessantly about critical aspects of their religious lives: infant baptism,

---

[168] Southcombe, "The Responses of Nonconformists to the Restoration in England" 190.

an inner light, the sufficiency of scripture, and the destiny of dying infants. Embracing an errant theology was a matter of life and death for many in the seventeenth century. The baptized believers in Lincolnshire and Norfolk ordained Thomas Grantham to represent and defend them with voice and pen, and he was always willing to champion their cause in the great debates of the day.

Chapter 5

God, Government, and King: Grantham's Loyal Dissent

King James I of England identified the symbiotic relationship between the crown and the prelacy with his famous line, "No bishop, no king."[1] The execution of Charles I only seemed to affirm his father's remark, for as Neil H. Keeble pointed out, it was "fidelity" to a distinctly non-episcopal vision for the Church of England that impelled those who executed the king.[2] The regicide ushered in a decade-long period of instability, which included numerous parliamentary failures, the rise and fall of the Protectorate, and the multiplication of religious sects. Thus, the restoration of kingship in 1660 was an "aspiration" mixed with hope and uncertainty.[3]

There was good reason in April 1660 to look favorably upon the return of a king. In his "Declaration from Breda," Charles II attempted to assuage the fears of those who may have been skeptical of the restoration of monarchy by promising a "general pardon" to his father's enemies and a "free parliament."[4] In the same statement, however, Charles's plan to

---

[1] James uttered these words at least twice at the Hampton Court Conference in 1604, and is reported to have said further that if he desired to live under a presbyterian system he would simply return to Scotland. For a recent introduction to the reign of King James, see Pauline Croft, *King James* (New York: Palgrave Macmillan, 2003).

[2] Neil H. Keeble, *The Restoration: England in the 1660s* (Malden MA: Blackwell Publishing, 2002) 116.

[3] Jonathan Scott, *England's Troubles: Seventeenth-century English Political Instability in European Context* (New York: Cambridge University Press, 2000) 6.

[4] For the text of the document see Gerald Bray, ed., *Documents of the English Reformation* (Minneapolis MN: Fortress Press, 1994) 544–45. Charles announced

offer "liberty to tender consciences" was a foreboding proposal for those committed to the established church and a ray of hope to those with "tender consciences."[5] It was generally assumed by those in positions of power and influence that granting greater latitude to Dissenters of any stripe would inevitably effect a decline in the peace and stability of the nation.

Barrington R. White identified several reasons for the strong reaction to, and ultimate rejection of, Charles's plan for religious toleration. Three of White's "causes" are particularly relevant to the present study.[6] First, many in England believed that only a single, unified church could alleviate the pressures and solidify the foundation of their troubled nation. A second factor was the common notion that on account of their rejection of prevailing religious norms, the sectarian religious factions that appeared in the 1640s and 1650s promoted and bred political instability or even sedition. A final and related cause was the idea that loyalty to the established church is performed best when joined with loyalty to the monarchy. The causes given by White may be better understood as a working set of assumptions held by many local magistrates and gentry in the late 1650s and early 1660s, but it is important to remember that such assumptions were not universally affirmed in England. Baptists, for example, claimed on numerous occasions that, despite their absence in the established church, they were loyal to the king and harbored no desire for insurrection.[7]

---

his acceptance of the English crown in April of 1660 in a statement commonly known as the "Declaration of Breda." For this study, the Declaration is significant because in it Charles outlined his conditions for assuming the throne. For background and context of the Declaration of Breda, see Paul H. Hardacre, "Genesis of the Declaration of Breda, 1657–1660," *Journal of Church and State* 15, no. 1 (Winter 1973): 65–82.

[5] Bray, *Documents of the English Reformation*, 544–45.

[6] Barrington R. White, *The English Baptists of the Seventeenth Century* (London: The Baptist Historical Society, 1983) 96.

[7] Several examples of such claims will be examined in this study. There was good reason to associate some Baptists with radical and possibly revolutionary ideas. White drew attention to "undeniable evidence" of folks linked with Baptists who had, in fact, sought to upset the Restoration (*The English Baptists of the Seventeenth*

Dissenters were never a majority in England's religious life,[8] so Baptists were probably relieved to hear that Charles II had promised to tolerate their own "tender consciences." In reality, however, the Restoration created an environment in which Dissenters routinely faced harassment and persecution. The possibility of political violence was a reality for many people in England during the 1660s, 1670s and 1680s. No large-scale violent outbursts actually occurred during these decades, but the consistent threat of conspiracy, invasion, assassination, and rebellion disquieted many citizens and magistrates.[9] During these decades of open and intermittent hostility against Dissenters, Thomas Grantham provided important leadership for the General Baptists in three distinct ways: (1) he represented the Lincolnshire General Baptists before Charles II in 1660 and 1672; (2) he favored accepting government-issued licenses for preaching and meeting places; and (3) he

---

Century, 102). Among the regicides executed, two had clear Baptist connections: John Carew and Thomas Harrison. Mark R. Bell has shown that there were clear connections between Baptists and the Fifth Monarchists (*Apocalypse How? Baptist Movements during the English Revolution* [Macon GA: Mercer University Press, 2000] 163ff). See also, Thomas K. Gulley, "The General Baptists in early Stuart and Revolutionary England," (PhD diss., University of Wisconsin-Madison, 1994) 604ff. Timothy George wrote that Baptists "were among the most militant of the godly" in the 1640s and 1650s ("Between Pacifism and Coercion: The English Baptist Doctrine of Religious Toleration," *Mennonite Quarterly Review* 58, no. 1 [January 1984]: 48). White also addressed Baptists in the revolutionary context in a two-part article: "English Baptists and the Great Rebellion, 1640–1660, Point 1," *Baptist History and Heritage* 8, no. 1 (January 1973): 16–27; and "English Baptists and the Great Rebellion, 1640–1660, Point 2," *Baptist History and Heritage* 9, no. 1 (January 1974): 16–29. See also the dated but helpful work of Louis F. Brown, *Baptists and the Fifth Monarchy Men in England* (Oxford: Oxford University Press, 1912).

[8] See Michael R. Watts, *The Dissenters: From the Reformation to the French Revolution*, 2 vols. (Oxford: Clarendon Press, 1978) 1.3. The Compton Census of 1676 revealed that out of a population of around 2.25 million, only about 100,000 were Dissenters. For more on the Compton Census, see Anne Whiteman, ed., *The Compton Census of 1676: A Critical Edition* (London: Oxford University Press, 1986).

[9] Paul Seaward, *The Restoration* (New York: St Martin's Press, 1991) 2–4.

wrote treatises that affirmed a qualified loyalty to the crown. The pages to follow will address each of these aspects of Grantham's relationship to the government in order to illustrate how he was a major component of General Baptist efforts to settle and solidify congregations in Lincolnshire and Norfolk.

Grantham and King Charles II

Grantham personally represented the baptized believers in Lincolnshire before Charles II in 1660 and again in 1672.[10] The document from the audience in 1660 survived and reveals a great deal about the hardships faced by Lincolnshire Baptists during the earliest months of the Restoration. In the aftermath of Thomas Venner's uprising in January 1661, Grantham was a signatory on two petitions presented to the king that aimed to refute any suggestion that Lincolnshire General Baptists were guilty of sedition. In 1672 Grantham presented "A Humble Address, or Remonstrance," which is no longer extant, to the king on behalf of the Lincolnshire Baptists.[11] Thus, an examination of the context, content, and import of Grantham's audiences with Charles II is in order. Taken together, these episodes indicate that from the beginning of his ministry, among the Lincolnshire General Baptists, Thomas Grantham filled a specific and important leadership role. Among other things, his tasks included drafting public statements on behalf of local baptized congregations at critical times and presenting those statements to the appropriate ruling authorities.

Grantham and the Narrative and Complaint, *26 July 1660.* When Charles II returned to England as king in May 1660, there was

---

[10] Grantham was a signatory on *The Third Address* (Thomas Grantham, et al, *The Third Address of Those Persons, Known by the Name of Anabaptists, in the County of LINCOLN* [London, 1661]) from the Lincolnshire Baptists delivered to Charles II on 23 February 1661. Grantham almost certainly did not deliver it in person since he was imprisoned in the Lincoln jail at the time.

[11] Thomas Crosby's *The History of the English Baptists*, 4 vols. (London, 1740) 3.83, included what amounts to a paraphrase of *A Humble Address and Remonstrance*. See Appendix G for Crosby's paraphrase of the address.

widespread jubilation and celebration.[12] Charles's acceptance letter from Breda had given Dissenters reasons to hope for toleration, but in the localities the return of the king signaled the likely return to power of many royalists who had suffered countless indignities during the civil wars and interregnum. In addition to the embarrassments they had endured, these royalists had accrued debt and lost land. For these reasons, Clive Holmes wrote, many royalists sought revenge against those responsible for their sad state: those who had replaced them in local government, Puritan ministers, and religious radicals.[13] Dissenters were undoubtedly easy targets for revenge. Rodney Ambler noted that the breakdown and abolition of ecclesiastical courts during the civil war years and interregnum fostered a sense of freedom among many citizens, but the restoration of the monarchy also amounted to a restoration of ecclesial courts.[14] When royalist justices of the peace were chosen in Lincolnshire in early 1660, almost immediately the tenor of local politics shifted. This was evidenced by the arrests of numerous Quakers and the interruption of Baptist meetings.[15]

---

[12] Keeble, *The Restoration: England in the 1660s*, 40–46. Keeble also wrote of the skepticism which the restoration of monarchy aroused, 46ff. Christopher Hill described the jubilation as "bought cheers" and finds "plenty of evidence for different sentiments among the populace" (*The World Turned Upside Down* [New York: Penguin Books, 1991] 354).

[13] Clive Holmes, *Seventeenth-Century Lincolnshire* (Lincoln UK: Society for Lincolnshire History and Archaeology, 1980) 220. Richard L. Greaves and Robert Zaller, in their editorial introduction to the three-volume *Biographical Dictionary of British Radicals in the Seventeenth Century*, described the rather anachronistic and broadly applied term "radicals" as those who "defended change on the grounds that they were merely reaffirming fundamental ideas and institutions which had been perverted," 3 vols. (Brighton UK: Harvester Press, 1982) 1.vii.

[14] Rodney W. Ambler, *Churches, Chapels and Parish Communities of Lincolnshire 1660–1900* (Lincoln UK: Society for Lincolnshire History and Archaeology, 2000) 9.

[15] Ibid. Justices of the peace had been "the principal organ of local government" under Elizabeth I, James I, and Charles I. For a discussion of the role of local justices of the peace in Stuart England, see J. H. Gleason, *The Justices of the Peace in England, 1558–1640* (Oxford: Clarendon Press, 1969) 68ff. For details of

Henry Jessey's *The Lord's loud call to England* illustrates well how quickly the situation transitioned from possible toleration to certain persecution for Baptists in Lincolnshire. In August 1660 Jessey published several narratives and documents pertaining to the harassment and imprisonment of various Dissenters.[16] Among the documents included in his short treatise was a portion of a *Narrative and Complaint*. The petition to the king described the "Gross Abuses to many Good peaceable People in Lincolnshire."[17]

H. Leon McBeth found that direct appeals to the king in the form of petitions were the most common form of Baptist publications from 1659 to the mid 1660s. The *Narrative and Complaint* was the first of three such direct appeals from the Lincolnshire General Baptists to the king in 1660 and early 1661.[18] Robert Kershaw underscored the distinctly local nature of this *Narrative and Complaint* by pointing out that the twenty-

---

the Quaker arrests, see Susan Davies, *Quakerism in Lincolnshire* (Lincoln UK: Yard, 1989).

[16] Henry Jessey, *The Lords Loud Call to England* (London: Printed by H. J., 1660). The introductory letter is dated 13 August 1660.

[17] Henry Jessey, *The Lords loud call to England*, 15–16.

[18] H. Leon McBeth, *English Baptist Literature on Religious Liberty to 1689* (New York: Arno Press, 1980) 216. Other petitions from Baptists in 1660 and 1661 include the *Apology of some called Anabaptists, in and about the City of London* (London, 1660); *The Humble Apology of Some Commonly Called Anabaptists* (London, 1661); and *A Declaration of Some of those People in or Near London* (London, 1660); *To the King of these Nations* (London, 1661); *The Humble Petition and Representation* (London, 1661) and *Sions Groans for Her Distressed* (London, 1661). There were also three petitions from the General Baptists in Lincolnshire (discussed below). Other Dissenters were active petitioners as well. For example, the Quakers submitted *A Declaration from the Harmles & Innocent People of God called Quakers* (London, 1660/1) and *For the King and both Houses of Parliament Being a Short Relation of the Sad Estate and Sufferings of the Innocent People of God Called Quakers* (London, 1661). The Congregationalist Joseph Caryl submitted *A Renuntiation and Declaration of the Ministers of Congregational Churches* (London, 1661).

four identifiable signatories were all from the South Marsh region of Lincolnshire where Thomas Grantham was a pastor.[19]

A short document of only two small pages, the *Narrative and Complaint* describes the dire situation in Lincolnshire for the baptized believers in 1660. The signatories claimed that local magistrates attempted to discharge Baptist meetings, a command the Baptists "durst not receive."[20] When the baptized believers in Lincolnshire refused to disband or to submit to the authority of those "who sate on the Bench of Justice,"[21] the situation became quite uncomfortable. Baptists endured many hostilities: they suffered verbal abuse when walking in public; they were stoned on the way to congregational meetings; enemies beat on their doors and threw stones at their windows. In addition, they were fined twenty pounds per month—and even imprisoned—for absence from Church of England services. It appears from this brief narration that enemies of the Baptists in Lincolnshire became openly hostile in the months following the Restoration. These Baptists appealed in vain to the local magistrates for "redress," so they decided to plead their case before Charles II.

Charles II arrived in London on 29 May 1660. In the first months of his reign the king received countless guests. Noted writer John Evelyn (d. 1706) apparently found it difficult to meet the king in June on account of the presence of "all sorts of people" waiting to do the same.[22] Given the crowded and frenzied nature of the newly restored royal court, it seems remarkable that two representatives of the Baptist "sort" were able to obtain an audience with Charles II in July 1660.[23] The representatives chosen to deliver the *Narrative and Complaint* to the king were Thomas

---

[19] Robert Kershaw, "Baptized Believers: Lincolnshire Baptists in Times of Persecution, Revolution and Toleration, 1600–1700" (Master's thesis, University of Nottingham, 1995) 33. There were thirty-three signatories total, and for all but nine something is known of their background or location.

[20] Jessey, *The Lords Loud Call to England*, 15.

[21] Ibid., 16.

[22] John Evelyn, *The Diary of John Evelyn* (London: Macmillan, 1908) 204. This entry is dated 4 June 1660.

[23] Jessey, *The Lords Loud Call to England*, 15–16.

Grantham, pastor of the South Marsh congregation, and Joseph Wright, a messenger of the Westby congregation. It is not altogether clear how Grantham and Wright succeeded in meeting Charles II, but Thomas Crosby ascribed the meeting to the assistance of an unnamed "honourable Member of Parliament."[24]

While before the king, the two representatives also submitted for the king's attention *A Brief Confession or Declaration of Faith* signed by forty "elders, deacons and brethren" and representing more than 20,000 supposed "Anabaptists" in England.[25] Grantham was not a signatory to the original *Confession*, which had been composed just a few months earlier in March. An intriguing part in all this was that Grantham, only twenty-six years old at the time and not yet himself a messenger of the General Baptist churches, was chosen to represent his fellow Baptists before the king. Grantham's relative youth could explain why Wright accompanied the young pastor to London. Nevertheless, that a persecuted and harassed association of Baptist congregations was willing to commission a young pastor to carry out such an important task suggests that Grantham was already recognized as a precocious minister with considerable discernment in religious and political matters.

Charles responded favorably to the Lincolnshire petitioners and assured them of the following:

> That it was not his minde, that any of his good Subjects, who lived peaceably, should suffer any trouble upon the account of their judgements or opinions in point of Religion, and that hee had declared the same in several Declarations. Hee promised us also that (upon our declaring our grievances) that hee would have particular care over us, that none should trouble us upon the account of our consciences in things pertaining to Religion. And (while wee were present before him) hee ordered an honourable Member of Parliament to go to the Lord Chancellor, and Secretary, and get something done to that purpose; the

---

[24] Crosby, *The History of the English Baptists*, 2.19.

[25] Ibid.

> Member of Parliament promised that hee would do as the King had ordered him.[26]

Such assurances from Charles II illustrated well the ruler's ostensible intentions regarding those with tender consciences. The king promised to protect his "peaceable" subjects and went so far as to remit the matter to Lord Chancellor Hyde.

The impact of Charles's official advocacy in Lincolnshire remains an open question, but if the release of imprisoned Quakers is any indication, Charles's sympathy for his peaceable subjects likely assuaged some of the pressures for Grantham's Baptists.[27] At the very least, the petition delivered by Grantham and Wright certainly alerted the king to the plight of his loyal subjects in the South Marsh area of Lincolnshire.

The progress toward implementing the Restoration was slow in the localities, as was the Convention Parliament's work to pass the Act of Oblivion and Indemnity. The relative toleration enjoyed by Quakers, Baptists, and other Dissenters in the second half of 1660 disappeared with the brief but frightful uprising led by Venner in January 1661. In this renewed atmosphere of fear and misunderstanding, Thomas Grantham was again called upon to declare the innocence of the Lincolnshire General Baptists.

Grantham and the "Second" and "Third" Addresses, 1661. The religious establishment of seventeenth-century England was not prone to making fine distinctions between the radical religious groups, so when the Fifth Monarchist Thomas Venner led a small revolt in London from 6–9 January 1661, the precarious freedom enjoyed by many Dissenters throughout England quickly disappeared. On 10 January 1661, Charles II

---

[26] Jessey, *The Lords Loud Call to England*, 17.

[27] Adam Taylor assumed that the audience with Charles II provided some relief (*The History of the English General Baptists*, 2 vols. [London: T. Bore, 1818] 1.188). According to Davies, twenty-one Quakers were released in Lincolnshire (*Quakerism in Lincolnshire*, 18–19). See also Holmes, *Seventeenth-Century Lincolnshire*, 221.

issued a proclamation forbidding the assembly of Anabaptists, Quakers, Fifth Monarchists, and other religious radicals.[28]

Venner and his cohorts may have been an "aberration," but it was not long before any religious dissenter was thought to be capable of similar actions.[29] Thus, it was commonly assumed that religious dissent and nonconformity were inextricably linked to sedition and revolution. In *The Humble Apology of some commonly called Anabaptists*, published on 28 January 1661 and presented to the king, Baptists throughout England issued a joint disavowal of the "late wicked and most horrid and most treasonable Insurrection and Rebellion acted in the City of London."[30] *The Humble Apology* reports that Venner's uprising in London created a situation in which to be called an Anabaptist was tantamount to being a criminal, "or at least a ground sufficient to question his Loyalty and fidelity to the Kings Majesty."[31] *The Humble Apology* goes on to inform the king that those represented therein had no foreknowledge of the insurrection nor did they participate in it. The signatories, most of who were from the London area, included the notable Particular Baptist William Kiffin and the General Baptist Henry Denne.[32] It seems likely that the Lincolnshire General Baptists at least agreed with the *Apology* based on Grantham's decision to include the full text in *Christianismus Primitivus* (1678).[33]

---

[28] See the Calendar of State Papers Domestic for Charles II, 1660–1661 (10 January 1661), "Proclamation for restraining all seditious meetings..." http://www.british-history.ac.uk/report.aspx?compid=54648 (accessed on 6 October 2008). See further, Norman Penney, ed., *Extracts from State Papers Relating to Friends, 1654–1672* (Philadelphia: H. Newman, 1913) 117–27.

[29] Meic Pearse, *The Great Restoration: The Religious Radicals of the 16th and 17th Centuries* (Carlisle UK: Paternoster Press, 1998) 235.

[30] *The Humble Apology of Some Commonly Called Anabaptists* (London: Printed by Henry Hills, 1661) title page. Hereafter referred to as *The Humble Apology*. It is worth noting that Henry Hills, Sr. (d. 1688/89), in addition to his role as a printer, was also an interesting Particular Baptist during this period.

[31] *The Humble Apology of Some Commonly Called Anabaptists*, 6.

[32] Ibid., 14.

[33] Thomas Grantham, *Christianismus Primitivus* (London, 1678) 3.7ff.

The situation in Lincolnshire was comparable to other Baptist contexts in early 1661, for it appears that local magistrates needed little motivation to enforce the royal prerogative. The late General Baptist historian Adam Taylor recorded that during these days "thousands" of Baptists were "stripped of their possessions, and thrown into prison; or obliged to flee from their habitations, and forsake their callings and families."[34] Struggles with the authorities in Lincolnshire prompted the General Baptists there to draft their own petition for the king in January 1661.[35]

In late January, the king received a "Second Humble Address of those who are called Anabaptists in the County of Lincoln."[36] The document, submitted in close chronological proximity to *The Humble Apology*, maintained that "in this Tottering Age" the Baptists in Lincolnshire were the king's loyal subjects. While providing little in the way of detail regarding the nature of persecution in Lincolnshire, the petition did mention the king's "Imprisoned and Distressed Subjects."[37] The baptized believers in Lincolnshire then called upon Charles to remember his "Letter from Breda" and distinguish properly between the just and the unjust when meting out judgment, "lest the Cryes of the Innocent and their ruined Families come up before the Lord." The baptized believers in Lincolnshire boldly expressed in no uncertain terms

---

[34] Taylor, *The History of the English General Baptists*, 1.194.

[35] There is disagreement over the dating of this document and its submission to Charles II, though the confusion is of little consequence. The confusion may date to Taylor's comment that a paper was submitted to the Lords of the Privy Council on 23 January 1661 to "strengthen" the petition from Lincolnshire (*The History of the English General Baptists*, 1.192). Taylor did not specify whether *The Second Humble Address* was also presented on 23 January or sometime earlier. William T. Whitley listed the date for *The Second Humble Address* as 16 January 1661 (*Minutes of the General Assembly of the General Baptist Churches in England*, 2 vols. [London: Kingsgate Press, 1909], 1.xxxv). Kershaw gave the date as 23 January 1661 ("Baptized Believers," 33).

[36] *The Second Humble Address of those who are Called Anabaptists in the County of Lincoln* (London: Printed by Simon Dover, 1661). This document is a single-page petition.

[37] *The Second Humble Address*.

that royal refusal to ameliorate the present situation would lead to God's displeasure.

That Thomas Grantham's name headed the list of thirty signatories is itself an important fact. Based on Whitley's list of General Baptist leaders in the seventeenth century,[38] *The Second Humble Address* seems to have been a "county-wide" petition.[39] No information is given regarding how the document made its way to the king, but it is possible given his recent favorable audience with Charles II that Grantham could have been the courier.

Charles's reaction to the petition was not recorded, but based on the submission of a third appeal to the king on 23 February 1661, it is clear that *The Second Humble Address* did not have the desired effect. Sometime after the delivery of *The Second Humble Address* in January but before 23 February, Thomas Grantham's name headed a list of eight "Heads" of Baptist congregations in Lincolnshire who had recently been imprisoned in the "Common Gaol at Lincoln."[40] All eight men had signed *The Second Humble Address*. Similar to *The Second Humble Address*, a survey of the geographical distribution of the leaders suggests a countywide representation of Baptist "Heads" jailed together in Lincoln.[41]

The address itself called upon Charles to orchestrate the release of the innocent Baptist prisoners for the "Glory of God" and the "renown of your Princely Majesty." Furthermore, the signatories pledged on behalf of the congregations that owned "that Confession of Faith presented to your Princely Hands, July 26, 1660" that they would never disturb the peace. Furthermore, the assenting congregations and their leaders promised to "cheerfully (as much as in us lieth, when lawfully called

---

[38] Whitley, *Minutes of the General Assembly of the General Baptist Churches in England*, 1.xxxv–xlvii.

[39] Kershaw, "Baptized Believers," 33.

[40] *The Third Address of those Persons, Known by the Name of Anabaptists, in the County of LINCOLN* (London, 1661).

[41] Whitley, *Minutes of the General Assembly of the General Baptist Churches in England*, 1.xxxv–xlvii.

thereunto) defend Your Majesties Person, Crown, and Dignity...." Finally, *The Third Address* requested that Charles allow the baptized believers to worship freely, but it also reminded him that they would continue to meet for worship according to the dictates of scripture regardless of the laws and statutes imposed upon them.

There is no record of how this petition reached the king's hand, but a note to the reader stated that Charles expressed his confidence in the innocence of the "Lincolnshire Petitioners" and his intention to "preserve" them. It is also recorded that Lord Chancellor Hyde spoke of the imminent completion of an "Instrument" that would protect and preserve those in such constraints. Despite such encouraging reactions, the promises made by Charles and Hyde proved to be hollow and had little positive effect in Lincolnshire. Local magistrates continued to persecute Dissenters of all stripes; Grantham remained in Lincoln jail for at least two Assizes, but in 1663 he was brought before the bar and dismissed without charge after fifteen months of imprisonment.[42] In vain did Grantham and his fellow Baptists attempt to secure religious toleration for their assemblies, but the unity and countywide cooperation of the General Baptists revealed in *The Second Humble Address* and *The Third Address* are important. Grantham may have personally delivered only one of the three petitions from the Lincolnshire General Baptists in 1660 and 1661, but he certainly provided important representational leadership during a period in which Baptists were accused of disloyalty and sedition. His own imprisonment testifies to his stature within and without the General Baptist communities in Lincolnshire during these years

Grantham and "A Humble Address, or Remonstrance," 1672. The Declaration of Indulgence in March 1672 offered considerable freedom to those who chose to register for licenses, but it did not ensure the cessation of hostility. In direct defiance of the Indulgence, Mr. Whately, a local justice in Lincoln, actually levied fines against worshippers

[42] For a more detailed discussion of the imprisonment, see the biographical and literary sketch in "A Man and His Remains."

meeting in a licensed assembly. John Maitland, Duke of Lauderdale and member of the king's Cabal, prosecuted Whately on the grounds that he had acted in "high contempt of his majesty's declaration."[43] It is probable that the Whately affair and similar situations prompted the Lincolnshire General Baptists to send Grantham (with another unknown messenger) to wait on the king with "A Humble Address, or Remonstrance" in 1672.

The details surrounding Grantham's next audience with Charles II in 1672 are largely unavailable, and what can be known is found only in secondary sources.[44] Though it is no longer extant, a few details of this document are available in Crosby.[45] One significant difference between the audience in 1660 and the appearance in 1672 is that Grantham had been ordained to the office of messenger in 1666. Thus, his status and reputation among the Baptists in Lincolnshire had certainly grown since his encounter with Charles some twelve years before.

In "A Humble Address, or Remonstrance" the Lincolnshire Baptists first expressed their gratitude to the king for allowing public assemblies. Grantham and his companion expressed concerns, however, over the ways in which the king's declaration still "infringed that liberty" that the Baptists felt they had a God-given right to enjoy. Based on Crosby's account, it appears that the Lincolnshire Baptists faced some resistance at the local level when attempting to exercise their "spiritual gifts of prayer" and "preaching." They urged the king to allow room for worship according to the dictates of scripture and affirmed that nothing less "would satisfy the church of God."[46] No account of the king's response is given, and it is likely that this was Grantham's final appearance before the king.

---

[43] Quoted in Frank Bate, *The Declaration of Indulgence, 1672: A Study in the Rise of Organised Dissent* (London: University Press of Liverpool, 1908) 102.

[44] Crosby provided an account of the encounter (*The History of the English Baptists*, 3.83).

[45] Crosby, *The History of the English Baptists*, 3.83. Crosby's account of the address reads more like a paraphrase than a quotation, though there is no reason to doubt his accuracy (*The History of the English Baptists*, 3.83–84).

[46] Crosby, *The History of the English Baptists*, 3.83.

It is clear that Grantham's role as a messenger of the General Baptist churches required that he actively defend and support the Baptist cause in Lincolnshire. In the early 1670s he fulfilled his ordained role in a rather public manner by debating the Quaker John Whitehead and the Anglican William Fort. In addition to speaking for the Baptists in theological disputes, Grantham's audience with the king in the wake of the Indulgence demonstrates that he continued to serve as a trusted liaison to the royal court. The Lincolnshire General Baptists valued this minister who was able to not only gain an audience with the king but also to articulate their concerns in a convincing and efficacious manner.

Grantham provided important leadership for the General Baptists of Lincolnshire at critical times. In 1660 and again in 1672 the baptized believers of his country sent him to wait on the king and secure royal protection. Grantham was a signatory on two 1661 petitions delivered to the king on behalf of the Baptist congregations in Lincolnshire. That Grantham played such a crucial role before being ordained to the office of messenger suggests he possessed considerable leadership ability at a young age.

Ambler argued that the ability of the Lincolnshire congregations to join together for local addresses and national statements suggests that Baptists in the county had organized effectively around capable leaders. Grantham's budding influence among the sectarian General Baptists seems to confirm Ambler's conclusion. That Grantham was not a signatory on the original *A Brief Confession or Declaration of Faith*, which was signed by forty leaders representing more than 20,000 Baptists nationwide, or *The Humble Apology*, might indicate that as of 1661 he was not yet a recognized figure in the larger General Baptist movement. One notes, however, that during the critical moments of the Restoration in 1660 and 1661, all known documents drafted specifically on behalf of the Lincolnshire General Baptists for the king bore Grantham's name. The apparent expansion from the local to countywide distribution of signatories represented in the three petitions in 1660 and

1661 suggests that Grantham's influence in Lincolnshire was growing.[47] Furthermore, that he was among the eight "Heads" of the local congregations arrested and imprisoned after Venner's uprising implies that he was recognized as an important leader of the General Baptists in Lincolnshire.

These petitions also reveal that the baptized believers in Lincolnshire were comfortable appealing over the heads of their local magistrates for redress of grievances. While it is certainly true that the king's court was a "remote" governing body for most people in seventeenth-century England,[48] Grantham's audiences with the king and the addresses he signed suggest that the king and his counselors were accessible to, and discursive with, at least some Dissenters. An understanding of the local issues facing Baptists during the 1660s and early 1670s is important, but it is equally necessary to point out that Charles's desires for toleration as expressed in the Declaration from Breda (1660) and Declaration of Indulgence (1672) were not taken as distant declarations by Dissenters in the countryside. Grantham's Baptists took the king's word and called upon Charles repeatedly to make good on his promises.

Finally, what conclusions can be drawn regarding the means by which Grantham and his fellow Baptists were able to gain multiple audiences with Charles II? As we have seen, Taylor suggested that their success was due to an unnamed but honorable member of Parliament. It is certainly possible, and quite likely, that there was a small number of those in the Convention Parliament (1660) and the Cavalier Parliament (1661–79) that were sympathetic to the plight of Dissenters. It is also possible that Grantham's family heritage played some role. He was, he claimed, from the ancient and esteemed Grantham family of Lincolnshire.[49] Lincolnshire had sent two men by the name of Thomas

---

[47] Ambler, *Churches, Chapels and Parish Communities of Lincolnshire 1660–1900*, 24.

[48] Barry Coward, *The Stuart Age: England, 1603–1704* (New York: Pearson Education, 2003) 96.

[49] Grantham, *Christianismus Primitivus*, 1.1.

Grantham to Parliaments in the first half of the century.[50] It seems there is no clear answer to the question of how they obtained the audiences, but the next section will show that Grantham was ever willing to take advantage of the rare governmental provisions for "tender consciences."

Licensing the Baptists, 1672 and 1688/9. Grantham accepted a government-issued license and encouraged other Baptists to do the same. The following pages will examine Grantham's interaction with the government by focusing on his reaction to the Declaration of Indulgence in 1672 and the Toleration Act of 1689. In both contexts, Grantham saw in the toleration offered by the king an opportunity to expand and solidify the General Baptist churches.

The Declaration of Indulgence, 1672. Charles II's efforts to provide some level of toleration in the early 1660s had been thwarted, but on 15 March 1672 he issued a Declaration of Indulgence in an attempt to garner support for a war with the Dutch and to fulfill a promise made to Louis XIV of France.[51] In 1670 Louis and Charles had agreed in the so-called "Secret Treaty of Dover" to make war against the Dutch. In addition, Charles promised to declare himself a Roman Catholic "as soon as his country's affairs admit" in exchange for French financial and military support.[52] Thus, the Indulgence was an attempt to offer, in a limited fashion, toleration to Catholics. It is possible that Charles thought the "country's affairs" were sufficiently in order for his open reconciliation with Rome. He was wrong.

The terms of the Indulgence did not require an oath of allegiance, but they did insist that Dissenters apply for licenses. Three basic types of

---

[50] See Holmes, *Seventeenth-Century Lincolnshire*, 140 and 205.

[51] Charles proclaimed the Indulgence while Parliament was prorogued. For the full text of the declaration, cited in Bate's *The Declaration of Indulgence, 1672* (76–78).

[52] For the full text, see Andrew Browning, *English Historical Documents, 1660–1714* (London: Eyre & Spottiswoode, 1953) 863–67. For the context of the treaty, see Coward, *The Stuart Age: England, 1603–1704*, 305–11; and Seaward, *The Restoration, 1660–1688*, 50–52.

licenses were offered under the Indulgence: (1) one could register for a license as a teacher, preacher, or minister of a particular group in a place named; (2) one could register to teach in any licensed place; and (3) one could register one's home as a meeting place for worship conducted not in accordance with the prescribed customs of the Church of England.[53]

The introduction of this tolerant policy posed a dilemma for Dissenters. Many were afraid that it might open the door for a revival of Catholicism. For others, it was a question of whether an application for a government-issued license amounted to tacit affirmation of the government's right to permit or restrict religious expression. Quakers as a whole refused on principle even to apply for licenses.[54] Presbyterians had mixed reactions, but they accounted for more licenses than any other group.[55]

Baptists did not react uniformly to the offered Indulgence. In sum, approximately 200 Baptists obtained preaching licenses.[56] Baptists in the far northern counties seem to have been disinclined to accept licenses. Not a single one was issued to a Baptist in the northern counties of Northumberland, Durham, Cumberland, or Westmoreland. In other northern counties such as Lancashire and Yorkshire, Baptists accounted for few licenses.

---

[53] Bate, *The Declaration of Indulgence, 1672*, 95. Bate noted that "meeting place" licenses were not initially granted for churches, chapels, or other large structures, 96.

[54] Watts, *The Dissenters*, 1.248. Some Presbyterians were unsure about the impact licenses would have had on their attempts at comprehension in the established Church of England.

[55] George L. Turner, *Original Records of Early Nonconformity under Persecution and Indulgence*, 3 vols. (London: T. F. Unwin, 1914) 3.732–36. See also Geoffrey F. Nuttall and Owen Chadwick, eds., *From Uniformity to Unity* (London: Society for Promoting Christian Knowledge, 1962) 209ff.

[56] An exact count is difficult. Bate puts the number at 200 (*The Declaration of Indulgence, 1672*, 99); Turner counts 210 (*Original Records of Early Nonconformity under Persecution and Indulgence*, 3.732–36).

Whitley traced the reticence among some Baptists to a "disdain" for requesting that which they held to be a right.[57] Michael Watts, relying on Whitley's assessment, concluded that a good number of Baptists adopted an identical position to Quakers with regard to licenses.[58] While it is true that many Baptists did not accept licenses, the evidence suggests that roughly half of the known Baptist ministers did take advantage of the protection a license offered.[59] John Spurr attributed the positive reaction to licenses by some Baptists to the voluntary nature of Baptist life.[60]

Of the 200 or so licenses issued to Baptists teachers or preachers, more than eighty were sent to Kent, Somerset, Lincolnshire, Wiltshire, and Norfolk.[61] In Lincolnshire, Baptists, who comprised the largest dissenting group in the county, were awarded a total of twenty-two licenses.[62] Of those, seventeen licenses were designated for "Teachers."[63] Of the seventeen Baptists in Lincolnshire who categorized themselves as "Teachers," fifteen also registered their homes as Baptist meeting

---

[57] William T. Whitley, "The Baptist Licenses of 1672," *Transactions of the Baptist Historical Society* (1908–1909): 156.

[58] Watts, *The Dissenters*, 1.248.

[59] Of Baptist hesitancy Douglas R. Lacey wrote, "The conclusion of religious historians that a large number of Baptist ministers did not apply is based upon a comparison of the number who did apply, which was 210 or more, to the number of Baptist ministers there presumably were, which is thought to have been about 420" (*Dissent and Parliamentary Politics in England 1661–89* [New Brunswick NJ: Rutgers University Press, 1969] 291 n. 89). Lacey's figure of 420 was taken from Whitley, *A History of British Baptists* (London: Kingsgate Press, 1932) 123.

[60] John Spurr, *England in the 1670s* (Malden MA: Blackwell Publishers, 2000) 35.

[61] Bate, *The Declaration of Indulgence, 1672*, 98. Rodney Ambler has shown that not all areas in Lincolnshire with a large number of Baptists are represented in the distribution of licenses (*Churches, Chapels and Parish Communities of Lincolnshire 1660–1900*, 21–24).

[62] Turner, *Original Records of Early Nonconformity under Persecution and Indulgence*, 2.730–31. See Ambler, *Churches, Chapels and Parish Communities of Lincolnshire 1660–1900*, 21.

[63] Turner, *Original Records of Early Nonconformity under Persecution and Indulgence*, 2.730–31.

places.[64] These numbers indicate that the Baptist leaders in Lincolnshire who registered as teachers also used their homes for congregational worship.

Thomas Grantham, unsurprisingly, registered himself as a Baptist "Teacher." That he did so in the neighboring county of Leicestershire to the southwest, however, is rather curious. William Whitley believed that Grantham's ministry had taken him as far west as Market Harborough, a market town in the county of Leicestershire, though it is unclear where he obtained this information. Public records show that Thomas Grantham took out a license at "Raiston" (or alternately "Rouston") under the Indulgence. Whitley's study of Baptist licenses drew attention to the unexpected location of Grantham's license and notes the paucity of information regarding his ministry in the county.[65] Assuming this was the same Thomas Grantham of Lincolnshire, the license raises important questions: was Grantham residing in Leicestershire, simply ministering there, or was there some other reason for his taking a license in the county?

Questions concerning Grantham's possible residence in Leicestershire come from a close reading of Turner's analysis and the issuance and delivery of the license itself. Turner noted, perhaps mistakenly, in his analysis that Grantham took out a license for a meeting place in 1672.[66] There is good reason to question Turner at this point since Frank Bate did not list Grantham among those in Leicestershire who registered a meeting place.[67] On the other hand, it is clear that as late 1666 the Baptist congregation that Grantham pastored in

---

[64] Ibid.

[65] Whitley, "The Baptist Licenses of 1672," 159. Whitley also recommended that "Raiston" be taken as an alternate spelling for "Rolleston" or "Rouston." For a helpful study of General Baptist beginnings in Leicestershire, see Alan Betteridge, "Early Baptists in Leicestershire and Rutland: General Baptists," *Baptist Quarterly* 25, no. 8 (October 1974): 354–78. Grantham did not appear in Betteridge's study.

[66] Turner, *Original Records of Early Nonconformity under Persecution and Indulgence*, 1.771.

[67] Bate did not have Grantham taking out a license for a meeting place (see Appendix VI in *The Declaration of Indulgence, 1672*).

Lincolnshire met in his home.[68] More compelling evidence for a possible lengthy stay in the county is found in the details of Grantham's preaching license itself, for which Turner included two separate entries. The first entry has a license specified for Thomas Grantham of Raiston as a Baptist "Teacher" in December 1672.[69] A second entry had a license being issued to Thomas Grantham of Rouston as a Baptist "Teacher" in February 1673.[70] The two entries suggest that Grantham's license was issued in December but delivered in February.[71] If this was the case, then at the very least, Grantham must have been present in Leicestershire in December 1672 and February 1673.

Grantham debated the Quaker John Whitehead in Lincolnshire sometime prior to November 1672; in 1673 Grantham debated William Fort at Blyton, Lincolnshire. There seems to be no extant reference to Grantham's presence or ministry in Leicestershire, nor are there church records from the area that mention Grantham or his presence in this region neighboring Lincolnshire. Thus, it seems highly unlikely that Grantham ministered in Lincolnshire while based in Leicestershire. Yet, it is reasonable to expect that in fulfilling his duties as a General Baptist Messenger he found reason to travel west and minister in that county. Was he perchance traveling back and forth with some frequency for the purposes of ministry? Such a scenario would help explain his application for a license in Raiston, Leicestershire.

The experiment with licenses was short-lived. Since Charles II was involved in an expensive war and low on funds, he was forced to recall Parliament in 1673. Parliament turned its attention rather quickly to the legality of the Indulgence issued a year earlier. Charles was caught between a need to secure additional money for the Dutch war and a

---

[68] Thomas Grantham to John Connould, 21 April 1691. The letters passed between Grantham and Connould are housed at The Beinecke Rare Book and Manuscript Library, Yale University Library, New Haven CT.

[69] Turner, *Original Records of Early Nonconformity under Persecution and Indulgence*, 1.579.

[70]Ibid., 1.58.

[71]Whitley found that the most of the licenses for Leicestershire were issued on 8 August and 9 December 1672 ("The Baptist Licenses of 1672," 159).

desire to legitimate his Indulgence. The need for financing prevailed, and in March Charles withdrew the Indulgence.[72] It was another two years before the licenses were recalled.[73] The king's decision to back down from his declaration negatively affected the Baptists and other Dissenters, who faced considerable hardships in the later 1670s and much of the 1680s. In 1689, however, William III enacted a similarly tolerant approach known as the Toleration Act. It is in this context that a clear example of Grantham's utilitarian approach to government licenses becomes evident.

Grantham and Toleration Act of 1689. Whiggish history has been prone to laud the Revolution of 1688 as a "Glorious" triumph for religious toleration, but in many ways the so-called Toleration Act enacted during the early reign of William III was deficient when compared with the Indulgences of James II in 1687 and 1688.[74] Technically speaking, the Toleration Act of 1689 was a compromise that provided no laws or licenses to protect Dissenters.[75] Furthermore, Dissenters were still excluded from public office and universities. The

---

[72] For the political context of the rescission, see Spurr, *England in the 1670s*, 36ff.; Lacey, *Dissent and Parliamentary Politics in England 1661–89*, 47–70; and Bate, *The Declaration of Indulgence, 1672*, 122–40.

[73] Bate, *The Declaration of Indulgence, 1672*, 140.

[74] For an introduction to the Indulgences of 1687 and 1688, see Richard E. Boyer, *English Declarations of Indulgence 1687–1688* (The Hague, The Netherlands: Mouton & Co., 1968). Hugh Trevor-Roper also detailed the limitations and shortcomings of the Toleration Act, "Toleration and Religion after 1688," in *From Persecution to Toleration*, eds. Ole P. Grell, Jonathan I. Israel, and Nicholas Tyacke (Oxford: Clarendon Press, 1991) 389–408.

[75] Ambler pointed out that William's plan for toleration amounted to a reluctant "acceptance of the failure of the Church of England to achieve the monopoly of religious practice envisaged for it in 1662" (*Churches, Chapels and Parish Communities of Lincolnshire 1660–1900*, 47).

act did, however, repeal the punishment for dissent under certain conditions.[76]

Dissenters could avoid facing punishment in civil and ecclesiastical courts for their unscrupulous behavior if they made certain public oaths. For those Quakers and sundry Baptists who opposed oaths, they could earn impunity by publicly confessing faith in the Trinity and belief in the inspiration of the scriptures. "Anabaptist" ministers were required to sign most of the "Thirty-Nine Articles," with the twenty-seventh article on baptism being the exception. Dissenters were given the latitude to worship publicly, with the doors unlocked, but only after they registered their meeting place with the local bishop or the Quarter Sessions. Instead of licenses, Dissenters were given a copy of the record of their oath or registration. Furthermore, dissenting citizens were theoretically protected from the ire of bitter local magistrates since the latter were not allowed to reject or deny anyone intent on meeting the requirements.

In February 1692 Nicholas Knowles recounted in a letter the early success and struggles of the General Baptist presence in King's Lynn, Norfolk, following the issuance of the Toleration Act.[77] Sometime in late 1688 or 1689, James Marham and Grantham began working to establish a General Baptist presence in King's Lynn. Marham secured a temporary meeting place in the Town Hall, where many "attentive Auditors, like hungry and thirsty Souls" attended to hear Grantham preach.[78] Grantham was so "exceedingly pleased" with the progress that he instructed Marham to secure "some convenient Place" in order that the "Meeting might be continued" in King's Lynn.[79] The pulpit was filled with various preachers in the following months: Grantham, ministers from Whittelsey

[76] The official title of the 1688 act was "An Act for Exempting their Majestyes Protestant Subjects dissenting from the Church of England from the Penalties of certaine Lawes."

[77] *The Lyn Persecution* (n.p., 1692/3) 6–14. This short document was published anonymously.

[78] *The Lyn Persecution*, 11.

[79] Ibid.

in Cambridgeshire, and William Long, who was sent to Norwich to assist Grantham.[80]

Grantham sent Long to minister in King's Lynn for a short time beginning in January 1690 in order that the new congregation "might taste the Kindness of the London Brethren."[81] The congregation grew under Long's leadership, and local magistrates soon took notice. City leaders sent undercover informants to Baptist meetings, and subsequently accused the congregation of unlawful assembly and levied fines: twenty pounds for the meeting place, twenty pounds for the preacher, and five pounds for those who attended the meetings.

The magistrates did not know whom to charge for the supposed violation of the Conventicle Act, so they called in Marham to find out who "hired" the meeting place.[82] Marham admitted that he was responsible for securing the meeting place, to which his accusers replied that he must pay the twenty pounds for housing the worship of "new religion."[83] Furthermore, they promised to discontinue the meetings and drive Marham out of the city if he persisted. Marham produced his copy of the record of the registration, but the magistrates' energies were unabated by the legality of the proceedings and the fines were imposed regardless. Marham's troubles continued for some time. He was jailed, his possessions were impounded, and his legal fees became more than even three Baptist congregations could pay.[84] Marham's case had not been resolved when *The Lyn Persecution* was printed in late February 1692.[85]

The narrative outlined above provides key insights into the nature of Grantham's leadership and understanding of Dissent. The extent of Grantham's personal compliance with the Toleration Act is not known.

---

[80] Ibid., 12.

[81] Ibid.

[82] Ibid.

[83] Ibid.

[84] Ibid., 15.

[85] *The Lyn Persecution* was published in order to alert Baptists in England to Marham's situation and garner support for his relief.

Given his own appeals to the king, his request for a license in 1672, and his support of taking oaths in civil affairs,[86] it seems likely that he would have seen the Toleration Act as a means to solidify and protect his ministry in Norfolk. This conclusion is confirmed by Grantham's decision to encourage Marham to take advantage of toleration by officially registering a location for Baptist meetings. Grantham's advice to Marham to register a meeting place was intended to foster Baptist permanence in the city. In the short term, the legal and official means by which Marham obtained a meeting place were disregarded by local authorities who sought to disband the Baptists. In the long run, however, Grantham's efforts were somewhat successful, for there was a General Baptist presence in King's Lynn in contact with the General Assembly as late as 1801.[87]

The local nature of harassment and persecution is also noteworthy in this episode. The events in King's Lynn illustrate well how latent local tensions over religiously tolerant royal policy could affect a young Baptist congregation. The earliest efforts of Grantham, Marham, and Long resulted in growth and an established General Baptist presence in King's Lynn. Consequently, Marham, who was not a native of Norfolk, shouldered much of the responsibility for defending the young congregation against attacks. As seen already, Grantham had also faced persecutions in Norfolk in the early 1690s.[88] Whereas Grantham, also new to Norfolk, was accused of stealing sheep and other immoral behavior,[89] Marham was pressed on the legality of Baptist meetings. Grantham's efforts to clear his name by the testimony of witnesses resulted in his exculpation by the authorities in Norwich. Marham, on the other hand, produced all the necessary proof that his Baptists met legally

---

[86] Grantham, *Christianismus Primitivus*, 3.23–28.

[87] Whitley, *Minutes of the General Assembly of the General Baptist Churches in England*, 1.xxxv–lxiii.

[88] See "A Man and His Remains." See also George Southcombe, "The Responses of Nonconformists to the Restoration in England" (DPhil thesis, University of Oxford, 2005) 177–78.

[89] See *The Slanderer Rebuked* (n.p., 1691) and *The Grand Imposter* (n.p., 1691).

yet he received no justice at the hands of the magistrates in King's Lynn. Grantham obviously understood that the Toleration Act provided significant freedom and potential for growth, but he may have also overestimated the practical level of toleration resulting from the act. Baptists had not been given "equal liberty" with Anglicans as Grantham wrote in 1691,[90] and local magistrates were not always willing to recognize what little liberty Dissenters had been given.

Grantham and the Government

The Loyal Baptis*t and* Christianismus Primitivus. Baptist contributions to the struggle for religious liberty have been well documented.[91] H. Leon McBeth's survey of seventeenth-century Baptist writings on religious liberty found that the most significant Baptist literature on religious liberty in the seventeenth century was published before 1673.[92] Moreover, McBeth determined that Baptists published little between 1673 and 1689 of any permanent significance in "content or influence."[93] A thorough investigation of Grantham's writings during these years, however, suggests that McBeth's negative conclusion regarding Baptist

---

[90] Thomas Grantham to John Connould, 17 April 1691.

[91] W. K. Jordan's four-volume *The Development of Religious Toleration in England* (London: George Allen and Unwin, 1932–40) provided important context. For studies focused on Baptists in particular, see J. D. Hughey, Jr., "Baptists and Religious Freedom," *Baptist Quarterly* 17, no. 6 (April 1958): 249–55; William R. Estep, *Revolution within the Revolution: The First Amendment in Historical Context* (Grand Rapids MI: Eerdmans, 1990); Walter B. Shurden, ed., *Religious Liberty* (Macon GA: Smyth & Helwys, 1997); and John Coffey, "From Helwys to Leland: Baptists and Religious Tolerance in England and America, 1612–1791," in *The Gospel in the World*, ed. David Bebbington (Waynesboro GA: Paternoster Press, 2002) 13–37.

[92] McBeth, *English Baptist Literature on Religious Liberty to 1689*, 256.

[93] Ibid., 256–57. McBeth attributed this decline to several factors: an increase in harsh, restrictive laws; Baptists found it difficult to get their works printed; Baptists appealed frequently to previously published materials; toleration was gradually becoming acceptable; Baptists shared in the spiritual decay of the period. His analysis of the documents from this period focused on the confessions issued and the writings of Thomas Delaune, Grantham, and Benjamin Keach.

thought on religious liberty in the fourteen-year span was perhaps too sweeping.

Where Grantham is concerned, McBeth's research focused on *The Prisoner against the Prelate* (1662), *The Baptist against the Papist* (1663), *Christianismus Primitivus* (1678), *A Friendly Epistle* (1680), and *The Baptist Complaint against the Persecuting Priests* (date unknown).[94] McBeth concluded that Grantham did not deal extensively with the topic of religious liberty, yet such a conclusion can be challenged on several grounds. First, McBeth failed to address the full gambit of Grantham's positions as presented in *Christianismus Primitivus*. He rightly drew attention to Grantham's distinction between "natural" religion and "positive" religion, but there was no discussion of Grantham's views on civil freedoms related to assemblies, marriage, burial, and poor relief. Second, McBeth's study made no mention of *The Loyal Baptist*, which Grantham published in 1674 and again in 1684. What follows will show that *Christianismus Primitivus* and *The Loyal Baptist*, when taken together, constituted a legitimate and significant theoretical contribution to seventeenth-century General Baptist ecclesio-political life and thought. From the historian's perspective, they also reflect the parameters of civil life in which Baptists struggled following the withdrawal of the Declaration of Indulgence in 1673.

The Loyal Baptist, *1674 and 1684*. Grantham's assertion in 1674 that Baptists were "loyal" to the king could be said of most Dissenters of the period. The typical dissenting attitude toward the state in the seventeenth-century was one of loyalty, but those in positions of power were not usually capable of recognizing this. Events in London often precipitated persecution in the localities,[95] so the failed attempt by the House of Commons to pass a bill providing relief for Protestant dissenters and the withdrawal of the Indulgence in March 1673 left many

---

[94] McBeth, *English Baptist Literature on Religious Liberty to 1689*, 239–44 and 264ff.

[95] Seaward, *The Restoration, 1660–1688*, 58.

"loyal" Dissenters vulnerable to retaliation.[96] It was in this context of toleration extended and withdrawn that Grantham published *The Loyal Baptist: Or An Apology for the Baptized Believers* (1674).[97]

Grantham argued in favor of a qualified loyalty to the king in 1674 when he published *The Loyal Baptist.* The treatise consists of two sermons (or discourses) on 1 Peter 2:17: "Honour all men. Love the brotherhood. Fear God. Honour the king" (Authorized Version of 1611). Grantham argues that these four duties are incumbent upon all Christians, and he was not alone in emphasizing the relevance of 1 Peter 2 in matters pertaining to a Christian's responsibility to civil magistrates.

Dissenting preachers and teachers often appealed to the thirteenth chapter of Romans when discussing the appropriate attitude toward governing authorities.[98] Another key passage, at least for General Baptists during the Restoration, was 1 Peter 2:13–20. Article XXV of the *Brief Confession or Declaration of Faith* (which came to be known as the *Standard Confession*) Grantham delivered to Charles II in 1660 cited 1 Peter 2:13–14 when speaking of the necessity and limits of Christian obedience to civil rulers:

> We believe that there ought to be civil Magistrates in all Nations, for the punishment of evil doers, and for the praise of them that do well, I Pet. 2.14. and that all wicked lewdness, and fleshly filthiness, contrary to just

---

[96] See Bate, *The Declaration of Indulgence, 1672*, 130. In 1673 a pamphlet titled *Mr. Baxter Baptized in Blood* was published in England alleging that Baptists in Boston, New England, had killed the Anglican minister Josiah Baxter because he had triumphed in a debate. *Forgery Detected and Innocency Vindicated* (London, 1673), an anonymous denial of the charges by the Baptists in England soon appeared. The charges were proven to be false in a court of law, but it demonstrates the ways in which Baptists were publicly portrayed by opponents in 1673. See David Benedict, *A General History of the Baptist Denomination in America*, 2 vols. (Boston MA: Lincoln and Edmands, 1813) 1.206–7.

[97] Thomas Grantham, *The Loyal Baptist: Or An Apology for Baptized Believers* (London, 1684). Hereafter cited as *The Loyal Baptist.* The only accessible edition of this treatise was published in 1684. In that edition, Grantham included the title page from the 1674 edition immediately following the 1684 title page.

[98] Evelyn D. Bebb, *Nonconformity and Social and Economic Life 1660–1800* (Philadelphia: Porcupine Press, 1980) 77.

> and wholesome (Civil) Laws, ought to be punished according to the nature of the offences; and this without respect of any Persons, Religion, or profession whatsoever; and that all men are obliged by Gospel rules, to be subject to the higher powers, to obey Magistrates, Tit. 3.1 and to submit to every Ordinance of man, for the Lord's sake, as saith Peter 2.13. But in case Civil Powers do, or shall at any time impose things about matters of Religion, which we through conscience to God cannot actually obey, then we with Peter also do say, that we ought (in such cases) to obey God rather than men; Acts 5:29.[99]

The importance of 1 Peter 2:13ff. was apparent in the excerpt quoted above, for it established the authority of civil rulers, the need to obey civil rulers, and the circumstances under which civil rulers are to be disobeyed. The *Brief Confession or Declaration of Faith* was repeatedly approved by the Assembly of General Baptists in the seventeenth century and became their "Standard Confession." Similarly, article XLV of the General Baptist *Orthodox Creed* (1678) affirmed the importance of civil magistrates and, among other scriptures, cited 1 Peter 2:13, 17.[100] Given its repeated appearance in General Baptist confessions of faith, 1 Peter 2 undoubtedly became recognizable as an important text for articulating a theology of the Christian's responsibility to civil magistrates. The consensus was that Baptists were commanded by scripture to be loyal to civil magistrates, but loyalty is always filtered "through conscience to God."

Grantham's own thinking on the nature and extent of loyalty to civil magistrates was quite similar, and by using 1 Peter 2:17 in particular, he expanded the discussion of religious liberty by arguing that freedom brings responsibility. The first duty of any loyal Baptist was to honor and esteem all people. Grantham offered three reasons why Christians must honor everyone. First, all humans are "Equals by Creation, the Workmanship of the Hands of God."[101] Second, God honors all humans

---

[99] William L. Lumpkin, *Baptist Confessions of Faith* (Philadelphia: Judson Press, 1959) 233.

[100] Ibid., 331.

[101] Grantham, *The Loyal Baptist*, 7.

through acts of providence, redemptive activity, and the preaching of peace.[102] Third, honoring others was an "effectual" means of convincing others of the veracity of Christianity.[103] Grantham concluded his thoughts on honoring all people with a warning to those who would "set up their Religion by Violence, Blood, and Treachery." Those who abused religion by employing violence on its behalf know neither Christ nor the "Divine Power of Christianity."[104]

Grantham interpreted love for the "brotherhood" to be a "more special kind of love" than Christians have for the world's general population. More specifically, Grantham takes "the brotherhood" in two senses. In a broader sense it includes all who "…hold to the Bible as the only rule of faith; believe in the Trinity; believe that Jesus died and was resurrected in order to justify sinners; and live sober lives according to the dictates of Christianity."[105] In a more narrow sense, "the brotherhood" includes "truly constituted and well-governed Societies of Christians." In this stricter sense Grantham assumed that God "undoubtedly" desires that Christianity be established in "all Nations."[106] On a practical level, Grantham encouraged his readers to "love the brotherhood" through practices such as praying, defending reputations, meeting physical needs, and preserving peace and prosperity.[107]

"To fear God," Grantham claimed, "is indeed a Duty incumbent upon all Men, and not upon Christians only."[108] What Grantham meant by this was that all people should "stand in awe" of God's majesty and splendor. Those who fear God rightly will be freed from fear of others and will give to God that which belongs to God (i.e., religious obedience). Where obedience to princes is concerned, Grantham wrote

---

[102] Ibid., 8–10. Grantham argued for a broad conception of "humanity." In this section he took all humans to be part of a "humane Fraternity," that was "antecedent" to any secondary association.

[103] Grantham, *The Loyal Baptist*, 11.

[104] Ibid.

[105] Ibid., 12.

[106] Ibid., 13.

[107] Ibid., 17.

[108] Ibid., 20.

that those with a healthy fear of God "Will not resist the power of princes; yet will he do what God commands, tho all the Princes in the World forbid him; nor will he do what God forbids, tho all the Princes in the World should command it."[109] While Grantham denied the prince any claim to religious obedience, it is clear that he thought princes were obligated to "promote the Interest of Religion" and offer "Encouragement to the Lovers of it."[110] For Grantham, then, the church and the government were not necessarily two separate spheres that were never to interact. In fact, he argued it was the duty of all rulers appointed by God to foster an environment in which Christianity could flourish.

The fourth and final section of *The Loyal Baptist* addressed directly the issues of kingship and the nature of loyalty to earthly rulers. In this discussion, Grantham laid out a defense of government and kingship. He noted that the command to "honor the King" in 1 Peter 2:17 did not refer to any king of Israel or Jesus, but rather it referenced a "heathen king."[111] In addition to 1 Peter 2, Grantham also cited Romans 13:1 in support of his claim that "Christians are bound by Gospel-Rules to be good Subjects to Princes, to honour their Persons, and conscientiously to obey their Authority."[112] This did not mean, however, that princes ruled independently of God.[113]

Grantham also addressed several possible objections to his views on obedience by listing those actions appropriate for loyal Christian subjects. Should Christians only obey those governing authorities established by God? There were apparently some whom Grantham encountered that thought so, but he would have none of this. Grantham ultimately grounded all secular authority and governing power in God's decision to establish or topple human regimes. Thus any government, regardless of the type or quality, was to be obeyed since it had been established by God.

---

[109] Ibid., 24–25.
[110] Ibid., 26.
[111] Ibid., 3.
[112] Ibid.
[113] Ibid., 26.

Did Grantham believe Christians were to obey rulers who acted inappropriately and oppressed their subjects? Grantham argued that the only "remedy" for such circumstances was "patient suffering."[114] Grantham did allow for "humble Supplication, to seek for Favour," much like what he presented to Charles II in 1660 and 1672, but beyond that the Christian has no recourse.[115] "Rebellion," Grantham stated unequivocally, "must by no means be admitted."[116] Even if a ruler decided to "entrench upon the Civil Rights" of loyal subjects, Grantham forbade retaliation. Grantham even warned against "dreaming" about regime change. For Grantham, then, there was no limit to the obedience and submission of Christian citizens to ruling authorities. Kings should extend religious liberty and toleration, but Christians should not seek to obtain their freedom at the expense of loyalty to those who rule over them. In this regard Grantham's theological theory of resistance and revolution is shown to have been different from that of the Baptists who had cooperated with the Levellers or Fifth Monarchists of years past.

Grantham's message regarding loyalty was not always expressed in negative terms. Going in a more positive direction with regard to loyalty, Grantham urged his fellow Baptists to esteem the king, honor him in love, and refrain from speaking evil of him.[117] Furthermore, Christian subjects were to remember always their position in the divinely ordained hierarchy, "for Obedience seldom issues from a lofty Mind."[118] Based on *The Loyal Baptist*, Grantham conceived of a three-tiered system with God at the top: God > Rulers (Grantham did not assume these always to be Christian authorities) > Subjects (which included Christians and non-Christians). By calling his fellow General Baptists to value all people, love the brotherhood, fear God, and honor the king, Grantham provided his persecuted seventeenth-century parishioners with a comprehensive

---

[114] Ibid., 30.

[115] Ibid.

[116] Ibid.

[117] Ibid., 31–32.

[118] Ibid., 33.

model of civil behavior. Moreover, he portrayed the General Baptists as a loyal group of Christians who sought the best for country and king.

A second edition a *The Loyal Baptist* appeared a decade later, in 1684. Did Grantham publish a second edition because he was pleased with the first? Had the first of *The Loyal Baptist* been so popular that it sold out and more copies were needed? Whatever other reasons there may have been for a second edition, the legal situation facing many Baptists in 1684 was similar to that of 1674: persecution. Persecution of Dissenters intensified in the aftermath of the discovery of the so-called Rye House Plot in 1683. Regardless of whether the plot was a reality, anti-Catholic conspirators were accused of planning to assassinate Charles II and his brother James (both of whom had Catholic sympathies). The supposed plan was foiled, but in the aftermath the recusancy laws normally used against Catholics were increasingly employed against Protestant dissenters. Dissenters were accused of rioting when the government elevated efforts to collect fines. Reaction in some areas became so volatile that dragoons were almost called upon to suppress the Dissenters.[119]

It is not clear what changes, if any, Grantham made in terms of the content of *The Loyal Baptist* between 1674 and 1684, for only a copy from 1684 survives. Since the 1684 edition included the original title page from 1674, it is possible that the 1684 publication was a second printing and not a revision. The one significant addition in 1684 was an appended document titled *The Second Part of the Apology* where Grantham critiqued Nathaniel Taylor's arguments in favor of infant baptism.[120]

The 1684 edition of *The Loyal Baptist* concluded with personal pleas to the Baptists and Charles II. Regardless of whether the same

---

[119] John Miller, *Popery and Politics in England 1660–1688* (New York: Cambridge University Press, 1973) 191–93. Watts described the increased persecution of Dissenters following the dissolution of the Oxford Parliament in 1681 (*The Dissenters*, 1.255ff.). There was no relief until James II dispensed with the Test Act and issued a general pardon to Dissenters in 1686.

[120] The two documents probably circulated together.

pleas were present in the 1674 edition, they were equally applicable in the similarly difficult circumstances of 1684. Grantham encouraged his fellow Baptists to "humble themselves" and "suffer patiently what Trials it shall please God to exercise you under."[121] Grantham hoped a copy of *The Loyal Baptist* would find its way into the hands of the king, and if it did, Charles would have read this personal appeal regarding the plight of the Baptists: "O let our Lord the King consider, that this is the greatest strait that any honest Christian can be put upon, either to deny what he believes to be true, or profess that to be true, which he believes to be otherwise."[122]

Christianismus Primitivus, *1678. Christianismus Primitivus* is generally considered to be Grantham's crowning literary and theological achievement. Joseph Ivimey thought it to be Grantham's "principal" work, while Whitley called it "a repertory of learning for [Grantham's] denomination."[123] William H. Brackney boldly asserted that it "may be fairly accorded first place chronologically among Baptist 'systematic' theologies."[124] McBeth described Grantham as the "greatest" General Baptist of the seventeenth century and claimed *Christianismus Primitivus* was the "greatest" Baptist writing of the seventeenth century, yet he did not seem to consider Grantham's discussion of religious liberty and toleration in *Christianismus Primitivus* (or *The Loyal Baptist*) to be a significant contribution similar to the Baptist documents that appeared before 1673.[125] The preceding discussion of *The Loyal Baptist* showed

---

[121] Grantham, *The Loyal Baptist*, 39.

[122] Ibid., 40.

[123] Joseph Ivimey, *A History of the English Baptists*, 4 vols. (London, 1814) 2.277. See also William T. Whitley, *A History of British Baptists* (London: Kingsgate Press, 1932) 134–35.

[124] William H. Brackney, "Thomas Grantham, Systematic Theology, and the Baptist Tradition" in *From Biblical Criticism to Biblical Faith: Essays in Honor of Lee Martin McDonald*, eds. William H. Brackney and Craig A. Evans (Macon GA: Mercer University Press, 2007) 216.

[125] McBeth, *English Baptist Literature on Religious Liberty to 1689*, 239 and 264. Grantham was certainly a dominant personality among General Baptists in the

that McBeth's conclusions need revision, and the following analysis of *Christianismus Primitivus* demonstrates this need more emphatically.

The Loyal Baptist predominantly addressed freedom of religion and the duties of Christians toward civil magistrates in abstract ways. In *Christianismus Primitivus*, however, Grantham developed in greater detail the practical and theological foundation for a Christian subject's interaction with authority. The bulk of the material related to the relationship between religion and government is found in the third book, "Of divers Cases of Conscience." Grantham basically divided his attention between issues related to the "rulers of this world"[126] and those matters pertaining to "Duty of all Christians to Civil Governors and Government."[127]

Grantham delineated the parameters of magisterial authority in several ways. He affirmed the basic equality of magistrates to their subjects by pointing out that all people are stewards, but some were appointed by God to be stewards of a "higher Rank."[128] He thought those who had been given this esteemed position had the responsibility to enact prudent laws, administer justice, and act mercifully. Where the laws were concerned, Grantham plainly rejected basing legislation on biblical principles: "as to the particular Laws for the Civil Government of such or such Nations, the Scriptures cannot be the Platform."[129] Grantham rejected the idea that the New Testament was "written as a Form of Government for any one Nation…much less to be a Form of Government to all Nations," and he is similarly hesitant to claim that the Law of Moses is "fitted for the civil policy of all nations."[130] Grantham did not intend that the scriptures be ignored in making laws; he did mean that any law that passed was in no way to contradict God's law or reason.

---

years after the Restoration, but other influential figures in the century would have included personalities like Henry Denne and Edward Barber.

[126] Grantham, *Christianismus Primitivus*, 3.12.

[127] Ibid., 3.1.

[128] Ibid.

[129] Ibid., 3.13.

[130] Ibid., 3.18.

It is helpful at this point to explore the relationship between civil statutes and God's law. Grantham clearly distinguished between "Natural Religion" and "Positive Religion." It is not clear where or when he picked up this notion of religious distinction, though he may have encountered the terms in conversations concerning the increasingly popular Deistical idea that intrinsic to all humanity is a basic and primitive natural religion (a direction in which some General Baptists were moving during this period). Herbert of Cherbury (1583–1648) pioneered this kind of thinking, and his ideas were later developed by thinkers such as John Locke (1632–1704) and Matthew Tindal (1657–1733). Though Deism did not reach its peak until after Grantham's death, many of the ideas circulated during his lifetime.[131] By the eighteenth century, "natural religion" had come to mean that all rational beings could infer the presence of a creator by observing the design of the world. "Positive religion," on the other hand, involved the particular claims to truth made by the various religious sects. Chris A. M. Hermans defined the distinction clearly when labeling natural religion as the genus and the sundry religious expressions as conceptualized species of the one genus.[132]

While Grantham never described what he considered "Positive Religion," he did use Romans 1:21 to define the natural sense of religion common to all people, a common sense that knew and recognized "one God, the Maker, and Preserver of all things; whom therefore all are bound to love, and serve, by being thankful for the Blessings they receive daily at his Hands, and to glorifie him only as their God."[133] For Grantham, then, it followed that since this natural religion was discernable by all people, the enforcement of its principles was included

[131] Peter Gay found that Deism in England was strongest from about 1690–1740 (*Deism: An Anthology* [Princeton NJ: Van Nostrand, 1968] 9–10).

[132] Chris A. M. Hermans, *Participatory Learning: Religious Education in a Globalizing Society* (Boston MA: Brill, 2003) 149. See also Nicholas Lash, *The Beginning and the End of "Religion"* (New York: Cambridge University Press, 1996) 15–16.

[133] Grantham, *Christianismus Primitivus*, 3.16.

in the duties of civil magistrates.[134] In short, if all have access to natural religion, then all are to be held accountable for transgressing it. Punishable violations of natural religion for Grantham included "open idolatry" and "worshipping and serving a Creature" instead of the creator.[135] Grantham did not speak specifically regarding additional problems, but he did allude to "vice and debauchery" as the "Enemy" of all religion.[136]

Grantham was clearly calling for the freedom to worship according to commands of God, but he was not interested in a latitudinal society in which all citizens could do what they wish in the name of religious freedom. While McBeth was reluctant to admit that the large majority of seventeenth-century Baptists advocated anything less than complete religious liberty "for those of every religion or none,"[137] John Coffey was right to call for a more "nuanced and complex conclusion."[138] Grantham's views may have been more radical in his own day, but he did not seem to have owned ideas similar to more modern notions of freedom from religion. Grantham sought freedom *for* religion. Nonetheless, Grantham's larger point in this section of *Christianismus Primitivus* was that magistrates did have a role to play in religion, but their involvement was to be confined to those elements that fell under the category of "Natural Religion."

In keeping with his understanding of natural religion, Grantham wrote that rulers were to make laws preventing the "Ruine" of citizens and vindicate "the Civil Rights of all Men."[139] Magistrates were also to enforce laws with a strong sense of justice and mercy.[140] He called upon all rulers to rule justly by avoiding what he considered to be the three most common barriers to the successful dispensation of justice: lack of

---

[134] McBeth, *English Baptist Literature on Religious Liberty to 1689*, 266.

[135] Grantham, *Christianismus Primitivus*, 3.17. Grantham cited Job 31:26–27 in support of these claims.

[136] Grantham, *Christianismus Primitivus*, 3.17.

[137] McBeth, *English Baptist Literature on Religious Liberty to 1689*, 277.

[138] Coffey, "From Helwys to Leland," 21.

[139] Grantham, *Christianismus Primitivus*, 3.15–19.

[140] Ibid., 3.14–15.

courage, bribery, and partiality. Good rulers, according to Grantham, mingled justice with mercy. In this way, Grantham suggested that justice and mercy were indispensable aspects of a magistrate's duty to his or her subjects.

Grantham was not content to speak only in positive terms about civil authority. He called attention as well to two specific practices that fell outside the religious jurisdiction of civil rulers. The first was related to general assemblies, or church councils. Grantham wrote that it was a "most virtuous thing" for a ruler to convene a general assembly, but he denies the ruler the right to demand that the various local churches conform to the assembly's findings.[141] Here Grantham admitted the legitimacy of past councils like Nicaea, but he stopped short of granting them any absolute authority comparable to that of the scriptures. The independence of the local congregation was paramount, and Grantham went so far as to claim that it was the "Priviledge" of all local congregations to initiate a general assembly. For this reason, and since he did not consider Baptist meetings seditious, Grantham refused to admit that baptized believers should adhere to the demands of the Conventicle Act (passed in 1664 and renewed in 1670).[142] Second, Grantham contended that persecution on account of differing "Apprehensions about Christianity" is inexcusable.[143] As witnesses to such a claim, he appealed to the testimony of antiquity, the learned opinion of Dr. Jeremiah Taylor,

---

[141] Ibid., 2.138. Grantham did add that the Baptists would gladly attend such a meeting if allowed, 2.143.

[142] Grantham, *Christianismus Primitivus*, 3.48–50. This type of resistance was consistent with his claim that in cases where human law goes against that which God requires, Christians must choose the latter. Where the Conventicle Act was concerned, his claim was built on three conclusions. First, he claimed that obedience would imply that government had the right to divide assemblies as often as it saw fit. Second, he wrote that the act did not apply to Baptist meetings because they were not seditious. But if the government persisted in enforcing the act, Baptists were not to dissolve their meetings because, as the true Church, they had the right to meet regardless of the number. Grantham here appealed to the example of the practice of the churches in the New Testament.

[143] Ibid., 3.21.

and Charles's own letter from Breda.[144] In this argument it is clear that Grantham was mixing his views of the freedom and independence of local congregations with his conception of the general assemblies of Christian congregations. The ultimate guide in any assembly, large or small, he urged his fellow believers, was the clear teaching of the scriptures.

In *Christianismus Primitivus* Grantham also spoke to a range of practical civil issues pertaining to baptized believers. He was forthcoming about his strong belief that government was not to be obeyed because it is ordained by God for the benefit of all people, yet he cautiously warned his readers against collapsing the distinctions between the church and the state. He wrote, "Christ's Church consists not of Nations in gross…[The Church] must have a Government distinct from the Government of Nations, although she is to be as subject to National Government."[145]

Insistence on a clear distinction between church and government did not, however, preclude Christians from serving in the government. In fact, Grantham claimed that it was just as much a citizen's birthright to expect protection from civil rulers as it was to be the instrument by which others are protected.[146] There was a caveat for Grantham: "[T]hough a Christian may lawfully be a Magistrate, yet he is not this as he is a Christian, but as a Man, ordained of God to Rule Men as Men, and not as Christians: And though a Man be no Christian, yet being by God's Providence put into Authority, is as lawful a Magistrate as if he

[144] Grantham included excerpts from Jeremiah Taylor's *Theologia Eklektike. A Discourse of the Liberty of Prophesying. Shewing the Unreasonablenes of Prescribing to Other Mens Faith, and the Iniquity of Persecuting Differing Opinions* (London, 1647). When Joshua Toulmin edited Daniel Neal's *History of Puritanism*, he wrote that Taylor "stated the opinion of the Antipaedobaptists with such advantages of style and elaborate chain of argument, that he was thought to have said more for the Baptists than they were able to say for themselves," 5 vols. (Bath UK: R. Cruttwell, 1795) 3.521.

[145] Grantham, *Christianismus Primitivus*, 3.18.

[146] Ibid., 3.51–52.

were a Christian."[147] For Grantham, a Christian may have attained the highest civil office in the land, but that does not mean that upon installment the Christian ruler automatically assumed the authority to govern other Christians in religious matters. In other words, the assumption of exclusive civil authority by a Christian did not translate into religious authority. Likewise, the legitimacy of a magistrate's authority was not contingent upon his or her identification with Christianity.[148] One historian noted that this type of positive view of civil authority effectively created a space for "civic loyalty and religious conviction [that] enabled the Baptists to work for positive change within the political system."[149] Military service, conscripted or otherwise, was one particular avenue for civil involvement that Grantham affirmed.

On the subject of military service, Grantham wrote that Christians were first and foremost a people of peace. War between nations, he claimed, was a reflection of God's anger. As undesirable as war may be, Grantham permitted Christians to bear arms and, if need be, take the life of another human so long as it protected the "common justice."[150] Proof for his claim was found in the examples of John the Baptist and Cornelius. John the Baptist did not instruct his followers to resign their military posts, nor did Cornelius leave the Roman military upon his conversion. Grantham insisted that the causes for war and battle should be just and honorable, but the final determination in these types of circumstances rested with the civil ruler who was responsible for making such decisions and not the individual conscience of the citizen. Magistrates, then, in Grantham's mind, were invested with the authority to wage war; Christians were not exempted from service.

The English Baptists of the seventeenth century did not fully withdraw from parish life; some Baptists managed to find limited ways of participating in parish religious life while still attending their own

---

[147] Ibid., 3.19.

[148] Ibid.

[149] George, "Between Pacifism and Coercion," 47.

[150] Grantham, *Christianismus Primitivus*, 3.54.

conventicles.[151] But there were also other ways in which Baptists continued to interact and contribute to their communities. One of the ways English citizens testified to the truth was by taking an oath. Quakers were roundly criticized for their adamant refusal to take oaths; Baptists were more ambivalent.[152] Grantham argued that oaths, unlike murder and idolatry, were not sinful in and of themselves. Rather, an oath was a permissible method for testifying to the truth before a magistrate because it "seems to be part of that Religion which is Universal."[153] Grantham traced the controversy over oaths to two key biblical passages: Matthew 5:34 and James 5:12. He insisted that these passages do not abrogate the law established in the Pentateuch, and further supported the use of oaths by pointing out that God, angels, and various holy men all took oaths. He concluded his treatment of oaths by noting that the greatest attack on the practice of oath-taking had been the effort of some civil authorities to impose "grievous Oaths, even such as may neither be lawful for them to impose, nor for others to accept."[154]

Seventeenth-century English Baptist marriage practices were often quite restrictive. Grantham, like most Baptists, advocated endogamous marriage.[155] He was, however, equally averse to marrying "near of Kin"

[151] E.g., the Particular Baptist John Miles (d. 1683), a principal figure in establishing a Baptist presence in Wales, managed to exercise leadership in a Baptist congregation in Ilston while simultaneously receiving payment from the established church. Miles was ejected from his Anglican living following the Restoration of 1660, which amounted to a loss of position and payment. Miles's Baptist congregation left for America just a few years later.

[152] For a comparison of Baptist and Quaker reactions see Ted L. Underwood, *Primitivism, Radicalism, and the Lamb's War* (New York: Oxford University Press, 1997) 96–98.

[153] Grantham, *Christianismus Primitivus*, 3.25. By "Universal" Grantham could have been referring to "natural religion," but he could have also meant that oath-taking was universally practiced. It is possible that he had both in mind with the latter being a reflection of the former.

[154] Grantham, *Christianismus Primitivus*, 3.28.

[155] Ibid., 3.38. See Bill Stevenson, "The Social Integration of post-Restoration Dissenters, 1660–1725," in *The World of Rural Dissenters, 1520–1725*, ed. Margaret

and the dissolution of marriages on any grounds other than infidelity.[156] *Christianismus Primitivus* did not address directly the civil implications of Baptist marriages, but in 1689 Grantham published his thoughts on "the Manner of Marriages among the Baptized Believers" in a revealing postscript to *Truth and Peace* (1689).[157] The postscript elucidated the complicated situation under which Baptists developed their matrimonial theology.[158] Baptists were forced to oversee their own marriages since Anglican priests would not generally marry those guilty of dissent. In the absence of a government-sanctioned ceremony, Baptists defied established marital customs by marrying each other in a private ceremony with friends and family. To ratify the marriage, they apparently drew up their own marriage certificates and provided "Counsel or Instruction" to the new couple.[159]

Grantham also informed the reader that in Baptist marriages "no Man takes upon him the Office to marry any, that being the proper Act of the Parties themselves."[160] This phrase suggests that the ministers present

---

Spufford (New York: Cambridge University Press, 1995) 361ff. See also White, *The English Baptists of the Seventeenth Century*, 139–45.

[156] Ibid., 3.38–41. Grantham did not support dissolving a marriage in which one spouse became Baptist after the wedding.

[157] Grantham, *Truth and Peace* (London, 1689) 74ff.

[158] In his instructive study of clandestine marriage, R. B. Outhwaite identified varying degrees and types of clandestine marriage, *Clandestine Marriage in England, 1500–1850* (London: Hambledon Press, 1995) 19ff. Outhwaite's seven categories of clandestine marriage were: (1) marriage without Church or Priest; (2) marriage by Priest but without Church; (3) marriage by Priest in Church but without Banns or Licence; (4) "lawless" ceremonies; (5) prison marriages; (6) licensed and clandestine marriage; and (7) conscientious objector marriage. Baptists are discussed in the section on "conscientious objectors," 35–37.

[159] The text of the sample certificate included in the postscript is available as Appendix H. This raises intriguing questions about Baptist understandings of their own marriages. Did the situation described by Grantham amount to common-law marriage among certain "conscientious objectors," to use Outhwaite's category? It seems that the Baptists, by drawing up on their own certificates, may have been attempting to legitimate the unions in their own manner so as not to stand guilty of cohabitation. Such a practice was not unheard of during this period.

[160] Grantham, *Truth and Peace*, 75.

at Baptist marriage ceremonies had no official capacity or power to marry. A few pages later in the postscript Grantham made it even clearer: "we can find no ground to believe that to celebrate Marriage is a ministerial act (though a Minister may do it) yet we do not refuse the Ministers of the Church of England, because such, but because they will not ratify our Contracts unless we conform to such things as seem to us to be sinful."[161] Furthermore, Grantham pointed out that the scriptures imposed no particular ceremony for the marriage occasion. His point was that in the absence of any biblical mandate, "let no Man judge one another to be unlawfully married, because some Ceremonies devised by Men are not observed."[162] Marriages performed ceremoniously or unceremoniously were legitimate, Grantham argued; therefore, Baptist marriages were to be recognized.

The exclusion of persistent Dissenters from nuptial ceremonies highlights the social alienation many of them experienced in seventeenth-century England. Looking beyond the theological basis for endogamous marriage, it is not surprising that dissenters like Grantham's Baptists looked inward for suitable marriage partners. Moreover, Grantham's writings show that Baptists had taken important steps to support and certify new couples.

Evidence of Baptist alienation at the parish level is also apparent in Grantham's treatment of poor relief and burials. In the seventeenth century, poor relief was carried out by the vestry of the local parish; the vestry determined the rate of payment and the dispensation of aid.[163] In

---

[161] Ibid., 86.

[162] Ibid., 77.

[163] See Lynn A. Botelho, *Old Age and the English Poor Law, 1500–1700* (Rochester NY: Boydell Press, 2004) 21–22. See also Paul Slack, *The English Poor Law, 1531–1782* (New York: Cambridge University Press, 1995) 1–9, 27–39. Peter M. Solar has shown that English poor relief differed from continental relief in several ways "Poor Relief and English Economic Development before the Industrial Revolution" (The Economic History Review 48, no. 1 [February 1995]: 3–5). One, all parishes were responsible for organizing their own relief, which was to be available to all men and women. Two, poor relief in England was financed by a local property tax. Solar also found that poor relief was better organized in rural areas.

rural areas or smaller parishes applications were probably made in person, and one's fortune in securing relief could depend on several factors ranging from personal sympathy to how often one frequented the alehouse.[164] Grantham supported paying the parish taxes for the benefit of the needy, but he was upset that Baptists were denied access to these funds in their own time of need. He described poor relief as the "Birth Priviledges" of all citizens, and went on to characterize the neglect of the Baptist poor as "irrational."[165] In this same section Grantham attacked the practice of denying Baptists access to burial plots on the common land. "The Burial of the Dead," he wrote, "is a Moral duty." Again Grantham noted that it is "not rational" to expect Baptists to pay for the upkeep of cemeteries only to be barred from being buried there.[166] To illustrate the point, Grantham narrated how the corpse of Robert Shalder, a Baptist of Croft, had been removed from the ground and left unburied in front of his family's home.[167] Grantham's comments related to poor relief and burials demonstrate the extent to which Baptists participated in, and contributed to, the welfare of their local communities. They also illustrate that Baptists expected to share in the many benefits of parish life; these expectations often went unfulfilled.

Grantham, as his writing in *Christianismus Primitivus* shows, undoubtedly supported the government's role in maintaining peace and security in England. He recognized that rulers had particular duties in regulating religion, at least that natural religion that he considered accessible to all subjects. He affirmed a magistrate's duty to pass just laws and enforce them with fairness, impartiality, and mercy. Civil rulers had the authority to convene an assembly of Christians, but they were not to coerce their subjects to attend or accept the assembly's decisions as absolute authority on a par with the scriptures. Furthermore, rulers of this

---

[164] Botelho, *Old Age and the English Poor Law, 1500–1700*, 22.

[165] Grantham, *Christianismus Primitivus*, 3.55.

[166] Ibid., 3.56.

[167] See also Crosby, *The History of the English Baptists*, 2.239; and Watts, *The Dissenters*, 1.233.

world were not to trouble subjects by imposing divergent beliefs regarding the particulars of the Christian religion.

Grantham provided multiple reasons that Baptists were not to be considered revolutionary. At the same time, he detailed the reasons why, in some cases, Baptists were to disobey governmental demands. Grantham was trying to make the point that Baptists were opposed to revolution, yet he also clearly defined which areas of the establishment needed revision. In this way, he demonstrated that Baptists were both conservative and radical.

What he did not address in *Christianismus Primitivus* (or *The Loyal Baptist* for that matter) is also noteworthy. First, he did not speak to the difference between local and national magistrates. What is the appropriate course of action when local demands conflict with the king or Parliament? One answer, as we have seen, is that Baptists were willing to appeal over the heads of local magistrates. Second, Grantham did not speak to elections or voting. It is unclear what percentage of Baptists in the post-Restoration years would have been eligible to vote, but information related to seventeenth-century Baptist thoughts on the process would provide additional insights into their political theory and practice. Third, Grantham did not address the tension that would inevitably arise when Christian nations went to war against each other. What were the limits to be on Christian loyalty to civil rulers when taking the life of another Christian was involved?

These types of questions point to what George described as an "unresolved tension" in Baptist conceptions of the state in the seventeenth century.[168] Gary S. De Krey identified four prominent types of published arguments for liberty of conscience in the post-Restoration years during which Grantham ministered.[169] Writers such as John Owen, John Humfrey, and Philip Nye based their conclusions on natural law and "defended the historical claims of the English crown to authority

---

[168] George, "Between Pacifism and Coercion," 49.

[169] Gary S. De Krey, "Rethinking the Restoration: Dissenting Cases for Conscience, 1667–1672," *The Historical Journal* 38, no. 1 (March 1995): 53–83.

over a religious establishment."[170] What proponents of this position sought, then, was freedom not to embrace the established religious settlement. A second position promulgated by some focused on the idea that liberty of conscience is beneficial for the state. De Krey noted that authors were not confined to one approach by showing that Humfrey also argued this position. A third case for conscience voiced by the likes of Sir Charles Wolseley and William Penn worked from natural law arguments to deny the government any significant jurisdiction in ecclesiastical affairs. In this view, Christians have the responsibility and ability to determine whether their religious behavior is consistent with divine mandates. Furthermore, magistrates, who may or may not be Christian, are required by God to enforce natural religion. De Krey points out, however, that according to this line of thinking magistrates should not regulate particular doctrines or practices because a magistrate's temporal power begins and ends outside the church. A fourth and final case for conscience used the Hebrew and Christian prophetic tradition of millennial imagery to make the point that religious persecution signaled a coming judgment.

While examples from all four of De Krey's categories can be found in Grantham's writings, the third category seems to reflect best Grantham's position. The point here is not to pigeonhole Grantham but to situate him in his own context. Grantham employed arguments of natural law, affirmed the magistrate's duty to uphold that law, and denied the state any serious influence in the church's affairs. Grantham's assent to Christian service in the government and military was consistent with other Baptist sentiments of the period, but with such service the possibility of coercion in the spiritual realm is also introduced. Coffey finds that Baptist enthusiasm for toleration subsided towards the end of the seventeenth century, and Baptist writings were "far more cautious" in advocating complete toleration.[171] He ascribes this trend to an increased level of persecution that forced Baptists to concentrate on their survival. In some ways Grantham exemplifies this trend well. His arguments for

---

[170] Ibid., 57.

[171] Coffey, "From Helwys to Leland," 21.

religious toleration were securely fastened to an assumption that idolatrous or irreligious behavior would be punished. Moreover, he believed that civil rulers should create an environment conducive to the practice of Christianity. When seen in this light, Grantham and the Baptists he represented were not as radical as some accounts would suggest.

It is true that on many levels Baptists were quite different from their Catholic, Presbyterian, and Anglican neighbors. They refused to baptize their infants, bow before the altar, and make the sign of the cross. Historians are often tempted to emphasize the unique or unexpected at the expense of the ordinary or normal. Yet the kind of baptized believers Grantham describes in *The Loyal Baptist* and *Christianismus Primitivus* would have been, or desired to be, similar to their Conformist neighbors on many other levels: oaths, civil service, military service, marriage, payment and receipt of poor relief, and the use of public cemeteries. It is important to remember that for the many Baptists who continued to live and work within the parish structure of seventeenth-century England, loyalty meant contributing to the greater good of their communities and their country.

Grantham's major writings on religion and the government, *The Loyal Baptist* (1674 and 1684) and *Christianismus Primitivus* (1678), prove that at least one General Baptist was producing fresh, creative, and significant literature on religious freedom between 1673 and 1689. That McBeth's study found few others doing so during this period renders Grantham's contributions all the more important. In addition, the present study shows that *The Loyal Baptist* is a significant but overlooked Baptist treatise on the practical and theoretical nature of Christian interaction with the state.

Summary

Dissenters in seventeenth-century England did not act out of a single theory of the proper relationship between the Church and the State. Baptists themselves disagreed on the question. This examination of the writings and ministry of one General Baptist found at least two key insights related to "God, Government, and King" from 1660 to 1689. First, Grantham's writings provide one with valuable information regarding what some General Baptists *thought* about civil government and its many roles in society. Second, in his own travels and interactions one is able to see how some General Baptists actually *interacted* with civil government.

On a practical level, persecuted General Baptists in Lincolnshire actively sought to gain the king's sympathy in 1660, 1661, and 1672. On all three occasions Grantham was a central figure in writing, signing, and delivering petitions to Charles II. In 1672 large numbers of baptized believers took advantage of the Declaration of Indulgence and registered for licenses; Grantham was among them. In so doing, licensed Baptists joined many of their dissenting neighbors in declaring the usefulness of some governmental intervention in religious affairs. That roughly half of all Baptist ministers registered with the government under the provisions of the Indulgence in 1672 suggests that many Baptists were not opposed in principle to accepting governmental protection. In 1689 Grantham urged James Marham to register a meeting place for worship in Norfolk. Marham likely took an oath in order to complete the registration process.

Grantham's published treatments of Christian magistrates, military service, marriage, poor relief, and cemeteries imply that Baptists were fairly integrated into parish life. In all of this, Grantham personally supported and directed Baptist interactions with national and local magistrates in order to uphold the common good and protect Baptists from false accusations. While his efforts to protect Baptists from hostility were not always successful, Grantham consistently exhibited a willingness to cooperate with the government as much as possible.

Grantham's theo-political arguments are also instructive. Baptists, he argued, were to subjugate themselves to government because civil authority existed by divine decree. On numerous occasions he reported that his General Baptists were loyal English subjects who harbored no seditious desires. Yet, that there were limits to obedience is clear from this study. Grantham's own constructive framework concerning the government and the Christian's posture toward government is probably best described as a "qualified loyalty." Examples of this qualified loyalty were present in the petitions Grantham presented to Charles II, *The Loyal Baptist*, and *Christianismus Primitivus*. In all of these one finds an unmistakable and unabashed commitment to obey the commands of God even in the unfortunate event that they came into direct conflict with the laws established by earthly magistrates.

Grantham's efforts to convince the civil rulers that the Baptists were a peaceable and legitimate movement were integral to the culmination of his ministry as a messenger, debater, and apologist, making him one of the leading General Baptist figures from 1660 until his death in 1692. Grantham's legacy of appearing before the king lived on into the eighteenth century. Grantham Killingworth, Thomas Grantham's grandson, erected in Norfolk a memorial in honor of his grandfather that, among other things, recounted Thomas Grantham's successful audience with King Charles II: "...Who delivered to the King Charles II our declaration of faith, And also presented to him a remonstrance against persecution, Both were kindly received and redress of grievances promised."[172] Further recognition of Grantham's labors to exculpate the Baptists in the eyes of the government came in Thomas Crosby's *The History of the English Baptists* (1738–1740). In his *History*, which was the first serious attempt at a history of the Baptists, Crosby made special mention of Grantham's audiences with Charles II, including even the full text of *Narrative and Complaint*.[173] Grantham's historical significance is even more apparent when one considers that Thomas Crosby was working with manuscripts and notes originally collected and organized by the Particular Baptist Benjamin Stinton (1676–1719). Thus, historically minded Baptists in the first half of the eighteenth century seem to have valued Grantham's leadership, for in the seventeenth

[172] For the full text of the memorial see Appendix B. The text of the memorial is found in Charles B. Jewson's *The Baptists in Norfolk* (London: Carey Kingsgate Press Limited, 1957) 29.

[173] Thomas Crosby's *The History of the English Baptists*, 4 vols. (London, 1740) 2.19ff., 3.76–83.

century he was the one who "encouraged the churches under the sufferings, and chiefly directed them in all their proceedings."[174]

[174] Ibid., 3.90.

Conclusion

Much remains to be said about Thomas Grantham and the General Baptists in Lincolnshire and Norfolk during the second half of the seventeenth century. How Grantham's theological conclusions impacted the future of the Baptist movement is a question for others to answer, but theologians ought to explore more fully the breadth and depth of his theology. Attention should be paid both to the places of overlap with other Baptist and non-Baptist theologians of the period and his own theological idiosyncrasies.

Questions beyond the limited and stated scope of this study warrant the attention of historians. For example, some have speculated that the early General Baptist growth was largely regional in nature (i.e., Kent, Lincolnshire, London, etc.), yet insufficient attention has been given to the sectarian nature of the General Baptist phenomenon. Historians have yet to explore adequately the emergence and maturity of the General Baptist phenomenon in the region known as the Midlands. Why did some General Baptist congregations in the Midlands invest their messengers with considerably more authority than messengers in other contexts? And what were the socio-economic factors involved when Lincolnshire farmers like the Grantham risked the benefits of parish life for a dissenting existence?

This book is but a piece of the story of one man who lived and died among the General Baptists of Lincolnshire and Norfolk in the seventeenth century. Grantham voiced the concerns, proclaimed the innocence, and defended the faith of his fellow baptized believers in the presence of jailers, judges, and kings. In his labors to solidify the office of messenger, he defined and articulated General Baptist convictions over against other Dissenters and the established Church of England. In light of these accomplishments, it comes as no surprise that when Thomas Crosby decided to complete the first history of the Baptists in England, he recounted the ministry of that eminent General Baptist printer and preacher, Thomas Grantham.

APPENDIX A

Thomas Grantham's Will[1]

In the name of God Amen. The ninth day of May, 1690. I, Thomas Grantham of Sutterby in the County of Lincolne, Husbandman, have made and ordained this My last will and Testam*ent* in manner and & form following.

Imprimis (in the first place).
Into the handes of almighty God I commit my Soul, and to the earth my Body in hope of a Happie Resuerection to Life eternal through Jesus Christ. My estate consisting in a Little Land I give it as followeth: To Benjamin my Son I give all my Land in Hundleby in the County aforesaid to hold to him and his Heires according to the Tennor of the Deed by *wch* it was given to me & to Bridget my Late wife and to the Heires of *or* bodies and for want of such Heires then to the right Heires of me the said Thomas Grantham forever Item my will is that all my land in Ashby next Partney shall be sold and the money for wch it shall be sold to the divided as followeth, to Benjamin my Son before Named ten pound, and the residue of price of my said Land to be equally divided between my two Sons John and Abel, Item I give to my kinsman John Hill of Azarby [Azgarby] one and twenty pound to enable him or his Assignes to pay a debt of twenty pounds for wch he standes bound with Mary Grantham relict of Thomas Grantham Late of Ashby Aforesaid deceased, but in case the said Mary Grantham do well and truly pay the said Twenty poundes with interest for the same Then my will is that the said John Hill or his Assignes shall pay the said twenty poundes To Abner and Thomas the sons of Thomas Grantham aforesaid deceased to be equally divided between them when they shall attain the age of one

---

[1] Lincolnshire Archives, W1691/ii/255.

and twenty yeares. Finally I do hereby enable my Son in Law Mark Smith of Sutterby and my said kinsman John Hill of Azarby to sell my said Landes in Ashby aforesd. And to distribute the money for which they shall sell it as I have pvided in this my will And I do also empower & hereby enable my said son in Law Mark Smith and my said kinsman John Hill to sell all that my Close of pasture in Holton houlgate comonly called Hales Close, and with part of the money for which it shall be sould I do hereby enable the said John Hill to pay the said debtes of its twenty pound if the said Mary Grantham do not pay the same, or else to pay the said twenty pound to my two Gran-Children Thomas and Abner aforesaid as I have by this my will appoynted And for the remainder of the price of the said Hales Close if any be my will is that it be divided half to the four Children of Abner Grantham my son Late deceased and the other half to Pious and Charitable uses at the discretion of my said Son in Law Mark Smith and John Hill aforesaid.

Tho: Grantham
Signed Sealed Published
And declared in the presence of
George Hill (signs)
William Parrat (signs)
John Johnson (marked)
John Maltby (marked)

APPENDIX B

The Dying Words of Thomas Grantham[1]

Friends, I am in a very weak Condition: And as this is the Sabbath, with me it will be the Everlasting Sabbath; for now I am going off the Stage of this World. Therefore I recommend you to the Grace of God, that you would walk stedfastly in the Faith of Jesus Christ, as by the Grace of God I have done to this my Live's End; for, by the Grace of God, I have not defrauded or polluted any Person in the World, as now I am going to answer before God the Father. I came not amongst you for Riches or Honour, but to preach this Gospel of Jesus Christ, to spend and be spent for your Good, both by Preaching and Printing; which Words and Works I recommend unto you, to strengthen you, in which I have preached, (in which Faith I live and die) which have been according to the Gospel of Jesus Christ, in which I would have you stand stedfast to the End, not wavering; but fight the good Fight of Faith, lay hold on Eternal Life. I desire you for the Lord's sake, to talk together, and keep the Unity of the Spirit in the Bond of Peace, as Christ hath commanded you; Then are you my Disciples, if you love one another. Beloved, build up your selves in your most holy Faith, praying in the Holy Ghost: Keep your selves in the Love of God, looking for the Mercy of our Lord Jesus Christ unto Eternal Life, as I have told you before. Submit your selves to the Will of God, and to every Ordinance of Man, for the Lord's sake; and give Honour to whom Honour is due; and walk peaceably with all Men, and

[1] These words were transcribed into a manuscript copy of *Christianismus Primitivus* (1678) owned at the time by Richard Clarke . The manuscript is housed at the Millennium Library in Norwich, Norfolk, UK. Original editions of *Christianismus Primitivus* are also housed at Southwestern Baptist Theological Seminary, Fort Worth, Texas, and the American Baptist Historical Society, Atlanta, Georgia.

so shall no Man have cause to speak evil of you. As for my part, since I have been amongst you, I have been made a Scoff and Gazing-stock of many People, which I freely forgive them all, and heartily pray that God would forgive them, and shew them the Errour of their Ways; and I would desire that you would all pray for them, and not seek any Revenge. And to be short, I must leave you; do not grieve nor mourn for me; though I die, I shall rise to Glory, where I desire that we may all meet, and see one another's Faces at the last Day, knowing one another, and rejoice in Glory: For I have conquer'd the Infernal Enemy by this Faith, and have made the Way plain and easy to me. And now I commit you to the Grace of our Lord Jesus Christ; and the Love of God, and the Communion of the Holy Ghost, be with you all. *Amen*.

APPENDIX C

A Memorial to Thomas Grantham[1]

Dedicated to the singular merits of
A faithful confessor and laborious servant of Christ,
Who with true Christian fortitude endured persecution
Through many perils, the loss of friends and substance,
And ten imprisonments for conscience sake,
A man endued with every Christian grace and virtue,
The Rev. Mr. Thomas Grantham,
A learned messenger of the baptized churches,
And pious founder of this church of believers baptized,
Who delivered the King Charles II our declaration of faith,
And also presented to him a remonstrance against persecution,
Both were kindly received and redress of grievances promised.

---

[1] This text is found in Charles B. Jewson, *The Baptists of Norfolk* (London: Carey Kingsgate Press Limited, 1957), 29.

APPENDIX D

Acrostics Composed on the Occasion of the Death of Thomas Grantham[1]

Acrostic A

Thomas granthams dead, yet still he speaks & lives
His death the Last and Loudest Sermon gives
Our thoughts are drown'd at present, but lets view
More what Gods interest is, and ours too
And then Grieve if you can; for you shall see
Such Dispensation will work well for thee

Grantham is gone and now there is but few
Remains from whom such services are due
And yet what then, shall now our spirits sinke
noe. Always, when wee've brought to ruins brink
There's Help for Sion, fear not Jesus will.
Hasten his coming, to confound the skill
And cunning of his foes O blessed Day
Make hast blest Lord, oh come, oh come away.

Acrostic B

---

[1] This text is taken from a manuscript copy of Grantham's *Christianismus Primitivus* held in the Norfolk Heritage Centre, located in the Millennium Library, Norwich. The acrostics are handwritten and are reproduced here as they appear in the manuscript. Samuel Hester also found a poem written about Grantham in Benjamin Miller's personal copy of *Christianismus Primitivus,* held at the American Baptist Historical Society, Atlanta, Georgia. See Hester, "Advancing Christianity to its Primitive Excellency" (ThD dissertation, New Orleans Baptist Theological Seminary, 1977) 184-85.

Though I doe mourn and weep, my sorrow still
Hath such reboundings, that my heart doth fill
Oh my dear friend is gone, & left me here
My heart doth grieve for him I lov'd most dear
And all my Griefe & sorrow seems in vain
Seeing I cannot bring hime back again.

God hath remov'd him, and he hence is gone
Reason must rule my great Affection
And I must Learn to stoop under the Rod
Not murmuring at the Righteous hand of God
True wisdom is in him, his works are pure.
Hee doth in righteousness always Indure
All wee must die, but he doth still remain
My friend he will restore to Life again.

APPENDIX E

Epitaphs for Thomas Grantham[1]

The Epitaph

Under this Earth here Thomas Grantham lies
the death of whom made many watry eyes
He Laboured Hard, and now his work is done
He resteth till the resurrection
Then he shall rise, and with all saints ascend
To live with the most High world without end
singing High praise to God, and to Adore
our Glorious Jehovah Evermore. Amen

The Epitaph

Within this Tomb, here Lies inclosed a guest
which was with universall Love possest
Its famous grantham, whoe is dearly mist
A preacher, Bishop and Evangelist.
Of his great worth can none but Angells
Hasten to him, and them, and soe farewell.

---

[1] The text is taken from a manuscript copy of Grantham's *Christianismus Primitivus* held in the Norfolk Heritage Centre, located in the Millennium Library, Norwich. The epitaphs are handwritten and reproduced here as they appear in the manuscript.

APPENDIX F

"Of Discourse,"[1] from a poem by Thomas Grantham

In thy discourse and talke with men
still very carefull be;
Speak little but of things of God
or of necessity.
Relate no faults of other men
In a backbiting way;
But pitty sinner, loath their sins
And go not thou astray
Before thou speak bethink thy selfe
What glory God will have
And men, what profit by thy words
Are likely to receive
Remember God doth hear and write
Down all that men do say
And every idle word shall bee
Accounted for one day.

---

[1] This text is taken from the thirteen-stanza poem entitled "The Christians dayly Exercise," which only appears in handwritten form in John Clarke's personal copy of Grantham's *Christianismus Primitivus*. Clarke's manuscript is held in the Norfolk Heritage Centre, located in the Millennium Library, Norwich. "The Christians dayly Exercise" consists of thirteen stanzas, or sections. I have reproduced here, as an example, the text for the tenth stanza as it appears in the manuscript.

APPENDIX G

"A Humble Address, or Remonstrance" as Summarized by Thomas Crosby[1]

...[T]hey set forth, wherein they thought his royal declaration infringed that liberty, which as Christians they had a right to; and beseeching him to leave them to the light of scripture, with respect to the exercise of those spiritual gifts of prayer, and preaching in their assemblies, according to their abilities, for the edification of the church, where gifts are free; that they should continue in this practice till they obtain his permission; assuring his majesty, that not no less liberty than the scriptures express, would satisfy the church of God. And then they concluded with thanks to his majesty for all his lenity; praying that God would magnify grace in his princely soul, that whilst he reigned here on earth, he might excel in all true honour, and after this life enjoy a crown of immortality, and a throne of glory in heaven.

---

[1] Crosby, *The History of the English Baptists*, 4 vols. (London, 1740) 3.83.

APPENDIX H

A Sample Baptist Marriage Certificate[1]

We whose Names are subscribed, do testify, That the above-said A. B. and C. D. the Day and Year above-said, did mutually take each other into the State of Marriage, acknowledging the Contract and Covenant, and ratifying the same by Word, and by the Subscription thereof as above-said. In witness whereof, we do hereunto set our Hands the Day and Year above-said.

---

[1] This sample certificate is taken from *Truth and Peace* (London, 1689), 75.

APPENDIX I

Thomas Grantham through the Years: A Historiography

It is remarkable that a man with no formal training but who published prodigiously continues to be the subject of formal scholarly research. This essay is testimony to the fact that the life and writings of Thomas Grantham have not gone unnoticed. In his own lifetime he was attacked and credited for capable leadership and contributions as a General Baptist messenger. Still, the limited nature of the scholarly attention on Grantham makes the absence of sustained scholarly studies of his life and immediate impact on seventeenth-century Baptist life all the more surprising— and necessary.

Unhappy with Daniel Neal's (d. 1743) multi-volume treatment of the Baptists in *History of the Puritans* (published between 1732 and 1738), Thomas Crosby (d. circa 1749) took it upon himself to write a history of the Baptist movement. Crosby's four-volume *The History of the English Baptists* was published between 1738 and 1740. Crosby made mention of Grantham briefly in volume two in order to show how the unjust "storm" of persecution on the early English Baptists was felt in both the urban and rural areas.[1] In addition, the full text of *A Brief Confession or Declaration of Faith* was appended to volume two.[2] It was in volume three, however, that Crosby highlighted learned and influential early Baptists who were instrumental to the movement's survival, and Grantham was among those figures Crosby deemed critical as he surveyed the more than 100 years of English Baptist history. Setting a biographical pattern followed by later historians such Joseph Ivimey (d.

[1] Ibid., 2.149.

[2] Ibid., 2.76ff.

1834) and Adam Taylor (d. 1833), Crosby the story of Grantham primarily from the perspective of his conflict with theological opponents and local officials. Crosby underscored Grantham's successful petitions to Charles II on behalf of the harried General Baptists in Lincolnshire and included a section of text from *The Baptist Complaint against the Persecuting Priests* (1685). From the outset, then, Crosby unequivocally connected the ministry of Thomas Grantham with the spread and strength of General Baptist life in Lincolnshire.

In 1805, just over fifty years after Crosby's history appeared, William Richard wrote a fairly thorough introduction to the life and ministry of Grantham for the *Universal Theological Magazine* in order that the "name of this eminent confessor… should not be suffered to sink into oblivion."[3] Richard underscored Grantham's role in presenting confessions to the King during the Restoration, multiple persecutions, and enduring contributions to Baptist life in Lincolnshire and Norfolk. It is worth noting that the biography provides a fascinating glimpse of how one Baptist understood the differences between the General Baptist churches of Grantham's lifetime and those of the New Connexion church more than 100 years later.

Joseph Ivimey's two-volume *A History of the English Baptists* (1814) included an excellent appraisal of the life and writings of Thomas Grantham in a section devoted to important Lincolnshire ministers after the Restoration. Building on the work of Crosby, Ivimey spent considerable time and energy outlining Grantham's toils as a Nonconformist, pastor, and messenger. Ivimey's discussion of Grantham wove together his life and writings by including local Lincolnshire concerns and broader political and religious issues in England. Ivimey referenced several of Grantham's publications throughout, but three in particular received sustained attention: *Christianismus Primitivus* (1678), *The Loyal Baptist* (1684), and *Truth and Peace* (1689). *Christianismus*

---

[3] William Richard, "Biography of Thomas Grantham," *Universal Theological Magazine* 3, no. 13 (January 1805): 1. Richard wrote the biography in four parts, published in the January, February, March, and April editions of *Universal Theological Magazine* in 1805.

Primitivus was described as Grantham's "principal work,"[4] yet *Truth and Peace* was discussed in greater detail. Ivimey presented a fairly thorough introduction to Grantham, but did so primarily from the perspective of Grantham's interaction and conflict with government officials or religious opponents.

In *The History of the English General Baptists* (1818) Adam Taylor also spent considerable energy outlining General Baptist life in Lincolnshire, of which Grantham was a vital part. Taylor, too, relied heavily on Crosby's *History* and Grantham's own writings. Taylor apparently had access to many of Grantham's published documents, from which he worked to highlight Grantham's importance as a Nonconformist spokesperson, capable debater, and tireless Baptist leader. Grantham's death was a "heavy loss," Taylor wrote, for "none of his successors inherited an equal portion of his spirit and abilities, though several of them were assiduous and sincere."[5] In addition to the thorough treatment of Grantham's work in and around Lincolnshire, Taylor's history is noteworthy for its fairly detailed discussion of Grantham's published and unpublished writings.

William T. Whitley's (d. 1947) *A History of British Baptists* (1923) probably constitutes the earliest modern and systematic attempt at a comprehensive account of Baptist history. Whitley highlighted Grantham's contributions as author, evangelist, and church founder.[6] *Christianismus Primitivus* is singled out as "a repertory of learning for [Grantham's] denomination."[7] Whitley also called attention to *Six Principles of the Christian Religion*, in which Grantham "laid his finger

---

[4] Joseph Ivimey, *A History of the English Baptists*, 4 vols. (London, 1811–30) 2.277.

[5] Adam Taylor, *The History of the English General Baptists*, 2 vols. (London: T. Bore, 1818) 2.316. Just nine years after Taylor's published history of the Baptists, Richard Knight's *History of the General or Six Principle Baptists, In Europe and America* (1827; repr., New York: Arno Press, 1980) credited Grantham with establishing a General Baptist presence in the South Marsh of Lincolnshire, 33–34.

[6] William T. Whitley, *A History of British Baptists* (London: Kingsgate Press, 1923) 134–35.

[7] Ibid.

on the ultra-Calvinist weakness of condemning all unbaptized infants, and found himself drawn into a many-sided debate on kindred points."[8] Whitley went on to claim that the General Baptist expression lost one of its "unifying forces"[9] when Grantham died in 1693; thus, it is no wonder that Whitley associated Grantham's departure with the larger discussion of General Baptist decline.

Jesse Plumb's University of Sheffield thesis, "Early Nonconformity in Lincolnshire" (1940), included a biographical sketch of Grantham's life and ministry.[10] When surveying Dissent in Lincolnshire during the seventeenth-century, Plumb singled out Grantham as a pioneer among the Baptists of South Lincolnshire. Plumb highlighted the importance of Grantham's influential *Christianismus Primitivus* and numerous imprisonments.

Alfred C. Underwood's (d. 1948) *The History of the English Baptists* (1947) hailed Thomas Grantham as the General Baptists' "ablest writer."[11] Underwood's treatment of Grantham consists primarily of a biographical sketch, though no sources were included. Underwood emphasized Grantham's part in the debates concerning infant-baptism, limited atonement, and church Messengers. Regarding messengers in particular, Underwood observed that Grantham was so effective in mollifying objections to the office of messenger that messengers became an accepted part of General Baptist church polity. Likewise, the late Barrington R. White, in *The English Baptists of the Seventeenth Century* (1983), treated Grantham in the context of the messenger debate and highlighted the significance of *Christianismus Primitivus*.[12]

---

[8] Ibid., 168.

[9] Ibid.

[10] Jesse Plumb, "Early Nonconformity in Lincolnshire" (Master's thesis, University of Sheffield, 1940).

[11] Alfred C. Underwood, *A History of the English Baptists* (London: Baptist Union Publication Department, 1947) 53. Ollie Latch's *History of the General Baptists* ([Poplar Bluff MO: General Baptist Press, 1972] 80) mentioned only Grantham's appearance before Charles II in 1661.

[12] Barrington R. White, *The English Baptists of the Seventeenth Century* (London: The Baptist Historical Society, 1983) 114–17. The section on messengers

Comprehensive studies of Baptist history in the second half of the twentieth century tended to devote less attention to Grantham, but by no means did they limit or downplay his significance. The late American Baptist historian Robert Torbet surprisingly made only brief mention of Grantham in *A History of the Baptists* (1973): "Among General Baptists, new churches had been planted and old ones were flourishing both in Lincolnshire and the adjacent counties under the able leadership of the reverend Thomas Grantham and of younger ministers."[13] While Torbet's description leaves the reader wishing for more detail, he affirmed Grantham's organizational importance in and around Lincolnshire.

In his 1980 contribution to the History of Lincolnshire series, Clive Holmes surveyed life in seventeenth-century Lincolnshire.[14] Holmes's excellent study adds significant insights related to Grantham's social and political contexts. Dissent and Nonconformity, in particular, characterize the discussions in which Grantham appears.

H. Leon McBeth, like Underwood and White before him, first referenced Grantham in the context of the messenger debates and noticed that Grantham taught the main function of messengers was to preach, plant churches, and ordain Elders.[15] McBeth's distinct addition to the Grantham portrait is found in his assertion that Grantham worked to distance himself and the General Baptists from the Fifth Monarchists and "Munster radicals," though the evidence for such a claim is unclear.[16] McBeth noted that in *Christianismus Primitivus* Grantham "expounded

---

remained unchanged in the 1996 edition of *The English Baptists of the Seventeenth Century*. Due to health issues, White was unable to prepare the final manuscript for publication, and so John F. W. Nicholson, the authority on Baptist messengers, prepared the final manuscript.

[13] Robert Torbet, *A History of the Baptists* (Valley Forge PA: Judson Press, 1973) 53.

[14] Clive Holmes, *Seventeenth-Century Lincolnshire* (Lincoln UK: Society for Lincolnshire History and Archaeology, 1980).

[15] H. Leon McBeth, *The Baptist Heritage* (Nashville TN: Broadman Press, 1988) 78–79.

[16] Ibid., 89.

Baptist theology, described Baptist worship, and set out Baptist views on several subjects."[17]

Thomas Grantham also appears as an important figure in numerous specific studies of seventeenth-century England. Ted L. Underwood spent considerable time in *Primitivism, Radicalism, and the Lamb's War* (1997) examining the Baptist-Quaker conflict in seventeenth-century England. Moving in a unique direction relative to general introductions to Baptist history, Underwood drew on Grantham several times, especially where the idea of the primitive church is concerned. When the discussion turned to the nature of religious authority, Underwood highlighted the tension – as represented by Grantham – that existed between the sufficiency of the Spirit and the sufficiency of scripture.[18] As Underwood took up the question of Christ's humanity, Grantham was again chosen as the Baptist voice in the debate. It is noteworthy that Underwood identified Grantham not only as an important voice within General Baptist circles, but also as a viable, informed, and capable defender of the Baptist movement in general. Furthermore, he highlighted the range of issues on which Grantham wrote and disputed.

Samuel E. Hester's 1977 dissertation at New Orleans Baptist Theological Seminary provided a brief biography and looked at Thomas Grantham's understanding of the "primitive church" as outlined in *Christianismus Primitivus*.[19] In a 1982 dissertation at the Southern Baptist Theological Seminary, Michael Atwol Smith included Thomas Grantham in a survey of several early English Baptists and their use of the Church Fathers.[20]

Robert Kershaw's 1995 thesis at the University of Nottingham addressed how Lincolnshire came to include a strong General Baptist

---

[17] Ibid., 117.

[18] Ted L. Underwood, *Primitivism, Radicalism, and the Lamb's War* (New York: Oxford University Press, 1997) 25.

[19] Samuel E. Hester, "Advancing Christianity to its primitive excellency: The quest of Thomas Grantham, early English General Baptist (1634–1692)" (ThD diss., New Orleans Baptist Theological Seminary, 1977).

[20] Michael A. Smith, "The Early English Baptists and the Church Fathers" (PhD diss., Southern Baptist Theological Seminary, 1982).

contingent in the late seventeenth century.[21] Kershaw examined a variety of key figures such as Hanserd Knollys, Samuel Oates, and Thomas Grantham. In addition to providing a fresh biographical sketch, Kershaw further proposed that Grantham was the most prominent Baptist in Lincolnshire after 1660 and that his ministry was crucial to the survival of the Baptist movement in Lincolnshire during the tumultuous years before Toleration.

Philip Thompson took a keen interest in Grantham in "A New Question in Baptist History: Seeking a Catholic Spirit among Early Baptists."[22] In this 1999 article for *Pro Ecclesia*, Thompson argued that contemporary Baptists have deviated from the path set forth by the early Baptists, who were "catholic in mind and spirit, and believed themselves to be speaking from within a tradition larger than any single communion."[23] Of particular interest here is Thompson's use of Grantham in support of his claim of a broad catholicity. In order to "reveal the catholic mind"[24] of early Baptists like Grantham on issues such as creeds, episcopacy, and the sacraments, Thompson drew heavily on *Christianismus Primitivus*, *St. Paul's Catechism*, *The Prisoner Against the Prelate*, *The Loyal Baptist*, and *Hear the Church*. Thompson noted that Grantham readily affirmed the church's ancient creeds, and even included the text of the Nicene Creed in *St. Paul's Catechism*. Where episcopacy was concerned, Thompson pointed to Grantham's status as a messenger among the General Baptist churches. Finally, Thompson directed the reader to *Christianismus Primitivus* and *The Loyal Baptist* as proof that "early Baptists possessed a sacramental understanding of baptism and eucharist."[25]

---

[21] Robert R. Kershaw, "Baptised Believers: Lincolnshire Baptists in Times of Persecution, Revolution and Toleration, 1600–1700" (Master's thesis, University of Nottingham, 1995).

[22] Philip E. Thompson, "A New Question in Baptist History: Seeking a Catholic Spirit among Early Baptists," *Pro Ecclesia* 8, no. 1 (Winter 1999): 51–72.

[23] Ibid., 71.

[24] Ibid., 64.

[25] Ibid., 66.

Similarly, Stanley Fowler's *More Than a Symbol* (2002) again brought Grantham into discussions of sacramentalism and the early Baptists. Citing *Christianismus Primitivus* and *A Sigh for Peace*, he showed how Grantham made baptism not "merely a sign, but an effective sign."[26] In the end, Fowler found that Grantham apparently said more about what did not happen to infants in baptism than what did happen to adults. The contributions of Hester, Kershaw, Fowler, and Thompson remain important and focused examinations of particular areas of Grantham's thought, but they were not – nor were they intended to be – comprehensive studies.

William H. Brackney has perhaps gone farther than any scholar towards establishing Grantham as a prominent—if overlooked—early (General) Baptist theologian. In his *Genetic History of Baptist Thought* (2004), Brackney acclaimed Grantham as the "first organized, comprehensive, published theologian of any of the Baptists."[27] The broad strokes with which Brackney painted in *Genetic History* called for a more detailed analysis, and in more recent essay, "Thomas Grantham, Systematic Theology, and the Baptist Tradition" (2006), he used *Christianismus Primitivus* to survey and assess the breadth of Grantham's theological thinking. In this article, Brackney outlined Grantham's positions on topics such as Nonconformity, creeds, scripture, Christology, ecclesiology, and worship patterns. Brackney's article further established Grantham as an important figure in the early Baptist evolutionary process who bequeathed to that process "a set of factors that qualified Baptists as a maturing evangelical Protestant tradition."[28]

---

[26] Stanley Fowler, *More than a Symbol: The British Baptist Recovery of Baptismal Sacramentalism* (Waynesboro GA: Paternoster Press, 2002) 28.

[27] William H. Brackney, *A Genetic History of Baptist Thought* (Macon GA: Mercer University Press, 2004) 114.

[28] William H. Brackney, "Thomas Grantham, Systematic Theology, and the Baptist Tradition" in *From Biblical Criticism to Biblical Faith: Essays in Honor of Lee Martin McDonald*, eds. William H. Brackney and Craig A. Evans (Macon GA: Mercer University Press, 2007) 199–216. In addition to my own recent historical work on Grantham ("Messenger, Apologist, and Nonconformist: An Examination of Thomas Grantham's Leadership among the Seventeenth-Century General Baptists"

George Southcombe, in an unpublished dissertation for Oxford University (2005), examined the variety of dissenting responses to the Restoration of 1660.[29] Among the case studies employed to demonstrate this variety was an analysis of Thomas Grantham. Southcombe saw in Grantham an evolving accommodation on the part of General Baptists with the Anglican Church and found that Grantham's ministry and move from Lincolnshire to Norfolk included a gradual shift in the Baptist minister's relationship with the Anglican establishment. Furthermore, he noted an increasingly irenic tone in Grantham's writings during the 1670s.

It is clear that historians in the eighteenth and nineteenth centuries (e.g., Crosby, Richard, Ivimey, and Taylor) were inclined to narrate the Baptist story by recounting the lives and exploits of influential figures. In the mid-twentieth century writers such as Underwood, White, and McBeth tended to emphasize important aspects of early Baptist life and employ various personalities as examples. More recently, theologians and historians have been looking to early Baptists like Grantham in order to develop a comprehensive picture of Baptist dissent, Baptist life at the county level, and evolving notions of a "Baptist identity."

In conclusion, this historiography demonstrates that scholars believe Grantham to have been among the most able, influential, and prolific of any of the early English Baptists.[30] Yet the absence of any broad treatment is equally apparent. The early testimonies of Crosby, Ivimey, and

[PhD diss., Baylor University, 2008]), Clint Bass completed a thesis on Grantham's theology ("Thomas Grantham and General Baptist Theology," [DPhil thesis, Regent's Park College, University of Oxford, 2008]). Access to Bass's thesis was not possible before the completion of this manuscript.

[29] George Southcombe, "The Responses of Nonconformists to the Restoration in England" (DPhil thesis, University of Oxford, 2005).

[30] Due to the best efforts of the censor Robert L'Estrange and others, it is a wonder that so many Baptists works managed to be published. For a helpful discussion of the printing and proliferation of Nonconformists texts, see Neil H. Keeble, *The Literary Culture of Nonconformity in Later Seventeenth-Century England* (Avon UK: Leicester University Press, 1987) 120ff. Citing the Baptists Benjamin Keach, John Spilsbury, and Grantham, Keeble also found that the social standing of many published authors was not very high, 145.

Taylor all affirmed that Thomas Grantham was a pivotal figure in the first century of English Baptist life. Furthermore, Grantham was deemed influential because of his tireless work to establish Baptist churches. One should not overlook, however, that all three historians explained Grantham's importance by elucidating his conflict with non-Baptist opponents. Ivimey, for example, consistently called attention to Grantham's conflict with ecclesiastical and governmental officials, almost to the exclusion of any intra-General Baptist dialogue. In time, however, those interested in the witness and legacy of the seventeenth-century General Baptists have begun to focus attention on leaders like Thomas Grantham.[31] As some contemporary Baptists debate the future of early Baptist history and identity, the work of Fowler, Thompson, and Brackney suggest that Grantham must remain an important figure in all such discussions.

Recent scholarship also agrees on Grantham's importance as a key General Baptist theologian in the second half of the seventeenth century. The essay by Brackney, perhaps more than any other study, solidified Grantham's place among the notable early Baptist theologians. Yet such an emphasis on Grantham's theological legacy may obscure the organizational aspects of his leadership. Therefore, this study sought to explore the ways in which that farmer and tailor Thomas Grantham, informed by his own theological convictions, established, ordered, and sustained a sectarian General Baptist presence in Lincolnshire and Norfolk.

---

[31] See, for example, a discussion centered on Grantham's soteriology at a 2011 event sponsored by the Baptist Center for Theology and Ministry, a research institute of New Orleans Baptist Theological Seminary. Published papers from the event include J. Matthew Pinson's "Thomas Grantham's Theology of the Atonement and Justification" (*Journal for Baptist Theology & Ministry* 8, no. 1 (Spring 2011): 7-21) and responses from Clint C. Bass ("RESPONSE to J. Matthew Pinson's 'Thomas Grantham's Theology of the Atonement and Justification,'" *Journal for Baptist Theology & Ministry* 8, no. 1 [Spring 2011]: 25-28), James Leonard ("RESPONSE to J. Matthew Pinson's "Thomas Grantham's Theology of the Atonement and Justification,'" *Journal for Baptist Theology & Ministry* 8, no. 1 [Spring 2011]: 29-33), and Rhyne Putman ("RESPONSE to J. Matthew Pinson's "Thomas Grantham's Theology of the Atonement and Justification,'" *Journal for Baptist Theology & Ministry* 8, no. 1 [Spring 2011]: 22-23).

Bibliography

Primary Sources

Unpublished Documents

Acrostics Composed on the Occasion of the Death of Thomas Grantham. Handwritten acrostics in John Clarke's personal copy of *Christianismus Primitivus* (1678). Norfolk Heritage Centre. Millennium Library, Norwich UK.

Bishop's Transcripts for Hatton, Lincolnshire, 1633/34. Lincolnshire Archives, Lincoln UK.

Bishop's Transcripts for Spilsby, Lincolnshire, 1633/34. Lincolnshire Archives, Lincoln UK.

Brief Notes Containing Memoirs of the Ministerial Acts, Particularly Such as Relate to the Writings of that Servant of Christ, the Reverend Mr. Thomas Grantham Messenger of the Baptized Churches in Lincoln Shire of Blessed Memory. Handwritten biographical manuscript (n.d.). Dr. Williams's Congregational Library, London UK.

Burgh & Monksthorpe Church Book, 1692–1825. Angus Library. Regent's Park College, Oxford UK.

Epitaphs Composed on the Occasion of the Death of Thomas Grantham. Handwritten epitaphs in John Clarke's personal copy of *Christianismus Primitivus* (1678). Norfolk Heritage Centre. Millennium Library, Norwich UK.

Letters to Thomas Grantham. The Beinecke Rare Book and Manuscript Library. Yale University Library, New Haven CT.

The Will of Thomas Grantham (9 May 1690). Lincolnshire Archives, Lincoln UK.

The Will of William Grantham (19 January 1657). Lincolnshire Archives, Lincoln UK.

Grantham, Thomas. "The Christians dayly Exercise." Handwritten poem in John Clarke's personal copy of *Christianismus Primitivus* (London, 1678). Norfolk Heritage Centre. Millennium Library, Norwich UK.

Mackerell, Benjamin. *St. Stephen's Parish In the City of Norwich, with some Observations on the Same.* N.p., 1737. Handwritten notes on the monuments and gravestones of St. Stephen's Church, Norwich, UK.

Published Primary Sources

A Brief and Plain Discourse upon the Decrees of God Wherein Mr. Grantham's Query Is Considered and Answered. London: Printed by T. Snowden(?), 1692.

A Declaration of Some of those People in or Near London. London: Printed by Thomas Milbourn, 1660.

The Humble Apology of Some Commonly Called Anabaptists. London: Printed by Henry Hills, 1661.

The Humble Petition and Representation. London, 1661.

The Lyn Persecution. N.p., 1692/3.

"A Memoir of Thomas Grantham." *General Baptist Repository and Missionary Observer* 4/44 (1 August 1825): 281–86; 4/45 (1 September 1825): 321–26; and 4/46 (1 October 1825): 361–67.

A True and Impartial Narrative of the Eminent Hand of God that Befell a Quaker and His Family. London, 1672.

Advice to the Men of Shaftesbury. London, 1681(?).

Apology of some called Anabaptists, in and about the City of London. London: 1660.

For the King and both Houses of Parliament Being a Short Relation of the Sad Estate and Sufferings of the Innocent People of God Called Quakers. London, 1661.

Forgery Detected and Innocency Vindicated Being a Faithful Account of the Seasonable Discovery of an Horrid and Detectible Slander Raised on the Anabaptists of New-England. London: Printed by J. D., 1673.

Mercurius Politicus. No. 559 (17–24 March 1659): 305–20.

Reformation in Religion, Greatly subservient to National Prosperity. London, 1763.

Sions Groans for Her Distressed. London, 1661.

To the King of these Nations. London: Simon Dover, 1661.

Barber, Edward. *A True Discovery of the Ministry of the Gospel*. London, 1645.

———. *A Declaration and Vindication of the Carriage of Edward Barber*. London, 1648.

Barret, John. *Fifty Queries, Seriously Propounded to those that Question, or Deny Infants Right to Baptism*. London, 1675.

———. *Much in a little, or, An Abstract of Mr. Baxters Plain Scripture-Proof for Infants Church-Membership or Baptism with a few Notes upon the Anti-Queries of T.G.* London, 1678.

Baxter, Richard. *Plain Scripture Proof of Infants Church Membership and Baptism.* London, 1651.

Benedict, David. *A General History of the Baptist Denomination in America.* 2 vols. Boston: Lincoln and Edmands, 1813.

Bilson, Thomas. *The Perpetual Gouernement of Christes Church*. London: Printed by Christopher Barker, 1593.

Caryl, Joseph. *A Renuntiation and Declaration of the Ministers of Congregational churches*. London: Peter Cole and Edward Cole, 1661.

Collier, Thomas. *The Right Constitution and True Subjects of the Visible Church of Christ*. London: Printed by Henry Hills, 1654.

Collinges, John. *The Intercourses of Divine Love*. London: Printed by T. Snowden, 1683.

Crosby, Thomas. *The History of the English Baptists*. 4 vols. London, 1738–40.

Danvers, Henry. *A Treatise of Baptism wherein that of Believers and that of Infants Is Examined by the Scriptures*. London: Printed by T. Snowden, 1674.

Denne, Henry. *ANTICHRIST Unmasked in two Treatises*. London, 1645.

———. *The Quaker no Papist*. London, 1659.

Edwards, Thomas. *Gangraena, OR A Catalogue and Discovery of many of the Errours, Heresies, Blasphemies and pernicious Practices of the Sectaries of this time.* London, 1646.

Eratt, William. *Anabaptism considered Wherein the Chief Objections of that Sect against Infant-Baptism, and the Manner of Baptizing by Aspersion, or Sprinkling, are Fairly Stated and Answered.* London: Printed by W. B., 1700.

Evelyn, John. *The Diary of John Evelyn*. London: Macmillan, 1908.

Everard, Robert. *An Epistle to the Several Congregations of the Non-Conformists*. Paris: 1664.

Evershed, William. *The Messengers Mission*. London: Printed by J. Brown, 1783.

Finch, Martin. *An Answer to Mr. Thomas Grantham's Book, Called, A Dialogue Between the Baptist and the Presbyterian*. London: Printed by T. Snowden(?), 1691.

Firmin, Giles. *The Answer of Giles Firmin, to the Vain and Unprofitable Question Put to Him, and Charged upon Him by Mr. Grantham, in His Book, Entituled, The infants Advocate*. London, 1689.

———. *Scripture-Warrant Sufficient Proof for Infant-Baptism: Being a Reply to Mr. Grantham's Presumption no Proof.* London, 1688.

Fisher, Samuel. *Baby-baptism meer babism*. London: Printed by Henry Hills, 1653.

Fox, George, et al. *A Declaration from the Harmles & Innocent People of God, called Quakers*. N.p., 1660/1.

Grantham, Thomas. *The Prisoner against the Prelate*. London, 1662.

———. *The Baptist against the Papist*. London, 1663.

———. *The Seventh-Day Sabbath*. London, 1667.

———. *The Paedo-Baptists Apology*. N.p., 1671.

———. *A Sigh for Peace*. London, 1671.

———. *The Loyal Baptist*. London, 1674.

———. *The Fourth Principle*. London, 1674.

———. *A Religious Contest*. London, 1674.

———. *Brief Animadversions upon Dr. Stillingfleet's Digressions about the Baptising of Infants*. London, 1674.

———. *The Quaeries Examined*. N.p., 1676.

———. *Christianismus Primitivus*. London, 1678.

———. *The Controversie about Infants*. London, 1680.

———. *A Friendly Epistle*. N.p., 1680.

———. *The Loyal Baptist*. London: Printed by Thomas Fabian, 1684.

———. *The Second Part of the Apology*. London, 1684.

———. *The Baptists Complaint against the Persecuting Priests*. N.p., 1685(?).

———. *Hear the Church: Or, An Appeal to the Mother of us All*. London, 1687.

———. *Presumption No Proof.* London, 1687.

———. *St. Paul's Catechism, or, A Brief and Plain Explication of the Six Principles of the Christian Religion, as Recorded Heb. 6., 1,2*. London, 1687.

———. *The Infants Advocate*. London: Printed by J. D., 1688.

———. *Truth and Peace*. London, 1689.

———. *The Infants Advocate: the Second Part*. London, 1690.

———. *A Dialogue between the Baptist and the Presbyterian*. London, 1691.

———. *The Forerunner toa Further Answer*. N.p., 1691.

———. *The Grand Imposter*. N.p., 1691.

———. *The Slanderer Rebuked*. N.p., 1691.

Grantham, Thomas, et al. *The Second Humble Addresse of those who are Called Anabaptists in the County of Lincoln*. London: Simon Dover, 1661.

———. *The Third Address of those person, known by the Name of Anabaptists, in the County of LINCOLN*. London, 1661.

Harrison, Joseph. *The popish proselyte the grand fanatick*. London, 1684.

Hooke, Joseph. *A Necessary Apology for the Baptized Believers*. London: Printed by R. Tookey, 1701.

———. *Creed-Making and Creed-Imposing*. London: Printed by J. Darby and T. Browne, 1729.

Horne, John. *The Cause of Infants Maintained. London, 1675.*

Howgill, Francis. *The True Rule, Judge, and Guide of the True Church of God Discovered*. N.p., 1665.

Ives, Jeremiah. *Rome is no rule, or, An Answer to an Epistle Published by a Roman Catholic who Stiles Himself Cap. Robert Everard*. London: Printed by *T. M., 1664.*

James, Ralph. *The Quakers Subterfuge*. London, 1672.

Jeffrey, William. *The Whole Faith of Man*. London: Printed by G. Dawson, 1659.

Jessey, Henry. *The Lords Loud Call to England*. London: Printed by H. J., 1660.

Knollys, Hanserd. *The Life and Death of that Old Disciple of Jesus Christ and Eminent Minister of the Gospel, Mr Hanserd Knollys*. London, 1692.

Lover, Thomas. *True Gospel Faith*. London, 1654.

Neal, Daniel. *History of the Puritans*. Edited by Joshua Toulmin. 5 Volumes. Bath: R. Cruttwell, 1793–97.

Petto, Samuel. *Infant baptism of Christ's Appointment*. London, 1687.

Poole, Matthew Poole. *The Nullity of the Romish Faith*. London: Printed by H. Hall, 1666.

Rider, William. *Laying on of Hands Asserted*. London, 1656.

Ruckhill, Robert. *The Quakers Refuge*. N.p., 1673.

Rudyard, Thomas. *The Anabaptists Lying Wonder*. London(?),1672.

Stillingfleet, Edward. *A Rational Account of the Grounds of the Protestant Religion*. London, 1665

Sutherland, James, ed. *Memoirs of the Life of Colonel Hutchinson*. New York: E. P. Dutton & Co., 1973.

Taylor, Jeremiah. *Theologia Eklektike. A Discourse of the Liberty of Prophesying. Shewing the Unreasonablenes of Prescribing to other Mens Faith, and the Iniquity of Persecuting Differing Opinions*. London, 1647.

Tombes, John. *An Addition to the Apology*. London: Printed by Henry Hills. 1652.
———. *Anti-Paedobaptism, or, The Second Part of the Full Review of the Dispute Concerning Infant-Baptism in which the Invalidity of Arguments*. London: Printed by Henry Hills, 1654.
———. *Anti-Paedobaptism, or, The Third Part Being a Full Review of the Dispute Concerning Infant Baptism*. London: Printed by E. Alsop, 1657.
Whiston, Joseph. *Infant-Baptism Plainly Proved*. London, 1678.
Whiston, William. *Memoirs of the life and writings of Mr. William Whiston*. 2 Volumes. London, 1753.
Whitehead, John. "Another Postscript to Ralph James." In Robert Ruckhill's *The Quakers Refuge*. N.p., 1673.
———. *The Written Gospel-Labours*. London: Printed by T. Sowle, 1704.

Secondary Sources

Dissertations and Theses

Bass, Clint C. "Thomas Grantham and General Baptist Theology." DPhil thesis, University of Oxford, 2008.
Gulley, Thomas K. "The General Baptists in Early Stuart and Revolutionary England." PhD diss., University of Wisconsin-Madison, 1994.
Hester, Samuel E. "Advancing Christianity to Its Primitive Excellency: The Quest of Thomas Grantham, Early English General Baptist (1634–1692)." ThD diss., New Orleans Baptist Theological Seminary, 1977.
Inscore Essick, John D. "Messenger, Apologist, and Nonconformist: An Examination of Thomas Grantham's Leadership Among the Seventeenth-Century General Baptists." PhD diss., Baylor University, 2008.
Kershaw, Robert R. "Baptised Believers: Lincolnshire Baptists in Times of Persecution, Revolution and Toleration, 1600–1700." Master's thesis, University of Nottingham, 1995.
Plumb, Jesse. "Early Nonconformity in Lincolnshire." Master's thesis, University of Sheffield, 1940.
Smith, Michael A. "The Early English Baptists and the Church Fathers." PhD diss., Southern Baptist Theological Seminary, 1982.
Southcombe, George. "The Responses of Nonconformists to the Restoration in England." DPhil thesis, University of Oxford, 2005.

Articles and Books

The Date Book for Lincoln and Neighbourhood. Lincoln UK: R. E. Leary, 1866.
"Two Association Meetings in Kent, 1657." *Transactions of the Baptist Historical Society* (1912–13): 247–50.

Adams, James Luther. *Voluntary Associations: Socio-Cultural Analyses and Theological Interpretation*. Chicago: Exploration Press, 1986.

Ambler, Rodney W. *Churches, Chapels and Parish Communities in Lincolnshire 1660–1900*. Lincoln UK: Society for Lincolnshire History and Archaeology, 2000.

———. "Church, Place and Organization: The Development of the New Connexion General Baptists in Lincolnshire, 1770–1891." *Baptist Quarterly* 37, no. 5 (January 1998): 238–48.

———. "Place and Structure: Lincolnshire General Baptists in the Seventeenth Century." In *La christianisation des campagnes*. Edited by J. P. Massaut and M. E. Henneau, 407–418. Rome: Brepols Publishers, 1996.

Barnes, Thomas. G. *Somerset, 1625–40*. Cambridge MA: Harvard University Press, 1961.

Bass, Clint C. "RESPONSE to J. Matthew Pinson's 'Thomas Grantham's Theology of the Atonement and Justification.'" *Journal for Baptist Theology & Ministry* 8, no. 1 (Spring 2011): 25-28.

Bate, Frank. *The Declaration of Indulgence, 1672: A Study in the Rise of Organised Dissent*. London: University Press of Liverpool, 1908.

Bebb, Evelyn D. *Nonconformity and Social and Economic Life 1660–1800*. Philadelphia: Porcupine Press, 1980.

Bell, Mark R. *Apocalypse How? Baptist Movements During the English Revolution*. Macon GA: Mercer University Press, 2000.

Betteridge, Alan. "Early Baptists in Leicestershire and Rutland: General Baptists." *Baptist Quarterly* 25, no. 8 (October 1974): 354–78.

Bitterman, M. G. F. "The Early Quaker Literature of Defense." *Church History* 42, no. 2 (June 1973): 203–28.

Blomefield, Francis and Charles Parkin, eds. *History of Norwich*. Vol. 4 of *An Essay towards a Topographical History of the County of Norfolk*. 2nd ed. London, 1805–10.

Botelho, Lynn. A. *Old Age and the English Poor Law, 1500–1700*. Rochester NY: Boydell Press, 2004.

Boyer, Richard E. *English Declarations of Indulgence 1687–1688*. The Hague, The Netherlands: Mouton & Co., 1968.

Brackney, William H. "Thomas Grantham, Systematic Theology, and the Baptist Tradition." In *From Biblical Criticism to Biblical Faith: Essays in Honor of Lee Martin McDonald*. Edited by William H. Brackney and Craig A. Evans. Macon GA: Mercer University Press, 2007.

———. *A Genetic History of Baptist Thought with Special Reference to Baptists in Britain and North America*. Macon GA: Mercer University Press, 2004.

———. *Christian Voluntarism in Britain and North America: A Bibliography and Critical Assessment*. Westport CT: Greenwood Press, 1995.

Bray, Gerald, ed. *Documents of the English Reformation*. Minneapolis MN: Fortress Press, 1994.

Broadie, Alexander. *Introduction to Medieval Logic.* New York: Clarendon Press, 1987.

Brown, Louis Fargo. *Baptists and the Fifth Monarchy Men in England.* Oxford: Oxford University Press, 1912.

Browning, Andrew. *English Historical Documents, 1660–1714.* London: Eyre & Spottiswoode, 1953.

Burgess, Glenn, ed. *The New British History.* New York: I. B. Tauris, 1999.

Bustin, Dennis. *Paradox and Perseverence: Hanserd Knollys, Particular Baptist Pioneer in Seventeenth-Century England.* Waynesboro GA: Paternoster Press, 2006.

Caffyn, John. *Sussex Believers: Baptist Marriage in the 17th and 18th Centuries.* Worthing UK: Churchman Publishing, 1988.

Cheney, C. R. *Handbook of Dates for Students of English History.* London: Offices of the Royal Historical Society, 1981.

Clifton, Robin. "The Popular Fear of Catholics During the English Revolution." *Past and Present* 52 (August 1971): 23–55.

Cobb, Ronald L. "George Fox and the Quaker-Baptist Controversy." *Foundations* 14, no. 3 (July–September 1971): 236–39.

Cockburn, J. S. *A History of English Assizes 1558–1714.* New York: Cambridge University Press, 1972.

Coffey, John. "From Helwys to Leland: Baptists and Religious Tolerance in England and America, 1612–1791." In *The Gospel in the World.* Edited by David Bebbington. Waynesboro GA: Paternoster Press, 2002.

Collinson, Patrick. *The Elizabethan Puritan Settlement.* Berkeley: University of California Press, 1967.

Coward, Barry. *The Stuart Age: England 1603–1714.* New York: Longman, 2003.

Croft, Pauline. *King James.* New York: Palgrave Macmillan, 2003.

Davies, Susan. *Quakerism in Lincolnshire.* Lincoln UK: Yard, 1989.

De Krey, Gary S. "Rethinking the Restoration: Dissenting Cases for Conscience, 1667–1672." *The Historical Journal* 38, no. 1 (March 1995): 53–83.

Durnbaugh, Donald F. "Baptists and Quakers—Left Wing Puritans?" *Quaker History* 62, no. 2 (Autumn 1873): 67–82.

Durso, Keith E. *No Armor for the Back.* Macon GA: Mercer University Press, 2007.

Estep, William R. *Revolution within the Revolution: The First Amendment in Historical Context.* Grand Rapids MI: Eerdmans, 1990.

Evans, Benjamin. *Early English Baptists.* 2 Volumes. London: J. Heaton & Son, 1864.

Fiddes, Paul S. *Tracks and Traces: Baptist Identity in Church and Theology.* Waynesboro GA: Paternoster Press, 2003.

Fowler, Stanley K. *More Than a Symbol: The British Baptist Recovery of Baptismal Sacramentalism.* Waynesboro GA: Paternoster Press, 2002.

Gauci, Perry. *Politics and Society in Great Yarmouth, 1660–1722.* New York: Oxford University Press, 1996.

Gay, Peter. *Deism: An Anthology.* Princeton NJ: Van Nostrand, 1968.

George, Timothy. "Between Pacifism and Coercion: The English Baptist Doctrine of Religious Toleration." *Mennonite Quarterly Review* 58, no. 1 (January 1984): 30–49.

Gleason, J. H. *The Justices of the Peace in England, 1558–1640*. Oxford: Clarendon Press, 1969.

Greaves, Richard L. and Robert Zaller, eds. *Biographical Dictionary of British Radicals in the Seventeenth Century*. 3 vols. Brighton UK: Harvester Press, 1983–84.

Grell, Ole P., Jonathan I. Israel, and Nicholas Tyacke, eds. *From Persecution to Toleration*. Oxford: Clarendon Press, 1991.

Hardacre, Paul H. "Genesis of the Declaration of Breda, 1657–1660." *Journal of Church and State* 15, no. 1 (Winter 1973): 65–82.

Harkness, Reuben E. E. "Early Relations of Baptists and Quakers." *Church History* 2, no. 4 (December 1933): 227–42.

Harris, Tim. *Politics under the Later Stuarts*. New York: Longman, 1993.

Haykin, Michael A. G. *Kiffin, Knollys, and Keach: Rediscovering Our English Baptist Heritage*. Leeds UK: Reformation Today Trust, 1996.

Hermans, Chris A. M. *Participatory Learning: Religious Education in a Globalizing Society*. Boston: Brill, 2003.

Hill, Christopher. *The World Turned the World Upside Down: Radical Ideas During the English Revolution*. 1972. Reprint, New York: Penguin Books, 1991.

Holmes, Clive. *Seventeenth-Century Lincolnshire*. Lincoln UK: Society for Lincolnshire History and Archaeology, 1980.

Horle, Craig. "Quakers and Baptists 1647–1660." *Baptist Quarterly* 26, no. 8 (October 1976): 344–62.

Hoskins, William G. *English Local History: The Past and the Future*. Leicester UK: Leicester University Press, 1966.

Hudson, Winthrop S. "The Associational Principle among Baptists." *Foundations* 1, no. 1 (January 1958): 10–23.

Hughey, J. D., Jr. "Baptists and Religious Freedom." *Baptist Quarterly* 17, no. 6 (April 1958): 249–55.

Ivimey, Joseph. *A History of the English Baptists*. 4 vols. London 1811–1830.

Jewson, Charles B. *The Baptists in Norfolk*. London: Carey Kingsgate Press, 1957.

_____. "The Old General Baptist at Norwich." *Baptist Quarterly* 1938-39): 430-32.

Jones, R. Tudor, ed. *Protestant Nonconformist Texts*. 4 vols. Burlington VT: Ashgate, 2006.

———. *Congregationalism in England*. London: Independent Press, 1962.

Jordan, W. K. *The Development of Religious Toleration in England*. 4 vols. London: George Allen and Unwin, 1932–40.

Keeble, Neil H. *The Restoration: England in the 1660s*. Malden MA: Blackwell Publishing, 2002.

———. *The Literary Culture of Nonconformity in Later Seventeenth-Century England*. Avon UK: Leicester University Press, 1987.

Kirkpatrick, John and Dawson Turner, eds. *History of the Religious Orders and Communities and of the Hospital and Castle of Norwich*. Yarmouth UK: C. Sloman, 1845.

Kliever, Lonnie D. "General Baptist Origins: The Question of Anabaptist Influence." *Mennonite Quarterly Review* 36, no. 4 (October 1962): 291–321.

Knight, Richard. *History of the General or Six Principle Baptists, In Europe and America*. 1827. Reprint, New York: Arno Press, 1980.

Lacey, Douglas. R. *Dissent and Parliamentary Politics in England 1661–89*. New Brunswick NJ: Rutgers University Press, 1969.

Langley, Arthur S. "Baptist Disputations of the Seventeenth Century." *Transactions of the Baptist Historical Society* 6 (July 1919): 216–43.

Lash, Nicholas. *The Beginning and the End of "Religion"*. New York: Cambridge University Press, 1996.

Latch, Ollie. *History of the General Baptists*. 1954. Reprint, Poplar Bluff MO: General Baptist Press, 1972.

Lee, Jason K. *The Theology of John Smyth: Puritan, Separatist, Baptist, Mennonite.* Macon GA: Mercer University Press, 2003.

Leonard, Bill J. *Baptist Ways: A History*. Valley Forge PA: Judson Press, 2003.

Leonard, James. "RESPONSE to J. Matthew Pinson's "Thomas Grantham's Theology of the Atonement and Justification."" *Journal for Baptist Theology & Ministry* 8, no. 1 (Spring 2011): 29-33

Lockyer, Roger. *The Early Stuarts: A Political History of England 1603–1642*. New York: Longman House, 1989.

Lumpkin, William L. *Baptist Confessions of Faith*. Philadelphia: Judson Press, 1959.

Manly, K. R. "Origins of the Baptists: The Case for Development from Puritanism-Separatism." *Baptist History and Heritage* 22, no. 4 (October 1987): 34–46.

Mason, F. J. "The Old Minute Book of Bourne Baptist Church." *The Baptist Quarterly* 15, no. 5 (January 1954): 226–28.

McBeth, H. Leon. *The Baptist Heritage: Four Centuries of Baptist Witness*. Nashville TN: Broadman Press, 1987.

———. *English Baptist Literature on Religious Liberty to 1689*. New York: Arno Press, 1980.

McGlothlin, William J., ed. *Baptist Confessions of Faith*. Philadelphia: American Baptist Publication Society, 1911.

Miller, John. *Popery and Politics in England 1660–1688*. New York: Cambridge University Press, 1973.

Mills, Susan B. "Sources for the Study of Baptist History." *Baptist Quarterly* 34, no. 6 (April 1992): 282–96.

Nicholson, John F. V. "The Office of 'Messenger amongst British Baptists in the 17th and 18th Centuries." *Baptist Quarterly* 17, no. 5 (January 1958): 206–25.

Nuttall, Geoffrey F. and Owen Chadwick, eds. *From Uniformity to Unity*. London: Society for Promoting Christian Knowledge, 1962.

Oldfield, Edmund. *A Topographical and Historical Account of Wainfleet and the Wapentake of Candleshoe, In the City of Lincoln*. Boston: Printed by John Noble, 1829.

Outhwaite, R. B. *Clandestine Marriage in England, 1500–1850*. London: Hambledon Press, 1995.

Page, William. *The Victoria County History of Lincoln*. 2 vols. London: Archibald Constable, 1906.

Payne, Ernest. "Baptists and the Laying on of Hands." *Baptist Quarterly* 15, no. 5 (January 1954): 203–15.

Pearse, Meic. *The Great Restoration: The Religious Radicals of the 16th and 17th Centuries*. Carlisle UK: Paternoster Press, 1998.

Penney, Norman, ed. *Extracts from State Papers Relating to Friends, 1654–1672*. Philadelphia: H. Newman, 1913.

Pinson, J. Matthew. "Thomas Grantham's Theology of the Atonement and Justification." *Journal for Baptist Theology & Ministry* 8, no. 1 (Spring 2011): 7-21.

Pollard A. W. and G. R. Redgrave. *A Short-title Catalogue of Books Printed in England, Scotland, and Ireland and of English Books Printed Abroad, 1475–1640*. 2nd ed. London: Bibliographical Society, 1976.

Putman, Rhyne. "RESPONSE to J. Matthew Pinson's "Thomas Grantham's Theology of the Atonement and Justification.'" *Journal for Baptist Theology & Ministry* 8, no. 1 (Spring 2011): 22-23.

Raymond, Joad. *Pamphlets and Pamphleteering in Early Modern Britain*. New York: Cambridge University Press, 2003.

Renihan, Michael T. *Antipaedobaptism in the Thought of John Tombes*. Auburn MA: B&R Press, 2001.

Richard, William. "Biography of Thomas Grantham." *Universal Theological Magazine* (January–April 1805): 1–10, 57–68, 109–17, 165–71.

Scott, Jonathan. *England's Troubles: Seventeenth-century English Political Instability in European Context*. New York: Cambridge University Press, 2000.

Seaward, Paul. *The Restoration*. New York: St. Martin's Press, 1991.

Shurden, Walter B., ed. *Religious Liberty*. Macon GA: Smyth & Helwys, 1997.

Slack, Paul. *The English Poor Law, 1531–1782*. New York: Cambridge University Press, 1995.

Solar, Peter R. "Poor Relief and English Economic Development before the Industrial Revolution." *The Economic History Review* 48, no. 1 (February 1995): 1–22.

Spufford, Margaret, ed. *The World of Rural Dissenters, 1520–1725*. Cambridge UK: Cambridge University Press, 1995.

Spurr, John. *England in the 1670s*. Malden MA: Blackwell Publishers, 2000.

Starr, Edward C., ed. *A Baptist Bibliography*. 25 vols. Rochester NY: American Baptist Historical Society, 1947–76.

Stassen, Glen H. "Anabaptist Influence in the Origin of the Particular Baptists." *Mennonite Quarterly Review* 36, no. 4 (October 1962): 322–48.

Stephen, Leslie and Sidney Lee, eds. *Dictionary of National Biography*. 63 vols. London: Smith, Elder, & Co., 1885–1901.

Stevenson, George. "Laker, Benjamin." *Dictionary of North Carolina Biography*. Edited by William Stevens Powell. Vol. 4, L–O, 6 vols. Chapel Hill: University of North Carolina Press, 1991.

Stone, Lawrence. "English and United States Local History." *Daedalus* (Winter 1971): 128–32.

Taylor, Adam. *The History of the English General Baptists*. 2 vols. London: T. Bore, 1818.

Thirsk, Joan. *English Peasant Farming: The Agrarian History of Lincolnshire from Tudor to Recent Times*. New York: Methuen, 1957.

Thompson, Philip. "A New Question in Baptist History: Seeking a Catholic Spirit Among Early Baptists." *Pro Ecclesia* 8, no. 1 (Winter 1999): 51–72.

Tolmie, Murray. *The Triumph of the Saints: The Separate Churches of London 1616–1649*. New York: Cambridge University Press, 1977.

Torbet, Robert. *A History of the Baptists*. Valley Forge PA: Judson Press, 1965.

Trevor-Roper, Hugh R. *Archbishop Laud, 1573–1645*. London: MacMillan & Co., 1963.

Turner, George Lyon, ed. *Original Records of Early Nonconformity under Persecution and Indulgence*. 3 volumes. London: T. F. Unwin, 1911–14.

Underhill, Edward B., ed. *Records of the Churches of Christ gathered at Fenstanton, arboys, and Hexham, 1644–1720*. London: Haddon Brothers, 1854.

Underwood, Alfred C. *A History of the English Baptists*. London: The Baptist Union Publication Dept., 1947.

Underwood, Richard A. "Child Dedication Services among British Baptists in the Seventeenth Century." *Baptist Quarterly* 23, no. 4 (October 1969): 164–69.

Underwood, Ted L. *Primitivism, Radicalism, and the Lamb's War: The Baptist-Quaker Conflict in Seventeenth-Century England*. New York: Oxford University Press, 1997.

———. "Baptist Henry Denne and the Quaker Doctrine of the Inner Light." *Quaker History* 56, no. 1 (Spring 1967): 34–40.

Walker, Michael J. "Baptist Theology of Infancy in the 17th Century." *Baptist Quarterly* 21, no. 6 (April 1966): 242–62.

Watts, Michael R. *The Dissenters from the Reformation to the French Revolution*. 2 Volumes. Oxford: Clarendon Press, 1978.

White, Barrington R. *The English Baptists of the Seventeenth Century*. London: The Baptist Historical Society, 1983.

———. "English Baptists and the Great Rebellion, 1640–1660, Point 2." *Baptist History and Heritage* 9, no. 1 (January 1974): 16–29.

———. "English Baptists and the Great Rebellion, 1640–1660, Point 1." *Baptist History and Heritage* 8, no. 1 (January 1973): 16–27.

Whiteman, Anne, ed. *The Compton Census of 1676: A Critical Edition*. London: Oxford University Press, 1986.

Whitley, William T. *A History of British Baptists*. London: Kingsgate Press, 1932.
———, ed. *A Baptist Bibliography, 1526–1837*. 2 vols. London, Kingsgate Press, 1916–1922.
———. "Associational Life till 1815." *Transactions of the Baptist Historical Society* (1916–17): 19–34.
———, ed. *Minutes of the General Assembly of the General Baptist Churches in England*. 2 vols. London: Kingsgate Press, 1909.
———. "The Baptist Licences of 1672." *Transactions of the Baptist Historical Society* (1908–09): 156–76.
Wing, Donald. *Short-Title Catalogue of Books Printed in England, Scotland, Ireland, Wales, and British America and of English Books Printed in other Countries 1641–1700*. 2nd ed. 4 Volumes. New York: The Modern Language Association of America, 1982.
Winter, E. P. "The Administration of the Lord's Supper among the Baptists of the Seventeenth Century." *Baptist Quarterly* 18, no. 5 (January 1959): 196–204.
Wright, Stephen. *The Early English Baptists, 1603–1649*. Rochester NY: Boydell Press, 2006.

Websites and Internet Sources

Burdick, Oscar C. "Grantham, Thomas (1633/4–1692)." *Oxford Dictionary of National Biography*, http://www.oxforddnb.com/view/article/11298?docPos=2 (accessed 3 September 2008).
Calendar of State Papers Domestic. "Proclamation for restraining all seditious meetings …," (Charles II, 10 January 1661). British History Online. http://www.british-history.ac.uk/report.aspx?compid=54648 (accessed on 6 October 2008).
Copsey, Richard. *The Medieval Carmelite Priory at Norwich: A Chronology*. http://www.carmelite.org/chronology/Norwich.pdf (accessed on 7 July 2008).
Cooper, Sheila M. "Horne, John (bap. 1616, d. 1676)." *Oxford Dictionary of National Biography*. http://www.oxforddnb.com/view/article/13790 (accessed 8 October 2008).
Greaves, Richard. "Whitehead, John (*c*.1630–1696)." *Oxford Dictionary of National Biography*. http://www.oxforddnb.com/view/article/29290?docPos=1 (accessed 19 September 2008).
Keyworth, Bryan. "History of Monksthorpe Baptist Church." Monksthorpe Baptist Church. http://homepage.ntlworld.com/bh.keyworth/History.htm (accessed 12 November 2008).
Mullett, Michael. "Lloyd, William (1627–1717)." *Oxford Dictionary of National Biography*. http://www.oxforddnb.com/view/article/16860?docPos=2 (accessed 10 July 2008).
Southcombe, George. "Everard, Robert (fl. 1647–1664)." *Oxford Dictionary of National Biography*.